FOR WANT OF
GOOD MONEY

For want of good money
The story of Ireland's coinage

Edward Colgan

Wordwell

First published in 2003
Wordwell Ltd
PO Box 69, Bray, Co. Wicklow
Copyright © The author

Cover design: Rachel Dunne.

ISBN 1 869857 61 5

British Library Cataloguing-in-Publication Data.
A catalogue record for this book is available from the British Library.

This publication has received support from the Heritage Council under the 2003 Publications
Grant Scheme.

Typeset in Ireland by Wordwell Ltd.
Repro: Niamh Power.
Editor: Emer Condit.

Book design: Nick Maxwell.

Printed by E.G. Zure Bilbao

Contents

Acknowledgements

The idea of writing this book goes back to a chance remark made by an assistant at the sales counter in the Central Bank of Ireland in Dame Street who, when asked about a commemorative medal to mark the 1000th anniversary of the first Irish coin, replied that she was not aware of any such medal, and anyhow Ireland's coinage only went back to the 1920s and certainly not a thousand years! I resolved there and then to set the record straight by writing this book.

This book charts the thousand-year-old story of Ireland's coinage, from the first pennies of the Viking rulers of Dublin, through the Anglo-Irish regal issues of the Normans and later English and British rulers, and the tokens of merchants and traders to the coins of the Free State and the Republic, and finally to the Euro-coins issued on 1 January 2002. It is, however, not simply a history of bits of metal but also a history of the Irish people and of how these bits of silver and brass over the last ten centuries have affected the lives of Irish men and women, not only in their everyday business transactions of buying goods and paying taxes, but also at some of the most defining and critical moments in Ireland's history.

In bringing this history of Ireland's coinage together, I have drawn on and acknowledge the original work and research of many numismatists, living and dead, including G. Brady, C. Challis, Michael Dolley, A. Dowle, Patrick Finn, C. Gallagher, W. O'Sullivan, Peter Seaby, W. A. Seaby, James Simon, John Stafford-Langan, F. W. Yeates and Derek Young. A detailed list of all the authors consulted in preparing this book is included in the bibliography.

I am grateful for the assistance I have received from the Department of Coins and Medals of the British Museum in supplying me with photocopies of articles and papers over the last five years.

A book on numismatics cannot work without illustrations, and just under 200 images have been included to give the reader a 'feel' for the coins described here. I am especially grateful for the permission received from May Sinclair of Spink & Sons Ltd, London, to use illustrations from the *Spink Numismatic Circular* (*SNC*). I am also grateful to Whyte's of Dublin for their permission to use illustrations from the Millennial Collection and other auction catalogues, and Dix Noonan Webb (DNW) of London and the Central Bank of Ireland for their permission to use illustrations and images. I am grateful in particular to the late Patrick Finn for his permission to use his Morbiducci group of patterns that featured in his 2000 list. Every effort has been made to identify and acknowledge the source of all illustrations used and to seek permission.

In writing this book and pursuing its publication I have received support and encouragement from a number of people, including Ian Whyte of Whyte's Auction House, Michael Kenny of the National Museum of Ireland, and John Mussell, editor of *Coin News*. I am particularly grateful for the encouragement I have received from friends and colleagues, particularly those of the Wessex Numismatic Society, including Peter Preston-Morley, Bill Petts and Walter Wilkinson.

I would like to thank the Heritage Council of Ireland and Christopher Webb of Dix Noonan Webb for their generous contributions towards the publication costs of this book.

I also wish to acknowledge the hard work of the Wordwell team, including publisher Nick Maxwell, his editor Emer Condit and Niamh Power, who was responsible for the reproduction and enhancing of the illustrations.

Finally, I wish to record my very sincere thanks to Dianne Poulton, without whom this book would never have been written.

Edward Colgan
Dowlish Wake, Somerset
28 April 2003

Introduction

The first coins are believed to have been made in Sardis in Asia Minor around 650 BC and were small bean-shaped pieces of electrum, a natural alloy of gold and silver, with some rough marks hammered into them. Over the next thousand years the use of inscribed pieces of metal as a currency, a means of exchange, was to spread through southern Europe and into Asia and Africa. Celtic tribes in central Europe first began to make their own coins, crude copies of Greek gold and silver coins, around 300 BC. Through trade and migration Continental Celtic coins were to make their way to Britain, where the British Celtic tribes in turn produced their own coins around 125 BC. In time, some of these Continental and British Celtic coins, with their abstract designs of horses and warriors' heads, were to find their way to Ireland.

Before the use of coins a wider range of objects and materials served as currency. Amongst the British and Irish Celts it is thought that 'ring-money', small rings of gold or gold-plated copper, may have circulated as a form of currency.

The westward march of the Roman Empire was to stop at Britain and the Romans were never to colonise Hibernia, the land of winter. Roman coins were, however, to make their way to Ireland through trade and raids.

Despite their mastery in the art of metalwork, the Irish seem to have had little need for coin; a man's or a woman's wealth in Celtic Ireland was measured in cattle. Irish traders had some need for coins in their dealings with Roman Britain and the Continent, but for most of the population coins were no more than a source of precious metal for making jewellery or a piece of bullion to be exchanged in trade. Some coins were used as votive offerings to the dead or the spirits, and offerings of Roman coins have been found at the great burial complex in Newgrange.

During the Dark Ages coins continued to find their way to Ireland, from Anglo-Saxon pennies from across the Irish Sea to the more exotic Islamic dirhams from as far away as Baghdad and Cairo, brought back in the purses and pouches of Irish traders and travellers. But, as in the past, these coins were more highly valued as raw material for intricately crafted jewellery and ornaments.

It was only at the end of the first Christian millennium in about 997 that the first coins were to be struck in Ireland, and these were not to be struck by the native Irish but by the merchants and traders of Viking Dublin...

To my parents, Tom and Mary Colgan
— and Marie, Pete, Christopher and Catherine

1. KINGDOM OF THE OSTMEN
The first Irish coins (997–1150)

Just over a thousand years ago in the Viking city of Dubhlinn, a metal-worker, a man possibly by the name of Eole, took a thin piece of silver, carefully placed it between two pieces of engraved iron, raised his arm and brought down a hammer — and with a resounding clash of metal upon metal began the story of Ireland's coinage.

The first Irish coin was struck in about 997 for Sitric III Olafson, the Viking king of Dublin, and was a silver *penningr* or penny, about the same size as a modern penny but much thinner and lighter.

The Vikings first arrived in Ireland in about 795 with a raid on Rathlin Island. Further raids followed, and soon no part of Ireland was safe from the Viking longboats. In about 840 the Viking fleets wintered for the first time in Ireland, and 'long-ports' or bases were established at Dublin and Annagassan. In time other long-ports were established at Cork, Limerick, Waterford and Wexford and grew into major trading centres through which passed Anglo-Saxon pennies, French Carolingian silver deniers, Kufic silver dirhams from the Volga and Arabic gold dinars from as far away as Cairo.

Viking fortunes ebbed and flowed in Ireland. The early Viking invaders, the Norwegian *Finn-gaill* or 'white foreigners', were in time displaced by the Danish *Dubh-gaill* or 'black foreigners', who in turn were defeated by a fresh wave of Norwegian Vikings. In about 871 the Danish Viking Ivar the Boneless established himself as ruler of the Vikings in Ireland and northern England. Over the next two centuries the Hiberno-Norse dynasty he founded was to provide kings not only of Dublin but also of Limerick, Waterford, the Isle of Man, the Scottish Isles and the northern English kingdom of Jorvik (York).

From the early tenth century Viking military power and political influence in Ireland began to wane. In 902 the Vikings or Ostmen were briefly expelled from Dublin, and over the next century the Hiberno-Norse successors of Ivar the Boneless saw the boundaries of their kingdom of Dyflinarskiri contract as Irish kings and chiefs reasserted their authority. Irish victories in 980 at the Battle of Tara and again in 999 at the Battle of Glenmama essentially ended the political ambitions of the Hiberno-Norse in Ireland. In some ways the Battle of Clontarf in 1014 simply underscored these defeats.

It was against this background of declining Viking fortunes that Sitric Olafson — *Silki-skegg*, 'Silkenbeard', as he is known to history (a reference to his youthful features) — issued the first Irish coins. Sitric had come to the throne in 989. In 995 he was removed by Ivar III Ivarson, the Hiberno-Norse ruler of Waterford, but re-established his authority a year later. It may well be that Sitric issued this first Irish coin as a political gesture to mark his return to his throne and his authority over the Dublin Ostmen. He was to rule his kingdom of Dyflinarskiri for another 40 years. A great-great-grandson of Ivar the Boneless, he was also, through his mother, Gormflaith, a grandson of Murchadh, the Irish king of Leinster. In time he was to be both the stepson and son-in-law of Brian Boramha (Boru), high king of Ireland (997–1014).

The coins issued by Sitric III were not the first coins to be struck by the Hiberno-Norse rulers of Dublin. In about 921 Sitric Caoch (921–7) ordered the striking of silver pennies in York for his kingdom of Jorvik. These first coins combined Christian symbols such as the name of Saint Peter, 'SCI PETRI MO', with the pagan symbols of the sword of Carlus, the ancient symbol of the Hiberno-Norse kingdom of Dublin, and the hammer of Thor! Later Hiberno-Norse kings of Dublin, Anlaf Guthfrithsan (939–41) and Anlaf or Olaf Sitricsson (941–3 and 948–52), were also to issue coins for their kingdom of Jorvik. Whilst struck for use in northern England, some of these coins found their way to Ireland and have turned up in Irish coin-hoards.

Coinage came later to the Viking kingdoms of Denmark, Sweden, Norway and Dublin. At the same time as Sitric III began to issue his first coins, other Viking rulers began issuing their own coins, all strongly influenced by English designs.

The need for coinage reflected a growth in trade. The Viking raiders had over time become adept dealers in a wide range of commodities, including slaves. At the turn of the first millennium Dublin reputedly had the largest slave-market in western Europe.

Coins were issued by the Hiberno-Norse rulers of Dublin for about 150 years and have been divided by archaeologists and numismatists into seven phases or periods on the basis of archaeological evidence from coin-hoards and the dating of Anglo-Saxon and Norman coins which served as models for almost all the early Irish coins. The first two phases broadly coincide with the reign of Sitric III from 995 to 1035.

The first Irish coins were imitations of pennies struck by the English king, Aethelred II, from about 971 to 997.

The Irish coins feature on the obverse a left-facing bust of the king holding a sceptre, with the legend around the border 'SIHTRICRE DYFLI' ('Sitric, king of Dublin'). The reverse of the coin features a short cross in the centre with the letters 'CRUX' in each quarter of the cross. The design is derived from a coin of Aethelred known as the 'Crux Penny'. The legend on the reverse included the

Fig. 1—Penny, Sitric III, Phase One, Eole of Dublin, 997. *SNC*, May 1995, No. 2737

name of the moneyer responsible for striking the coin and the word 'DYFLHI' or a variation in the rendition of the word Dublin. It is believed that this type of coin was struck between 995 and 1000.

Some 24 moneyers' names were to feature on the Dublin coins of Sitric, including AELFELN, ASCETEL, CAR, EDRIC, EIOMNS, EOLE, FAENEMIN, FAEREMIN, FASTOLF, GODRIC, GOLDSTEGN, LIOELF, LIOGOLF, NDREMIN, NIRIN, RINGULF, SIEL, SIULF, SIULT, STENG, STIREIN, ULFIAT, WULFGER and WULFIG. The name 'Dublin' was to appear in some seventeen different forms, from the more obvious 'DIFLIN' to shortened abbreviated forms such as 'DNI', 'DYE' and 'DY' or the less obvious 'HHO', 'IFIM' or 'NIO'.

Alongside these variations in the names of moneyers and the spelling of Dublin, other variations of these CRUX-type pennies appear with mismatched legends, having Sitric's portrait and titles on the obverse but with the name of an English moneyer or town on the reverse. Some have the English King Aethelred's title on the obverse and a Dublin moneyer's name on the reverse. In these instances it is assumed that the engravers simply copied the reverse or obverse of the English coins they had in front of them and did not make the necessary local amendments.

The names of some 30 English moneyers appear on these 'Dublin' coins, such as Godwine of Winchester, Giodric of Lincoln, Eadril of York and Lyfing of London. At least eighteen English towns and cities are referred to on the reverse of some of Sitric's coins.

The coins of this period and of the next five centuries were struck manually with a hammer. A flat round piece of silver or 'blank' was placed between two pieces of wrought iron with engraved designs at one end, the dies. The lower die, known as the 'pile', had a spike at its end so that it could be held steady in a block of wood when it was being used. The upper die, the 'trussel', had a flat top to absorb the hammer-blows of the moneyer.

The designs at the ends of the two dies, an engraved mirror image of the coin to be struck, were cut in reverse by a 'graver' who either 'stamped' or 'sunk' the design into the flat working surface of the die, using punches with elements of the design cut into them, or directly 'cut' or engraved the design onto the surface of the die. It is estimated that as many as 20,000 coins could be produced from one set of dies before they were worn flat.

A medieval mint, with a coiner producing coins in the bottom right-hand corner

In about 1000 a new type of design was introduced onto Sitric's coins, the Long Cross type. This was again based on the English King Aethelred's coins and features a left-facing bust of the king (with distinctive spiked hair and a cape gathered around his neck) with the legend 'SIHTRIC RE+ DYFLIN' ('Sitric king of Dublin') or a variation in wording on the obverse. The reverse featured a long voided cross, stretching to the edge of the coin, with the legend incorporating the name of the moneyer around the border of the coin. This coin was issued between 1000 and 1010. A number of variations exist. Coins of this type with mismatched legends throughout this first phase, in particular those with references to English towns, are extremely rare, if not, in some cases, unique.

Fig. 2—Penny, Sitric III, Long Cross type, Fiemen of Dublin, 997–1020. *SNC*, May 1996, No. 2157

One coin issued in this period bears the obverse legend 'DYMN ROE MNEGNI', which some early numismatists attributed to Donald, king of Monaghan, although there is no evidence to suggest that such a monarch existed or indeed issued coins. It has also been suggested that the 'Dymnroe' or Thymm coins, as they are sometimes known, may have referred to a possible Hiberno-Norse rival of Sitric III and could have been issued at a point when Sitric's rule, following the defeat at Glen Mama (999), was under threat.

Fig. 3—Penny, 'Thymm' or 'Dymnroe', Phase One, 997–1020. *SNC*, February 1998, No. 5

From about 1004 to 1010 a coin with a helmeted bust was also issued by the Dublin moneyers. The reverse continued to feature a long cross but superimposed over an ornamental square.

In about 1010 a further type or variety was introduced, featuring a smaller, left-facing portrait of the king within a circle and the usual legend of 'Sitric king of Dublin'. The reverse design, again copied from a coin of Aethelred's, featured a small cross within a circle, with the moneyer's name and the reference to Dublin forming the legend. As with the other earlier issues, versions exist which refer to mints in Chester, London or Shrewsbury.

The final coins to be issued in this first phase were based on a penny issued by the Danish King Cnut (Canute) of England (1016–35). They feature a portrait of the king within a quatrefoil design and on the reverse a long cross with two crescents in each quarter. It is believed that these coins were issued from about 1016 to 1020. A variety, as with some of the earlier coins, has an obverse with a reference to an English king, in this case Cnut, matched with a reverse featuring a Dublin moneyer's name and an abbreviated form of Dublin.

Fig. 4—Penny, Phase Two, 1015–35. *SNC*, February 1998, No. 6

The second phase in the history of the early Hiberno-Norse coinage, from 1015 to 1035, began to see a deterioration in the quality of the coin, both in design and in an increased blundering of legends. The coins were also to become smaller and lighter than the coins issued in the previous twenty years. During this period some of the coins were almost half the weight of those previously issued at twelve grains, although the majority were about two thirds of the previous weight. Sitric's earlier coins had weighed between 27 and 28 grains — the same weight as their English and Scandinavian equivalents. They were readily accepted by foreign merchants and saw wide circulation across Britain and Scandinavia. The later smaller and lighter coins were unacceptable for international trade and were only to circulate in Ireland. A rate of three Irish pennies to two English pennies was eventually established amongst merchants and traders.

This decline in the quality of Sitric's coins may reflect the further decline of the political and economic fortunes of the Hiberno-Norse kingdom of Dublin following Brian Boru's defeat of Sitric's supporters and allies at the Battle of Clontarf in 1014. Whilst Sitric had been one of the principal instigators of the events that led to the Battle of Clontarf, he did not fight in the battle. Despite the defeat of his Viking allies from Man and the Isles and the Leinster Irish, he was to retain his crown and Dublin. The last twenty years of his reign were, however, characterised by further battles and skirmishes with Irish kings and chiefs, marking a deeper decline in Hiberno-Norse authority.

The coins issued in this phase featured much cruder portraits of the king, and on the reverse a cruder rendering of the earlier long cross designs with the addition of a pellet in the quarters of the cross. Some varieties have symbols such as an 'E' (lying on its back) or spirals or stylised hands incorporated into the design.

In about 1035 Sitric was deposed by his nephew and went into exile, possibly to north Wales, where it is believed he died in 1042.

The third phase in the Hiberno-Norse coinage, from about 1035 to 1060, roughly coincides with the reigns of Margad Ranaldson (1035–8 and 1046–52) and the interim rule by Ivar IV Haroldson (1038–46). The dynastic struggles of the Hiberno-Norse kings and the increased intervention of Irish kings in the affairs of the city — including a period of direct rule by Murchad, the son of Diarmat MaelnamBo, the king of Leinster from 1052 to 1072 — possibly account for the further decline in the Hiberno-Norse coinage of Ireland during this period.

Fig. 5—Penny, Phase Three, 1035–60. *SNC*, February 1998, No. 15

The coins, although based on the earlier Long Cross coins, were even cruder in style and production, the legends often reduced to a meaningless series of strokes and spirals. The weight and size of the coins also continued to decline. Coins during this period mostly weighed between sixteen and twelve grains. Whilst the standard fineness of coins was not significantly to drop below .920 (despite reductions in weight and size), some coins have been found with a silver content of just above .500 fineness. This series of coins is commonly known as the

Long Cross and Hand coinage because of the incorporation of stylised hands along with pellets into the quarters of the cross on the reverse of the coin.

The blundering of the legends on these coins to a jumble of meaningless words, or a series of strokes and spirals, saw a number being ascribed by earlier numismatists, such as James Simon (1749) and John Lindsay (1839), to a range of Viking rulers in Dublin, Limerick and Waterford, as well as to Gaelic kings and princes.

Simon in his essay on Irish coins ascribed coins to a number of Viking rulers, and in some cases to mythical Irish kings and princes; he even attributed a coin with a helmeted portrait to Brian Boru, 'as he was a great warrior' (Simon 1749, 5). John Lindsay's contemporary, the numismatist John Akerman in his *Numismatic Manual* (1840, 395) similarly makes reference to 'several rude coins' being appropriated to the early Irish princes.

As late as 1921 the numismatist Henry Alexander Parsons authoritatively attributed a blundered Hiberno-Norse coin to a Southern O'Neill prince of Limerick. The coin was subsequently to be identified as a Scandinavian coin copied from a penny of Edward the Confessor.

The fourth phase in the Hiberno-Norse series, which covered about five years from 1060 to 1065, consists of the so-called 'scratched-die' coins, so called because of the method of production of the reverse dies. It would appear that the dies for these coins were produced using punches but with some parts of the design being 'scratched' on or cut directly into the die. In terms of design and quality of striking these coins are even cruder than the earlier Long Cross coins.

Fig. 6— Penny, Phase Four, scratched die coinage, 1060–5. *SNC*, February 1998, No. 21

This phase did, however, herald a major change in design. All the coins up to this date had featured, or had attempted, some form of rendering of the left-facing bust which had been used by Sitric III. During this phase the coins featured a similar bust but facing right, possibly an engraver's error, but the most significant change was the appearance of a front-facing head wearing a helmet with a triple-strand moustache made up of three lines. Whilst the obverse is a major departure from previous coins, the reverse features the long cross design with crudely engraved 'hands', pellets and crosses in the quarters.

Fig. 7— Penny, Phase Four, facing helmeted bust, 1060–5. *SNC*, February 1998, No. 25

This phase was the last to make any pretence of trying to follow the Sitric model introduced some 60 years earlier. With the exception of the brief rule of Gudrod Sitricson (1072–5), the Hiberno-Norse kingdom of Dublin was to be ruled by the local Irish kings and chiefs for the next 55 years. It is reasonable to assume that there was little dynastic or civic interest on the part of the native Irish rulers in producing coins. Coins were principally required by traders and merchants, not by the political authorities, and it is perhaps in this context that the next phase of Ireland's Hiberno-Norse coinage needs to be considered.

Fig. 8— Penny, Phase Five, 1065-5. *SNC*, February 1998, No. 26

This next or fifth phase, which was to last for about 30 years from 1065 to 1095, is characterised by the production of imitations of a wide range of coins of the late Saxon and early Norman rulers of England. The coins were exceptionally crude in production, with blundered legends and smaller than the original coins from which they were copied. Amongst the English coins to be copied were pennies of Aethelred II (including the earlier CRUX-type coin which had inspired Sitric's first coin), Canute, Harthacnut, Edward the Confessor and Harold II. The coins of the early Norman rulers of England, William I and William II, were also copied, as were coins of some Scandinavian rulers. One group of coins struck during this period may have been based on the 'Agnus Dei' coins of Aethelred II, which some numismatists believe to have been struck to mark the first millennium in about 1000–1010. The later Hiberno-Norse coins, struck almost a century later, feature on the obverse a creature more akin to a galloping horse than the Lamb of God; it is possible that these may be an imitation of the original Aethelred coin or an Irish copy of a Scandinavian copy of the original coin!

Fig. 9— Penny, Phase Five, copied from William I canopy-type penny with tribach of three birds on reverse, 1065-5. *SNC*, February 1998, No. 27

The sixth phase, from 1095 to approximately 1110, saw a return by Hiberno-Norse moneyers to copying even cruder versions or what are described as 'degraded imitations' of the earlier Long Cross coins of previous issues.

The final phase in the Hiberno-Norse series dates from 1110 to about 1150 and consists of a series of coins which are known as semi-bracteates and bracteates. These coins, whilst much larger than the previously issued Hiberno-Norse coins, were so thin that the design on one side could be seen inverted on the other. The semi-bracteates normally featured on the obverse a crude bust, and on the reverse a series of designs based on a cross design inspired by the previous Sitric III coins. Because of the thinness of the coins, the designs on both sides were struck separately on a piece of wood or leather rather than between a pair of iron

Fig. 10— Semi-bracteate, 1110–50. *SNC*, February 1998, No. 30

dies. Inevitably, traces of the design on one side of the coin showed through, resulting in poorly defined coins.

The bracteate coins, which were probably issued between 1130 and 1150, some time later than the semi-bracteates, are much finer in the quality of design. They featured a design on only one side, with an incuse version or shadow of the design appearing on the other side. All the designs on the bracteate coins have a cross as the central motif, with a range of abstract symbols; some twenty different designs are known in this series.

Bracteate coins are not unique to Ireland; the early Greeks had manufactured similar uniface coins or 'shadow' coins, which were buried with the dead to accompany them on their journey to the world of shadows. At the same time as bracteate coins were being struck in Ireland they were also being struck in Germany, where they were known as 'hollow pennies'. Because of their thinness the coins were very fragile and could easily be bent or damaged. It is unlikely that these coins saw any real circulation in Germany; they were probably struck for specific purposes, such as the payment of taxes or tithes or as ceremonial offerings to the church or a king.

The Irish bracteates are similarly fragile and this probably accounts for their extreme rarity.

Fig. 11— Bracteate, 1110–50. Seaby and Purvey 1984, No. 6193

With the collapse of Viking rule in eleventh- and twelfth-century Ireland, it is questionable how many of the coins issued from about 1110 to 1150 can be directly attributed to the Hiberno-Norse rulers of Dublin. The largest hoard of these bracteate coins was found in Castlelyons in County Cork, well away from the areas where Hiberno-Norse coins are known to have circulated.

A fleeting reference in the medieval text *Cambrensis Eversus* states that the Irish high king Turlogh Ua Conchobair (O'Connor) (1119–56) 'ordered silver to be struck at Clonmacnoise' (Dolley 1966, 142–3). Some numismatists believe that these bracteate coins, which are so different from the Hiberno-Norse coins issued over the last 120 years, could be the silver struck at Clonmacnoise, and as such might be the first native Irish coins.

Whether these bracteate coins were to mark the birth of a new Irish coinage will never be known. In early May 1169 a group of knights strode ashore at Bannow Island, just off the Wexford coast, and the next phase in Ireland's numismatic history was about to begin.

2. LORD AND KING
The coins of the early Normans (1185–1211)

In August 1170 the Norman adventurer Richard FitzGilbert landed in Ireland with an army of a thousand men to restore Diarmait MacMurchada, the exiled king of Leinster, to his throne. The earlier success of the offensive at Bannow and the seizure of Wexford by Robert FitzStephen and his force of Normans, Flemings and Welsh soldiers, provided the launching pad for a major invasion of Ireland. Waterford was seized within days, and within weeks FitzGilbert's and Diarmait's forces had taken Dublin and deposed Asculf MacTorkil, the last Hiberno-Norse king.

Within a year Diarmait was dead and FitzGilbert, or 'Strongbow' as he was to become known to history, had succeeded his father-in-law to the kingdom of Leinster.

It was the prospect of his feudal subjects establishing themselves as kings on the borders of his Angevin empire that prompted Henry II, supported by a fleet of 400 ships and the bull *Laudabiliter* giving papal authority for an invasion, to sail for Ireland in October 1171 and reassert his authority over his errant knights.

Over a period of eight months, Henry received the submission of Strongbow and his companions and regranted territories previously seized by the Norman knights. In a series of ceremonies, he also offered his protection to a number of Irish kings and chieftains who were willing to recognise his authority, although the Irish were soon to find that royal protection could not save them from the territorial ambitions of the Normans. Henry retained for the Crown the city of Dublin and the surrounding lands that ultimately formed the English Pale, as well as the old Viking port towns of Waterford, Wexford and Limerick.

In 1175 Henry's position in Ireland was further consolidated when Ruaidri Ua Conchobair, the high king of Ireland, recognised Henry's overlordship over the Anglo-Norman territories in Leinster and Meath in the Treaty of Windsor. In 1177 Henry created his nine-year-old son, John, lord of Ireland, a first step in establishing Ireland as a separate kingdom within the Angevin empire.

In March 1185 John arrived in Ireland to take personal control of his lordship. His eight months there proved to be a diplomatic disaster, as he alienated many of the Irish kings and chieftains, and some of the great Norman lords, who had sworn allegiance to his father thirteen years earlier.

Fig. 12—Halfpenny, John as lord of Ireland, first coinage, 1185. *Spink: Irish Coin Values* (1979), No. 35

The first coins to be issued by the Norman invaders were probably struck in 1185, the year Prince John as lord of Ireland made his first visit to Ireland. The coin was a silver halfpenny. On the obverse it featured a head facing left within a circle and the legend 'IOHANNES' (John). The reverse featured a cross potent with a lis and pellet in each quarter within a circle, with the name of the moneyer forming the legend. Four moneyers' names are to be found on this coin: ELIS, RAUL, BLUNT and ROGER. It is generally accepted that the names on these coins refer to three men rather than four — the 'RAUL' and 'BLUNT' being the forename and surname of one moneyer, Raul Blunt.

It has been suggested that the choice of a halfpenny, rather than a penny or denier, which was the principal circulating coin in England and Europe, may reflect the 'supposed inferior' or subordinate position of Ireland as a lordship within the Angevin empire, rather than a fully-fledged kingdom.

This first Norman coin is loosely based on the design of a penny issued by William the Lion of Scotland (1165–1214).

This first John halfpenny has also been attributed to another John, the Norman lord John de Courcy, lord or 'prince' of Ulster. De Courcy embodied Henry II's worst fears concerning his Norman knights. Arriving in Ireland in 1176, he amassed a force of 300 men and invaded the kingdom of Ulaid (Ulster) in 1177, deposing its king and bringing the modern territory of Down and Antrim under his control as lord of Ulster, or sometime self-styled prince of Ulster.

De Courcy, despite his personal ambitions, was to maintain an uneasy relationship with John and his lieutenants in Ireland from 1185 to 1195. Indeed, at times during this period he acted as justiciar or governor of the lordship on John's behalf.

De Courcy in his territories promoted his own personal devotion to St Patrick through the endowment of churches and monasteries. It also found an outlet in his coins, a series of silver halfpennies and farthings that he ordered to be struck in his capital of Downpatrick between 1185 and 1204. This series of coins are known as the 'St Patrick' coinage because of their reference to the saint on the obverse legends.

The halfpenny, which is now unique, featured on the obverse a crozier and a cross set in a circle with the legend 'PATRICUS' (Patrick). The reverse featured a cross pattée (a cross with annulets with a pellet at the end of each branch) with a pellet in each quarter within a circle, with the legend 'IOH'S DE CVRCI' (John de Courcy). The farthing, which is also extremely rare, featured on the obverse a cross pattée with a pellet in each quarter with the legend 'PATRICI' (Patrick). The reverse featured a voided cross within a circle with the legend 'GOAN D CVRCI' (John de Courcy).

Fig. 13—Halfpenny, John de Courcy, Downpatrick, 1185–1204. Seaby and Purvey 1984, No. 6223

A further issue of St Patrick farthings was made by de Courcy sometime after 1195; whilst following essentially the same design as the previous farthings, they make no reference to de Courcy and are known as the 'Anonymous' St Patrick's issue. The first farthing features on the obverse a processional cross or voided cross within a circle and the legend 'PATRICII' (Patrick). The reverse features a cross potent with a crescent in each angle within a circle with the mint signature of 'DE DÙNO' (of Downpatrick), a reference to the mint town.

Fig. 14—Farthing, Anonymous St Patrick coinage, John de Courcy, 1195–1205. *SNC*, February 1998, No. 38

Two further types of farthing exist in this series; they essentially follow the design of the Downpatrick farthing but feature two different types of cross on the reverse, as well as the legend 'CRAJ' (of Carrickfergus), the mint town of these farthings. All these latter farthings are also very rare. An example of the Downpatrick farthing sold at Whyte's Millennial Collection Sale (29 April 2000) for £IR2,800 and a Carrickfergus farthing for £IR2,600.

From 1201 de Courcy was increasingly to find himself at odds with the de Lacy brothers, John's principal representatives in Ireland. In 1204 his territories were invaded and he was overthrown.

In about 1190 a second series of coins, consisting of silver halfpennies and farthings, was issued in the name of Prince John. This second series is known as the Dominus coinage because the coins include the prince's title *dominus* (lord) as part of the obverse legend. These new coins were initially struck only in Dublin between 1190 and 1194. It is believed that minting was halted during 1194 when John de Courcy led a revolt against John's deputy, Peter Pipard, in the name of John's older brother, Richard Coeur de Lion. Production resumed once again in about 1195.

The halfpenny features on the obverse a 'man in the moon'-like portrait of the prince wearing a diadem or band on his head within a circle and the legend 'IOHANNES DOMIN YBER' (John lord of Ireland). The legend varies slightly on coins, with the prince's title being contracted in different ways. The reverse features a small cross potent (a cross with arms with short cross-bars on the end) with an annulet in each quarter within a circle. The reverse legend features the mint and the name of the moneyer. The Dublin coins bear the contracted mint signatures of 'DWE', 'DVVE', 'DW', 'DV', combined with the names of some eight moneyers: Adam, Huge, Nicholas, Norman, Rodberd, Tomas, Turgood and Willelm. The first halfpennies between 1190 and 1194 were struck on a large flan; subsequent issues after de Courcy's revolt were struck on a slightly smaller flan, from 1195 to 1198.

Fig. 15—Halfpenny, John as lord of Ireland, second coinage, 1190–9. *SNC*, February 1998, No. 32

A variation of the Dublin halfpenny features an obverse with the legend 'IOHANNES DE MO' rather than *dominus Hibernia*. This is believed to reflect the prince's title of count of Mortain, which was granted to John following his marriage in 1198 by Richard I.

A further Dublin variation featuring a small cross pommée instead of a cross potent on the reverse design was also struck between 1198 and 1199.

A second mint was established in Waterford in 1195 and mints were also established in Limerick and Kilkenny in about 1197. The Kilkenny mint was, however, to be short-lived and it is understood that production ceased within two years of its opening, possibly owing to a legal dispute regarding the burghal or civic status of the town and its right to mint coins.

Halfpennies similar in design to the Dublin small-flan issue were struck at mints in Waterford, Kilkenny and Limerick as well as at de Courcy's mints at Carrickfergus and Downpatrick from 1190 to 1199. The reverse legend on the coins in each case features the mint signature of the town and the moneyer.

On the Waterford coins the mint signature is abbreviated to 'WATER', 'WATE', 'WA' or 'VVA'. Eight moneyers operated out of the Waterford mint, including Davi, Gefrei, Geifri, Marcus, Robert, Walter, Willem, Willelmus and Willmus. In the case of Waterford, one type of halfpenny bears the obverse legend 'IOHANNES COMI' (Count John) which may date it to 1198 or later.

Kilkenny coins were distinguished on the reverse with the mint signature 'KIL' or 'KEN' and the names of the three moneyers, Andreh, Simund and Waltex.

Limerick halfpennies featured 'LIM' on the reverse legend and were all struck by one moneyer, Siward.

Halfpennies of similar design were also struck at Carrickfergus by the moneyer Roberd. These included John's title as lord of Ireland, but another variety include the obverse legend 'CAPUT IONIS PEGIS' (the head of King John). Halfpennies issued by the Downpatrick mint also bear the legend 'CAPUT IOHANIS PEG'. The Carrickfergus coins with the normal 'dominus' legend bear the mint signature 'CRAC' or 'CRAG' and the name of the moneyer Roberd. The later 'head of the king' coins feature the mint signature 'CCFECIG' or 'CRACFOR' and the names of the moneyers Salmo and Thomas. The Downpatrick coins all feature the 'head of the king' legend and have the mint signature 'DVNO' and the name of the moneyer Thomas.

It is assumed that the Carrickfergus and Downpatrick pennies were struck after 1199 when John succeeded to the English crown following the death of Richard Coeur de Lion. The 'caput' pennies of Carrickfergus roughly coincide with the last year of de Courcy's revolt against John's authority and it is thought that they may indicate an attempt by de Courcy to reconcile himself to the new king through a very public display of loyalty. It is possible, however, that these 'loyal' coins may have further provoked John's anger, as he may have seen their production as an infringement of his prerogatives and rights as de Courcy's liege lord.

A less likely interpretation is that the reference to 'king' on these coins may not have been an acknowledgement of John's overlordship but rather a reaffirmation of de Courcy's own position as independent ruler of Ulster!

Fig. 16—Mascle farthing, John as lord of Ireland, second coinage, Adam of Dublin, 1190–9. *SNC,* February 1998, No. 36

Alongside the Dominus halfpennies, small and crudely designed farthings were also issued. These did not include any reference to John as lord of Ireland or the mint town. The obverse of these tiny coins featured a mascle (a lozenge-shaped heraldic device) with trefoils (a flower-like device with three petals) at the corners, the design occupying all of the available space. The reverse featured a cross with four letters of the moneyer's name in the angles of the coin. From these abbreviated names it is possible to establish that farthings were struck in Dublin by the moneyers Adam (ADAM), Nicholas (NICO), Norman (NORM), Rodberd (ROBD) and Tomas (TOMA). Similarly farthings were struck at the Waterford mint by Marcus (MARC), Walter (WALT) and Gefrei (GEFR), and in Limerick by Siward (SIWA).

Whilst the Dominus halfpennies, particularly of Dublin and Waterford, are relatively common, all the Dominus farthings are rare. In 1970 it was believed that fewer than 30 of John's mascle farthings may have survived. It is possible that just under a hundred of these coins survive. These small, fragile coins, produced in small numbers, have been described as the 'numismatic workhorses' of their day, being used in most everyday financial transactions. The coins inevitably were quickly worn and chipped, and were of such low value that they were seldom hoarded. A mascle farthing of the Dublin moneyer Adam sold at the Whyte's Millennial Sale for £IR600.

The early years of the thirteenth century saw John and his Angevin territories drawn into a series of wars with King Philip II of France. John looked to his Irish lordship to provide men, supplies and, increasingly, money to finance his Continental campaigns. It was this need for money for his war chest that prompted John's third and final issue of coinage.

John's third coinage was issued between 1205 and 1211. It is known as the 'Rex' coinage because it features John's new title of king, *Rex*.

The new coinage was struck to the same weight and fineness as John's English coins (11oz. 2dwt or .925 fineness), making the coins acceptable in England and on the Continent. These new coins consisted of a silver penny, halfpenny and farthing, and this was the first time all three denominations were struck together. A three-denomination system of penny, halfpenny and farthing was not to be introduced into England for another 70 years. The penny was to weigh 22 grains, the halfpenny 10½ grains and the farthing 5½ grains, the slightly lower weight of the halfpenny and farthing reflecting the higher costs of manufacturing these coins.

The penny or 'denariis Hiberniae' features on the obverse a facing crowned portrait of the king holding a sceptre within a triangle (the three points of the triangle touching the edge of the coin) with the legend 'JOHANNE' or 'JOHANNES REX'. The use of the triangle on John's coins has been the subject of discussion. It has been suggested that the inverted triangle that appeared on the later coins of Edward I might have been a reference to the harp. The general consensus, however, seems to be that John's triangle was simply a device to differentiate his Irish coins from those of his English mints. The triangle device was to be copied in time by other medieval European rulers.

Fig. 17—Penny, John as king, Roberd of Dublin, 1207–11. *SNC*, February 1998, No. 39

The reverse design of the penny was a major departure from previous coins, featuring a stylised sun, moon and three stars within a triangle and a legend including the mint signature and the moneyer's name. Pennies were struck in Dublin with the moneyers' names Roberd, Iohen, Willem and Wilelm P, the 'P' possibly to differentiate between Wilelm and Willem.

The unusual sun, moon and stars device — all symbols of light — is believed to be a reference to the king's patron saint, John the Baptist, who according to the Gospel of St John was 'a witness to the light' (John I.VIII).

Pennies of a similar design were manufactured in Limerick with the moneyers' names of 'Wace' and 'Willem'. Pennies were also struck later at Waterford with the moneyer's name 'Willem'.

The later years of John's rule saw an increasing centralisation of control over the production of coins by the royal administration. The mint in Dublin was to be situated in the new castle that John had begun in 1204. Responsibility for the production and overseeing of the issue of coins shifted from the men who struck the coins or prominent citizens who oversaw their manufacture and issue to the great officers of state. John's moneyer on his Dublin coins from 1207 to 1210, Roberd, was Robert of Bedford, who was later to become bishop of Lismore. The names 'Willem' and 'Wace' that appear on Dublin, Limerick and Waterford coins are believed to represent another high official, William Wace, who was later to become bishop of Waterford.

Fig. 18—Halfpenny, John as king of Ireland, Roberd of Dublin, 1207–11. *SNC*, May 1995, No. 2761

The halfpenny featured on the obverse a facing crowned bust of the king within a triangle and the legend 'IOHAN REX'. The reverse featured a cross, moon and stars within a triangle and the legend 'ROBERD' or 'WILLEM ON DIVE', Roberd or Willem of Dublin. On some coins the Dublin mint signature is represented by 'DI' or 'D'.

Fig. 19—Halfpenny, John as king of Ireland, Willem of Limerick, 1207–11. *SNC*, February 1998, No. 44

As with the pennies, halfpennies were also struck at Limerick to the same design with the reverse legend 'WILLEM' or 'WACE ON LI', William or Wace of Limerick, and at Waterford with the reverse legend 'WILLEM VA', Willem of Waterford.

Like the pennies and halfpennies, the tiny farthings featured the king's portrait in a triangle with the legend 'IOHAN REX'. The reverse design featured a stylised sun in a triangle. The size of the coin meant that there was sometimes only space for the moneyers' name to appear without a mint signature. Two moneyers' names appear on John's Rex farthings — Roberd and Willem. Whilst the coins do not have a mint signature, it is assumed that they were struck at Dublin. Some farthings are known to exist which include a mint signature 'OND', 'of Dublin'.

Until recently it was generally assumed that farthings were only struck at the Dublin mint. However, in February 2001 a farthing with the mint signature 'WACON LI', 'Wace of Limerick', was identified for the first time, raising the question of whether, if farthings were minted at Limerick, they could also have been produced at Waterford.

The John Rex farthings are extremely rare. A farthing of Willem of Dublin sold at the Whyte's Millennial Sale for £IR1,500.

The new pennies soon found their way out of Ireland. Official documents, the Close Rolls of 1205, record a payment for the carriage of 400 marks of Irish pennies from Nottingham to Exeter and on to the Continent. A mark was a unit of account of 13s 4d or 160 pennies; this transaction alone saw 64,000 Irish pennies being transported out of Ireland to fund John's Continental campaigns. Whilst the pennies were principally for export, the smaller number of halfpennies and farthings were mainly for local use.

It is thought that an order was issued in 1207 to call in and demonetise the Dominus halfpennies and farthings issued before 1200. The old coins were melted down and recoined as new Rex coins. There is some doubt as to whether all the Dominus coins were withdrawn at this time. A small hoard of 22 Irish coins found in France in 1986 and probably hidden away by an Irish soldier fighting in the 1213–14 French campaigns included a mixture of Dominus and Rex coins, which would suggest that some five years after the order of 1207 both types of coins were continuing to circulate and be accepted.

In June 1210 King John made his second visit to Ireland to consolidate his authority over the Anglo-Norman barons and the Irish kings and chieftains. Over a period of nine weeks he re-established his control in Leinster, Meath and Ulster. It is possible that the mints at Limerick and Waterford were opened at this time to finance the king's Irish campaign. It is generally felt that minting operations were short-lived at these two sites, possibly a matter of months, production stopping once all local supplies of silver had been exhausted.

The early thirteenth century saw Ireland drained of its silver; as bullion supplies dried up production slowed down. This state of affairs is reflected in the surviving coins from that period, with the coins of Robert of Bedford produced in the early years of John's last recoinage being much commoner than the pennies of William Wace produced in 1210–11.

With the completion of John's recoinage in about 1211 no Irish coins were to be struck for another 40 years. The currency needs of England's Irish colony would be met by Irish halfpennies and farthings that would become increasingly worn and chipped, supplemented by English coins.

3. LIKE FATHER, LIKE SON
The coinage of Henry III and Edward I
(1251–1302)

Henry III ascended the throne at the age of nine following the death of his father, King John, in 1216. It was not until 1251, however, 35 years after his accession, that a coinage in the name of Henry III was struck for Ireland. For the early part of his reign the monetary needs of the Anglo-Irish territories and the main port towns were met by the coins of his father issued some 40 years earlier and imported English pennies. The introduction of this new Irish coinage, as with John's last coinage, followed a major recoinage in England in 1247.

Henry III's reign was characterised by the further extension of Anglo-Norman influence in Ireland into the lands of the native Irish and the consolidation of royal authority in his Anglo-Irish territories through a series of reforms to the central administration in Dublin Castle, including the establishment of a new chancery, expansion of the role of the royal treasury, and the introduction of English courts and legal systems. Like his father, Henry was to find himself engaged in a series of costly wars on the Continent.

It was this need for money to finance his wars which was to prompt the striking of a new coinage for Ireland in 1251. Some five years earlier, Henry, desperate for money, borrowed 10,000 marks (£6,667) from his younger brother, Richard, earl of Cornwall. In return Richard was granted the right to strike new money in the king's name in England, Ireland and Wales from the feast day of All Saints (1 November 1247) for twelve years. The king was also to receive a moiety, part of the profits from the production and exchange of the new coins. Despite this payment to his brother, it was estimated that the earl would make total profits from the scheme of £20,000, a threefold return on his loan.

Whilst coins were struck in England, none were struck in Ireland. On 8 May 1251 a further 'Licence to coin new money in Ireland in the King's name, for 12 years from the Feast of the Nativity of the Blessed Virgin' (8 September 1251) (Dykes 1963, 102) was granted to the earl of Cornwall in exchange for a further loan of 2,000 marks (£1,333) to the king. Richard was promised a generous share of the profits from the mint and the exchanges or *cambii* that would issue the new coins in exchange for old coins.

On 17 September 1251 Roger de Haverhull was appointed warden of the change (Cambii) throughout Ireland and master of the mint in Ireland. A mint was established in Dublin Castle and it is probable that whilst most of the unskilled workers were local men, the coiners who struck the coins were sent from London or brought over from the Continent. Roger de Haverhull was to receive payment of 40 marks and the church of 'Kyngeston' for his efforts.

A *cambium* or exchange was established in Dublin outside the castle walls, and 'mints' or *cambii* were established in Limerick and Carrickfergus. There is a view that these 'mints' were essentially currency exchanges as there are no records of minting equipment being supplied to them. Official documents record that coins took four days to be carried from Dublin to Limerick, where a house was rented as a mint at 4d a week for eighteen months from September 1252 to March 1254. Other records note £2,000 in coin (480,000 pennies) being sent to the Carrickfergus mint to meet the needs of Ulster.

Native Irish records similarly note some of the events around this recoinage. The Annals of Loch Cé state that in 1252 'new money was ordered by the king of the Saxons to be coined in Erinn, and the money previously in use was abandoned for it' (Dykes 1963, 102).

Fig. 20—Penny, Henry III, Davi of Dublin (Class 1A), 1251–4. *SNC*, May 1995, No. 2763

Henry's new coinage was to consist entirely of silver pennies and all were to be struck at Dublin, to the same weight and fineness (.925) as his English pennies.

The obverse was similar in design to John's Rex coinage, with a crowned facing portrait of the king holding a sceptre and a cinquefoil (a heraldic flower with five petals) to the right of the bust within a double triangle with the legend 'HENRICUS REX III' (King Henry III). The reverse design was based on the new 'long cross' coins which had been introduced in England in 1247 and featured a voided cross pommée stretching to the edge of the coin with three pellets in each quarter and a legend with the mint signature 'DAVI' or 'RICARD ON DIVELI' or 'DIVE': Davi (David) or Ricard (Richard) of Dublin.

Fig. 21—Penny, Henry III, Ricard of Dublin (Class IJd), 1251–4. *SNC*, May 1995, No. 2769

The moneyers referred to on the coins are believed to be David of Enfield and Richard Bonaventure. They were two prominent London moneyers who were responsible for supervising the preparation of the Irish dies in London and their conveyance to Dublin. They were also responsible for recruiting the coiners and other skilled craftsmen to work at the Dublin mint. Despite the linking of their names with the mint signatures of Dublin, it is questionable whether they directly supervised the production of the new coins in Dublin, or ever visited Ireland. It is estimated that some 500 obverse and reverse dies were to be used to produce Henry III's coinage. About three quarters of all the coins struck have the mint signature of Ricard and the remaining quarter that of Davi. A similar split in the proportion of coins produced by the two moneyers can also be seen in the coins attributed to them in England, which probably reflects some financial arrangement between the two men.

Nine varieties of the penny are known with minor differences to the obverse design, including the use of a single rather than a double triangle to frame the king's portrait, a sixfoil instead of a cinquefoil, three curls of hair instead of two, and small differences in the design of the crown and sceptre.

No halfpennies or farthings were struck during the reign of Henry III, although the penny's reverse design of the voided long cross lent itself to being cut into halves and quarters for use as halfpennies and farthings.

Pennies were struck between the autumn of 1251 and January 1254, when the Dublin mint again closed. The *cambium* continued to operate for a few months after the closure of the mint. The exchange of old coin for new coins was not without risk: a Carrickfergus clergyman was fined 28s 2d for producing old halfpennies which were newly clipped — whether it was the priest's doing or one of his parishioners passing them off in the collection box is not known!

The coin, with its high silver content, was to circulate not only in Ireland but also in England and on the Continent, and as a design it was to be copied as far away as Saxony in the Holy Roman Empire. Most of the pennies were to find their way out of Ireland. Almost half of all the surviving examples of Henry III's pennies are believed to originate from Continental hoards. One hoard found near Brussels in 1908 yielded 1,800 Irish pennies of Henry III.

It is estimated that £43,000 worth of pennies was to be produced, over ten million coins in 27 months. Richard de Haverhull as master of the mint in Ireland was principally charged with locating bullion to turn into coin. As an incentive he was to receive a commission on every pound of silver coined. By the time the Dublin mint closed on 8 January 1254 de Haverhull was £500 richer and Ireland's silver supplies were exhausted.

In the same year Henry III created his eldest son Edward lord of Ireland. Whilst Henry II had envisaged a separate lordship or kingdom of Ireland for his son John, Henry III was adamant that the lordship of Ireland should never be separated from the crown of England. Ireland, or that part of the island controlled by the Anglo-Irish, now found itself in a new constitutional position *vis-à-vis* England.

It was, however, to be another 22 years before Edward exercised his prerogative to strike coins for his lordship and by this point he was king of England, following the death of Henry III in 1272. Edward's first Irish coinage was issued between 1276 and 1279. The coins were a direct copy of the earlier Henry III 'long cross' pennies issued some 20 years earlier, even to the extent that they bore the late king's name. This practice of issuing coins in the name of a late monarch was not unusual; Richard I and John had issued English coins in the name of their late father, Henry II, and Edward I's first English coins were similarly struck with the name and titles of his father. It is possible that this reluctance to change designs was due to the fact that most of the population were illiterate at the time and probably wary of new coins with unfamiliar portraits and legends.

The coinage of Ireland at this time was in a very poor condition, mainly clipped or lightweight with 'five or six different sorts of base and mixed money being privately imported into England and Ireland and uttered for sterlings (pennies) though not worth about one half-penny' (Simon 1749, 14).

Fig. 22—Penny, Edward I in name of Henry III, Richard Olaf of Dublin, 1276–9. *SNC*, February 1998, No. 51

This first coinage of Edward I consisted entirely of pennies and was struck in Dublin under the supervision of the Dublin goldsmith Richard Olaf, who was appointed mint master in 1276. His name as 'Ricard' was to appear on the reverse of these pennies. A record in the Irish Exchequer Payments notes that Richard the Goldsmith was paid £3 6s 8d for various utensils and other necessary items for the mint in Michaelmas term 1275.

The obverse of the penny featured a crude crowned facing bust of the king holding a sceptre within a triangle and the legend 'HENRICVS REX III' (King Henry III). The reverse featured the long cross and pellets design of the previous coinage with the legend 'RICARD ON DIVE' (Richard of Dublin).

This later penny can be distinguished from the earlier pennies of Henry III because the portrait of the king has more realistic hair than the stylised curls of the earlier coinage. A variety of this penny occurs with the 'V' in the legend being replaced by a Lombardic 'U', the legends reading 'HENRICUS' and 'DIUE'. These first pennies of Edward I are very rare; most were intentionally melted down in the great recoinage of 1280, and it is possible that as few as twelve may exist. An example in the Whyte's Millennial Collection Sale (April 2001) sold for £IR1,300, and two years earlier another example sold for £IR1,150.

This coinage was to be short-lived. In 1279 Edward embarked on a major recoinage in England and Ireland; the coins of his father, Henry III, and his own first-issue coins were called in and melted down to be replaced by his second coinage, which was issued at intervals between 1279 and 1302.

Edward's reign, like those of his predecessors, was marked by further consolidation of royal authority, and increased revenues were required to support his campaigns in Wales, Flanders, Gascony and Scotland. The reign saw a further expansion of Anglo-Norman influence across Ireland into the west and the south-west, and the first attempted plantation of English peasants as colonists in Leinster, Meath and Munster, and as far as western Mayo and Dingle.

The responsibility for overseeing Edward's recoinage fell to Stephen de Fulbourn, the treasurer of the lordship of Ireland, and his brother Walter, the deputy treasurer. It was to be a major logistical exercise. An account in the royal records, the Pipe Rolls, refers to the Irish mint accounts from 1 May 1279 to Michaelmas 1286 'for wages and subsistence of 82 moneyers and workmen who went from London to Ireland £49 14s 8d, that is to say 13s 4d for each of the eight and 12s for each of the seventy four' (Dykes 1963, 103).

A series of accounts relating to the early 1280s and the recoinage can also be traced through the Irish Exchequer Payments records and provide some insight into the people involved and the working of the king's great recoinage. In 1281 reference is made to a payment of £6 13s 4d to Bartholomew the Goldsmith for services in the foundry and the mint, and to a payment of £124 16s 0d to Walter Unred and his associates in the mint for making dies, which might suggest that some of the early dies may have been engraved in Dublin rather than sent from London. A further payment of £10 0s 0d was made by the Irish exchequer to Walter Unred in 1283 for keeping the king's mint for three years at his own expense. A record of 1282 notes a payment of £2 0s 0d to Peter the Chaplain of Dublin Castle for his wages as keeper of the cutting of the king's coins from 25 March 1281 to 25 March 1283.

The new Irish coins were struck to the same standard as Edward's English coins (.925 fineness), the standard that was increasingly known as sterling silver; the penny weighed 20 grains, the halfpenny 10 grains and the farthing, which was slightly debased, 6–6½ grains.

Modern numismatists have divided the coins of Edward's recoinage from 1279 to 1302 into four groups or six issues. The first group comprises the three issues from 1280 to 1284, while the three other groups correspond to issues in 1294, 1295 and 1297–1302.

The first of Edward's six issues occurred in 1280. The obverse design of the penny featured a crowned facing portrait of the king within an inverted triangle with a trefoil of pellets on the king's breast. As mentioned in the previous chapter, it is thought that the use of the inverted triangle by Edward I may be an allusion to the Irish harp, as the earliest known reference to the harp as the heraldic symbol of Ireland dates from about the 1270s.

The obverse legend reads 'EDWR ANGL DNS HYB' (Edward, king of Ireland, lord of Ireland). The reverse features a long cross with three pellets in each quarter and, in a departure from the coins of Sitric, John and Henry III, the legend reads 'CIVITAS DUBLINIE' (city or town of Dublin). With Edward's second coinage, the practice of incorporating the name of the moneyer into the legend of the coin ceased. It is generally assumed that the dies were prepared in London and shipped to Dublin for the manufacture of these coins. Minor variations or mint marks (secret devices incorporated into the design of the coin) allowed officials to differentiate between the dies produced by various engravers.

The new coinage also included halfpennies and farthings, and both these coins were struck in Dublin in 1280. Both followed essentially the same design as the penny, although the farthing had a shortened obverse legend, 'ERA NG LIE' (Edward, king of England). An extremely rare version of this 1280 issue has the more detailed legend 'EDWARDUS REX' (King Edward).

It is believed that this first issue of coins was short-lived, the mint probably opening for only a few months. This issue was followed by the more substantial issue of 1281–2, which follows the same design as the first issue but with the incorporation of a pellet just before the start of 'EDWR' in the legend. The penny and the halfpenny were both struck at the Dublin mint.

In 1281 a second mint was opened at Waterford. It is possible that the first choice for a mint might have been Roscommon, but Stephen de Fulbourn, as well as being treasurer of Ireland, was bishop of Waterford, and the prospect of a seignorage or a proportion of the profits on every pound of silver coined that was due to the incumbent bishop may have influenced his decision to settle on Waterford. The Exchequer records indicate that the de Fulbourn brothers took a personal interest in the Waterford mint. One entry notes that Stephen de Fulbourn personally delivered £200 of silver by weight to the mint, and another records that Walter de Fulbourn at the Waterford mint received £97 1s 6d from the citizens of Cork. Whatever the reasons for its choice, minting operations at Waterford were to be short-lived. The mint closed in 1282, having exhausted local supplies of silver, but not before yielding a handsome profit. The Exchequer records of 1281–2 note a payment of £1,352 1s 6½d to the keepers of the Waterford mint. In 1286 Stephen de Fulbourn was appointed archbishop of Tuam. In turn, his brother Walter was made bishop of Waterford, ensuring that any future revenue from the Waterford mint was kept in the family!

The mint at Waterford issued pennies, halfpennies and farthings between 1281 and 1282. The coins essentially follow the same design as the Dublin coins, the reverse legend reading 'CIVITAS WATERFOR' (city or town of Waterford). Varieties exist which read 'VATERFOR'. The pennies produced at Waterford, in common with the Dublin coins of this issue, have a trefoil of three pellets on the king's breast and a pellet before the word 'EDWR' on the obverse legend. Two types of halfpenny were also produced by the Waterford mint, one with and one without a pellet before the obverse legend. The Waterford farthing, like the Dublin farthing, bore the abbreviated legend 'ERA NG LIE' (Edward, king of England).

Fig. 23—Penny, Edward I, Waterford, 1279–84. *SNC*, May 1995, No. 2776

Fig. 24—Halfpenny, Edward I, Waterford (Group Ib), 1281–2. *SNC*, May 1995, No. 2780

Fig. 25—Farthing, Edward I, Waterford, 1281–2. *SNC*, May 1995, No. 2792

The pennies of this second issue from Dublin and Waterford are probably the most common of all the medieval Irish coins available today.

Fig. 26—Penny, Edward I, Cork (Type III), 1295. *SNC*, February 1998, No. 56

A third issue of pennies and halfpennies occurred in 1283. These coins were only struck in Dublin. The pennies were distinguished by having a small cross before 'EDWR' in the obverse legend or a Lombardic 'n' in the reverse legend. The halfpennies of this issue, whilst featuring a pellet, can be distinguished from the second halfpennies because a Lombardic 'E' is used in the obverse legend.

A fourth issue of coins occurred in 1294. These can be differentiated from earlier issues as they featured a rosette or heraldic rose instead of three pellets on the king's breast. The lettering on these coins is also more irregular or cruder than the coins issued between 1280 and 1283. Pennies and halfpennies were struck at the reopened Dublin and Waterford mints, although minting operations were short-lived and the mint closed again in 1295. It is thought that the dies used in Waterford may have been locally engraved, either in Waterford or Dublin, rather than being sent from London.

A fifth issue of pennies and halfpennies took place in 1295. The pennies minted at Dublin can be distinguished from earlier issues as they have a pellet incorporated into the points or angles of the triangle on the obverse. These Dublin pennies are extremely rare. It is generally assumed that no halfpennies were issued by the Dublin mint in 1295, although in 1992 a halfpenny was identified with a pellet below the bust of the king and another in the upper left angle or point of the triangle which has been attributed to the Dublin issue of 1295.

Pennies and halfpennies were also struck at a new mint in Cork. It is believed that Thomas Fitzmaurice Fitzgerald, the new justiciar of Ireland, established the new mint of Cork deep in the heartland of his Desmond territories. Fitzgerald's decisions may have been influenced, like those of de Fulbourn, by the prospect of a seignorage on every coin struck in his territories!

The Cork coins followed the same design as the Dublin 1295 pennies, with the reverse legend of 'CIVITAS CORCAGIE' or 'CORCACIE' (city of Cork). Both the Dublin and the Cork pennies of this issue are very rare. It is thought that the dies for the 1295 coinage were produced in Ireland, possibly in Dublin, rather than being sent from London. The halfpennies issued by the Cork mint are extremely rare; it is believed that only six exist. One such halfpenny sold for £IR1,400 at the Whyte's Millennial Collection Sale.

The appointment of Sir John Wogan as the new justiciar of Ireland in place of Fitzgerald saw the closure of the Cork mint later in 1295. Wogan, mindful of King Edward's own prerogatives relating to the seignorage from the production of coins, which would accrue to the royal purse, moved against mints established either for personal feudal or ecclesiastical benefit. Production was to be centralised in Dublin, which continued to issue coins at intervals until 1302.

The use of local dies in the Dublin and Cork mints may have been a matter of necessity rather than some display of local independence on the part of the mint authorities. Records show that in about 1295 William de Wymundham, controller of the King's Exchange in England, sent 'twenty four stamps for coining money' to Sir William de Essenden. The stamps or dies were for the production of pennies, halfpennies and farthings, and were accompanied by 'John le Minor, Thomas Dowle and John de Shordich, clerks, members of the company of minters at London, to be by them used in the coinage of money' (Simon 1749, 15).

The sixth and final issue of pennies took place between 1297 and 1302. This series of coins can be distinguished from previous issues by the single pellet below a smaller portrait of the king and the smaller lettering used on the obverse of the coins, with larger lettering on the reverse. A number of minor varieties exist, including some with a pellet before the start of the obverse legend, others with small lettering on both sides and still others with the appropriate lettering but no pellet below the bust.

Two varieties of halfpenny were issued: one with and one without a pellet on the breast of the king. This final issue of pennies and halfpennies was only struck in Dublin.

There is some debate as to whether farthings were struck as part of this issue as William de Wymundham did supply dies for the striking of farthings in 1295. In 1992 an Edward farthing was identified with a single pellet below the bust and lettering similar to that used on the halfpennies issued between 1297 and 1302, which would seem to suggest that farthings also formed part of this last issue.

A number of pennies exist with a large oval pellet below the breast. It is believed that these are contemporary Continental copies of Edward's pennies. As with the pennies of Henry III, the strict adherence to the sterling standard meant that Edward's pennies had wide circulation, not only in Ireland but also in England and on the Continent, where they were widely copied.

Examples of Edward pennies are often found with blundered legends or mismatched obverses and reverses, incorporating English and Irish designs on the same coin. Many of these Continental imitations originated from the German city-states of the Holy Roman Empire.

The master of the Dublin mint who was responsible for overseeing the final issue of Edward's coinage was Alexander Normanni of Lucca. Italians from this part of Italy were commonly known as Lombards. Normanni was a prominent member of the Italian or Lombard merchant banking community that Edward I had encouraged to settle in England and Ireland. He was to continue as master of the Dublin mint until 23 August 1302. It is believed that he may have served as master at intervals from as early as 1281. Not only was the supervision of the Dublin mint in foreign hands at this time but records show that £75 0s 0d was paid to Philipuchius del Beck and 24 associates who went from London to Ireland to coin money. The general view is that del Beck and his 24 associates who assisted in the final coinage of Edward I were all foreign workers.

It is estimated that between 1294 and 1302 the mints of Dublin, Waterford and Cork produced £10,000 worth of coins, the bulk of them produced in Dublin under Wogan's governorship. Edward's reign had seen the economy of his Anglo-Irish colony in Ireland flourish: the presence of the Italian banking houses in Ireland and the growth of the colony's wool trade were just two indicators of this rapid economic growth.

In 1272, when Edward became king, his revenue from the lordship of Ireland totalled £2,085; by 1283 this had risen to £9,000. As in previous reigns, much of this revenue, in the form of silver pennies, was to find its way out of Ireland to finance the king's military campaigns. In 1283 almost all of the revenue from the Anglo-Irish colony was used to fund the king's campaign in north Wales. A further £30,000 was used in later years to build a string of castles to hold Edward's newly won Welsh lands.

De Fulbourn in the 1280s and Wogan in the 1290s were both to 'milk' the Irish 'cash-cow' almost dry. By the beginning of the fourteenth century, much of the wealth and produce of the colony had been creamed off and pressed into war service.

Silver supplies were exhausted, and what little silver was left by 1300 was of such poor quality that the minters in Dublin had difficulty in smelting it and turning it into good coin.

The economic miracle of the early years of Edward's reign was to be followed by a century of economic collapse, war, famine and plague.

4. GREATLY IMPOVERISHED
Black money, the Black Death and black rent
(1300–1460)

Even as Philipuchius del Beck and his associates grappled with the difficulties of refining poor-quality silver into good coin, the king's officials in Dublin Castle were turning their attention to another problem that was to be a feature of Ireland's numismatic history for the next 150 years — the lack of good money.

The halfpennies and farthings that remained in the country following King Edward's great recoinage were not sufficient to meet the needs of the Anglo-Irish colonists of the early fourteenth century. As silver continued to be drained from Ireland, good-quality coin became increasingly difficult to find. The gap was initially filled by a mixture of foreign coins, often lightweight or debased, and later by clipped and counterfeit coins.

As the Dublin mint was engaged in striking the last coins to be issued under Edward I, the first in a series of proclamations was issued in about 1300 which 'decryed' in Ireland the circulation of 'base and mixed monies called crocards and pollards, and other foreign coins called mitres, lionines, rosaries, rosanines, eagles, etc. from the stamp of figures impressed on them, which were privately brought from France and other parts beyond the seas and uttered here for pennies, though not worth half a penny' (Simon 1749, 15) on forfeiture of life and goods.

Wogan's quest for silver in the latter years of the reign of Edward I had essentially bankrupted Ireland. The early years of the fourteenth century were also to mark a change in the fortunes of the Anglo-Irish as the native Irish kings sought to re-establish their authority and reassert their independence. In 1315 the high kingship of Ireland was restored and the crown offered to Edward Bruce, the brother of Robert Bruce. Edward Bruce invaded Ulster in 1315 and waged a three-year campaign against the Anglo-Irish, ending in his death at Faughart in 1318. In the wake of the devastation of Bruce's campaign came famine, a breakdown in law and order, and a growth in brigandage and criminality. Whilst the Anglo-Irish were able to reassert their authority, a second invasion from Scotland in 1327 was in turn followed by bad weather, poor harvests and a further series of disastrous famines.

It was against this background of economic collapse that as early as 1311 the powerful Anglo-Irish lords were to win the promise from Edward II that revenue raised in Ireland should be spent within the lordship rather than going to fund the king's military campaigns.

The supply of good money, however, remained a problem throughout the reign of Edward II, and as late as 1331 the Irish Exchequer Payments records refer to debased and counterfeit money being received by the authorities!

In May 1336 John de Elleker, the treasurer of Ireland, issued an order announcing proposals for the introduction of a new coinage of pennies, halfpennies and farthings in the name of Edward III, who had ascended the throne in 1327. The proclamation went on to set the standard of the new coins, 'that a pound of mailes (halfpennies) by the standard of the exchange should contain twenty one shillings by tale, and the pound of farthings, twenty one shillings and eleven pence, and the pound aforesaid should contain ten ounces of pure silver' (Simon 1749, 16). This debasement allowed the equivalent of 252 pennies (21 shillings) to be made from every pound of silver, compared to the 240 pennies to the pound under previous reigns. A similar debasement of the silver standard was also to be found in the halfpennies and farthings issued in England from 1335 by Edward III.

The proclamation also instructed de Elleker to set in hand arrangements for the prospecting and mining of silver deposits in Ireland and for the establishment of a mint in Dublin. It is assumed that de Elleker's scheme to issue a new coinage floundered in 1336 because he was unable to obtain sufficient quantities of silver.

In the absence of any Irish coinage, foreign coins continued to fill the needs of most day-to-day transactions. In March 1338 a proclamation was issued relating to 'de moneta nigra', the black moneys called 'Turneys' (French deniers or double deniers of mixed metal struck at Tours in France, called Tournois, hence their nickname of Turneys), 'which before used to pass current here, were prohibited' (Simon 1749, 17), although permission was given that they could be received in payment until a new official coin was available to replace them. Further legislation of the period sought to restrict the movement of coin out of the country and the importing of 'false' or foreign coins into Ireland. In order to ensure that these laws were enforced, hostlers (innkeepers) were 'sworn' to search their guests for 'false money'!

In 1330, some two years after Elleker's proclamation, a new order was issued that 'eight pair of puncheons for pennies sterling, eight pair of puncheons for halfpennies and eight puncheons for farthings, shall be sent without delay to the attorney of master John Rees, clerk, treasurer of Ireland, in order that such pennies, halfpennies and farthings be immediately coined there for the convenience of the king and his people' (Simon 1749, 17). In early 1339 the dies were completed and carried to Dublin by Peter de Okeburn.

The urgency in preparing the dies and establishing a mint in Dublin to produce coins was now driven by the king's need for fresh funds to support his

Fig. 27—Halfpenny, Edward III, Dublin, 1339.
Seaby and Purvey 1984, No. 6269

military campaigns to seize the French throne. It is believed that minting operations began in Dublin in March 1339, coinciding with a further proclamation which proscribed the circulation of Turneys. Within three months, however, a further instruction was issued which allowed for the continued acceptance of Turneys as legal currency 'until the king shall have caused other money to be made'.

The Dublin mint probably only operated for five or six months. It is believed that production of coins stopped in August 1339, although the dies supplied by Peter de Okeburn were not formally returned to London by John Rees until November 1340. The short life of Edward III's Dublin mint was in all likelihood due to the continued absence of sufficient supplies of silver in Ireland.

The numismatic legacy of these six months of activity is just two halfpennies. The halfpenny of Edward III which was struck in Dublin sometime in 1339 is amongst the rarest of coins in the Irish series. It was struck to the same base silver fineness set out by de Elleker in 1336, of 10oz. fineness (.833), the same standard used for halfpennies and farthings in England between 1335 and 1343. The halfpenny incorporates a star mark on each side of the coin, which was also a feature of the English base silver coins and distinguishes the halfpenny from those struck by Edward I.

The halfpenny essentially follows the same design as those issued nearly 40 years earlier by Edward I, with a crowned facing bust of the king within a triangle and the legend 'EDWARDUS REX' (King Edward). The star mark is to be found at the start of the obverse legend before 'EDW'.

The reverse design features the long cross with the three pellets and the legend 'CIVI(TAS) DUBLIN(IE)', with the star between the words 'CIVITAS' and 'DUBLINIE'. One of the Edward III halfpennies forms part of the Ulster Museum's coin collection; the second was sold for £IR7,500 at the Whyte's Millennial Collection Sale.

The halfpenny of Edward III was first identified in 1951. It has also been suggested that a farthing of Edward III may exist in the National Museum of Ireland's collection which has normally been ascribed to Edward I, although in this case the tell-tale star is missing from both the obverse and reverse of the coin because of the badly chipped flan.

Despite the provision of dies for the production of pennies, it is generally assumed that only halfpennies and possibly farthings were struck in Dublin in

1339. Whilst there are no records to indicate the size of the mintage, it is reasonable to assume that only small amounts of base silver coins were produced because of the lack of silver, and that pennies which in all likelihood would have been struck to the higher sterling standard — as they were in England during this period — were not produced. The lack of significant numbers of coins from this period perhaps reflects the straitened circumstances in which the Irish economy found itself by the middle of the fourteenth century.

With the Dublin mint closed and coin production at an end, the currency needs of the Irish were to be met by worn and lightweight English pennies, often dating back to the reign of Edward I, and the French Turneys.

In the summer of 1348 the people and economy of Ireland were dealt a further blow with the arrival of the Black Death in the port towns of Drogheda and Howth. Within months thousands were dead. By the time the plague had run its course in 1349 it was estimated that between a third and a half of the population of Ireland were dead. In the aftermath of the plague the economy of Ireland collapsed, as towns were left deserted and the estates and farms of the Anglo-Irish lords abandoned. The onset of a prolonged depression in agriculture saw an inevitable rise in prices and in turn wages for those who survived the plague. Inflation set in.

The depression in the agricultural economy saw people leave the land and the first major wave of migration from Ireland to England. The accompanying collapse of the economy and civil society in the wake of the plague led to a rise in crime and disorder, and the native Irish chiefs took the opportunity to reclaim lands and reassert their independence. In 1361 Edward III sent his son Lionel, duke of Clarence, with an army to restore royal authority and Anglo-Irish fortunes.

Between 1361 and 1376 the English spent £91,000 in maintaining their army in Ireland, but now almost all the money to maintain the English lordship was coming from English taxpayers. Ireland had ceased to be a 'cash-cow' for the English Crown and had become a financial liability. The revenue from the lordship of Ireland in the 1370s totalled no more than £2,000 in any year. This level of subsidy could not be maintained, and by the 1380s Edward III's grandson, Richard II, could not even afford to pay his soldiers in Ireland.

The period was also marked by a steep rise in the price of silver and an accompanying debasement of coinage across Europe.

Inevitably the state of the coinage in circulation worsened; coins were clipped or sheared or melted down for their bullion value, and the few coins remaining in circulation were worn and chipped. The currency needs of the Irish were met by a variety of debased or light foreign coins, including Scottish groats, which principally circulated in Ulster, Sligo and Leitrim. The Scottish groats, whilst notionally valued at fourpence, only contained threepence worth of silver.

Fig. 28—'Light Groat', Robert II, Scotland, 1371–90

Although the same size and fineness as English groats, the Scottish groats of David II (1329–71) and Robert II (1371–90) were about 25% lighter in weight than the English coin.

In England official steps were taken to regulate the circulation of these 'light' groats; in Ireland it was left to the church authorities. On the Friday before the feast day of St Michael the Archangel in 1379, Miles Sweetman, the archbishop of Armagh and primate of Ireland, issued the following instruction to his church: 'that everywhere, for the liberty of the church and for the utility of the land, the groat of the money of Scotland shall not be tendered by an person to another, nor passed nor received save for the value of three pennies of silver of the money of England, and that such as shall do the contrary shall be by the authority of the present constitution automatically excommunicated with a sentence of greater excommunication and any territory to which offenders may resort shall automatically be placed under ecclesiastical interdict' (Gallagher 1967, 93).

In time these 'light' groats became scarce and were replaced by counterfeit groats produced by the local Irish. A hoard of these plated forgeries and the tools for making these counterfeit coins, found near Pettigo on the borders of Donegal and Fermanagh in the 1850s, may well be considered the first 'coins' to be produced by the native Irish!

In 1386 it seemed as if steps might be taken to remedy the shortage of good money in Ireland. Richard III granted to Robert de Vere, earl of Oxford, the right of 'coining money of gold and silver, and of all other kinds of money heretofore used in the said island (Ireland), so that the same be of the same alloy and assay, as the money of England' (Simon 1749, 18). Despite the grant de Vere was not to issue a new Irish coinage; it can only be assumed that the ongoing shortage of silver in Ireland meant that there would be little profit in the enterprise.

The absence of reasonable supplies of silver also probably explains why no coinage was struck by Richard II on his two visits to Ireland, in 1394–5 and again in 1399, to establish royal authority over the increasingly independent Anglo-Irish lords and the native Irish chiefs. Although his first visit, accompanied by 5,000 troops, saw royal authority quickly restored, it was not long before it was challenged again. In 1399 a second visit to Ireland was cut short by the invasion of England by the Lancastrian pretender to the throne, the future Henry IV.

Within months Richard II had been murdered and the first moves made in the great dynastic struggle which was to become known as the War of the Roses. In Ireland this conflict between two royal houses was to divide the great Anglo-Irish families, principally the Fitzgeralds, the earls of Kildare and of Desmond, and the Butlers, the earls of Ormonde. The dynastic struggle between these two noble families was to last almost two centuries.

The accession of Henry IV saw the financial fortunes of the Irish lordship probably reach their lowest point, with the annual revenue amounting to no more than £1,000. Royal authority also weakened as the boundaries of the lordship contracted to the royal shires of Dublin, Meath, Louth and Kildare. Within 50 years the territory of the lordship had shrunk further to cover an area surrounding Dublin which was to become known as the Pale. No Irish coinage was to be struck under Henry IV or his successor Henry V.

In 1425 John Cobham was appointed master of the mint of Ireland and the Irish parliament authorised the striking of a new coinage for Ireland. The new coins were to be struck to the same standard and weight as those in England. In 1412 the standard weight of coins in England had been reduced, allowing 32 pennies to be struck from an ounce of silver as opposed to the sterling standard of 20 pennies.

Fig. 29—Penny, Henry VI, 1425–6.
Seaby and Purvey 1984, No. 6270

There are no records to indicate the actual mintage of Henry VI's 1425 coinage but it is generally thought to have been small, and only three pennies have survived. These are sometimes known as the 'annulet' pennies because of the small ring which is incorporated into the design of the coin. The coins, which were struck to the English standard of 32 pennies to the ounce, are smaller than previous pennies, with an example identified in 1980 weighing about 10 grains.

The obverse design of these coins constituted a break with the past, the facing crowned bust of Henry VI with a star to the right of the portrait being placed within a circle rather than a triangle, with the legend around the border 'HENRICVS DNS HIBNIE' (Henry, lord of Ireland). There is an annulet at the end of the obverse legend similar to that found on Henry's English coins issued between 1422 and 1426. The reverse design features a voided long cross design with three pellets in each quarter and the legend 'CIVITAS DUBLINIE' with an annulet placed after the 'CIVI'. Whilst these coins bear the mint signature of the Dublin mint, it is believed that they were struck in London and exported to Dublin.

Two examples of these pennies are to be found in museums: one in the British Museum collection in London and the other in the Fitzwilliam Collection in Oxford. The third penny was identified in 1996 by the numismatist Patrick Finn and forms part of a private collection.

This issue of pennies was to have little, if any, impact on the state of Ireland's coinage. The reign of Henry VI was to be marked by a series of proclamations dealing with the clipping or counterfeiting of coins, which became so widespread in Ireland that by 1447 the Anglo-Irish parliament meeting at Trim issued the following proclamation: 'For that, the clipping of the coin of our sovereign lord, the king; hath caused divers men in this land of Ireland, to counterfeit the same coin, to the great damage and destruction of the said land, and is like to do more hereafter. Wherefore it is ordained and agreed by authority of this present parliament, that no money so clipped by received in any place of the said land from the first day of May next to come, nor the money called O'Reyly's money, or any unlawful money, so that one coyner be ready at the said day to make the coyn' (Dolley and Seaby 1967, 114).

Fig. 30—'O'Reilly's Money'. A clipped groat of Henry VI. Whyte's Millennial Sale, April 2000, No. 82

'O'Reilly's money' or 'le money del Oraylly' were counterfeit coins which were produced by the native Irish and were sometimes known as 'argent irrois', Irish silver. The 'coins' were produced by hammering a thin sheet of silver or foil over a coin, leaving impressions of the obverse and reverse of the coin, which were then cut out and soldered together onto a lead core, to give weight to the coin, producing a silver-plated coin of the appropriate weight but with nothing more than a coating of silver.

Why the name O'Reilly is attributed to these forgeries is uncertain. One suggestion is that there may have been a preponderance of these 'coins' in the Cavan and Meath area, the traditional home of the O'Raghallaigh sept. The 'coins' are mainly copies of clipped English and Scottish groats of the last half of the fourteenth century and the early part of the fifteenth century.

The ambitions of the Trim parliament were not to be realised: no new 'coyner' was to arrive and no new 'coyn' was to be made for Ireland. Instead, the numbers of clipped and counterfeit coins continued to increase.

Ten years after the Trim parliament had outlawed 'O'Reyly's money', a second parliament sitting in Naas on 'the Friday next after the Feast of All Saints' in 1457 found itself legislating against these forgeries again. 'As Ireland is greatly impoverished by daily exportation of silver plate, broken silver, bullion and wedges of silver, and by the great clipping of the coin by Irish enemies and English rebels, by which the coin is diminished and greatly impaired, and the Irish money called the O'Reyly's daily increases it is therefore enacted by the authority aforesaid, that every person who carries broken silver, bullion or wedges of silver out of this land, shall pay for custom to the king twelve pence for every ounce' (Dolley and Seaby 1967, 114).

In the end the authorities had to accept the pitiful state of the lordship's coinage. The standard coin circulating in Ireland in the later years of Henry VI's reign was the clipped English groat. The reverse of the full coin featured a cross and pellets design with two concentric circles or borders, the outer legend reading 'POSUI DEUM ADJUTOREM MEUM' ('I have made God my helper'), whilst the inner legend comprised the mint signature of the coin. The groat and other coins circulating in Ireland tended to be clipped or sheared back, one concentric circle with the outer legend missing, or 'double-sheared' so that both legends on the reverse were missing, leaving the central design of the cross and pellets on the reverse and the king's face on the obverse. These sheared coins remained in circulation in Ireland because they were unacceptable elsewhere, and even in Ireland it has been suggested that their use was limited to meeting a darker and more sinister need.

The late fourteenth and fifteenth centuries in Ireland, as in the rest of Europe, had been marked by a growth in crime and disorder in the wake of the Black Death. In Ireland the native Irish chieftains took advantage of the weakened position of the Anglo-Irish to exact protection money or 'black rent' from Anglo-Irish landlords, their tenants and even, on occasions, from entire towns. In 1392 the town of Castledermot was required to pay a chief of the MacMurroughs 84 marks in 'black rent'.

There is a view that the sheared groats, which were generally unacceptable for trading and business transactions, may have been used for paying the 'black rent'. Whether or not this was the case, the currency needs of the Irish colony had become so desperate that in 1460 the Anglo-Irish parliament meeting in Drogheda declared that 'The Gross (groat) of London, York and Calais, not clipped within the extreme circle (shall pass) at five pence, the Demy-Gross (Half-Groat) at two pence half-penny, the Denier (penny) at one penny farthing; the Gross clipped at fourpence, the Demy-Gross clipped at two pence, the Denier clipped at one penny' (Simon 1749, 79).

This legislation, however, confused rather than resolved the situation regarding clipped coins circulating within the lordship, and within weeks further legislation was passed, stating: 'As there is great variance in the receipt of the Gross, Demy-Gross and Denier, it is enacted, that the Gross and Demy-Gross having the second circle clear and not clipped, and if any writing appears above the said circle in two quarters, then that Gross shall pass for five pence, and the Demy-Gross for two pence halfpenny, and that all deniers, that pass in England, shall pass here for one penny farthing; that the Denier with the cross called Irelandes be utterly void' (Simon 1749, 75–80).

The Drogheda legislation also sought to regulate the circulation of gold coins within Ireland and declared 'That the English Noble of lawful weight shall pass in Ireland at the value of eight shillings and fourpence, the Half-Noble at four shillings and twopence, the Quadrant-d'or of the same coyn and weight at two shillings and one penny' (Simon 1749, 79).

The noble had first been introduced into England by 1344 by Edward III, with a value of 6s 8d. This magnificent coin, about the size of an old half-crown, featured the king standing in a ship with sword and shield on the obverse and an ornate cross on the reverse within a border of tressures or ornate ribbon.

Later legislation also regulated other foreign gold coins circulating in Ireland, 'the Rider of lawful weight pass at four shillings, the Duckat of full weight at four shillings and twopence, the Jean of full weight at four shillings and twopence, the Crown at three shillings and fourpence, the Burgoigne-Noble at six shillings and eight pence, the Salute at four shillings and two pence'. Legislation to regulate and set the value of foreign coins in Ireland was to become a regular feature and tool of the authorities over the next 300 years.

The regulation of gold coins and the desperate temporary measures of over-valuing illegally clipped coins was driven by merchants and traders anxious to keep as much circulating coin as possible within the lordship. A more permanent solution, however, was required for the colony's currency problems.

In 1449 Richard, duke of York, was appointed lieutenant of Ireland by his cousin Henry VI. The appointment, during what might be termed a 'truce' in the War of the Roses, was perhaps a poisoned chalice, but Richard turned it to his advantage. In a series of successful military campaigns in Ulster and Leinster he gained the submission of a number of Irish chiefs and the support of many of the great Anglo-Irish nobles, including the Fitzgeralds, who were to become the principal supporters of the Yorkist cause in Ireland for the next 30 years.

Ten years later Richard, now declared a traitor by Henry VI, found himself again in Ireland. The Anglo-Irish, striving for greater freedom from the English Crown, gave their support to Richard and his plans to invade England in return for a series of concessions which were to emphasise Ireland's sovereignty and independence. One of these measures was for the Anglo-Irish to issue a separate and distinctive coinage for Ireland.

At Drogheda the Anglo-Irish parliament, in Richard's presence, declared Ireland 'separate' from the realm of England and all 'the laws and statutes of England' and that the lordship should issue 'a proper coyne separate from the coyne of England'.

This new 'proper coyne', as set out in the 1460 Act, was to consist of 'one of the weight of a half-quarter of an ounce troy weight, on which shall be imprinted on one side a lyon, and on the other side a crown, called an Irlandes d'argent, to pass for the value of one penny sterling; the other of vij.ob of troy weight having imprinted on one part of it a crown, and on the other part a cross, called a Patrick, of which eight shall pass for one Denier. That a gross be made of the weight of three deniers sterling, and to pass for four deniers sterling, which shall have imprinted on it on one side a crown, and on the other wise a cross like the coyne of Calais, bearing about the cross in writing the name of the place where the coin is made; and that every person who brings bullion to the mint, ought to receive and have for every ounce of silver, troy weight, nine of the said grosses of the value of three deniers. That the coyne called the Jack be hereafter of no value and void, and that the above coyness be made in the castles of Dublin and Trymme'. Perhaps capturing the nationalist tone of this legislation it was further declared that 'This act to commence on St Patrick's day' (Simon 1749, 79).

There is a certain irony in the fact that this legislation which ignored Richard of York's treason and asserted Irish independence from England was passed in the name of Henry VI by men who were already actively engaged in plans to depose Henry and replace him with Richard.

In the summer of 1460, Richard and his Yorkist allies launched their attack on Henry VI. By the end of the year Richard was dead, killed at the Battle of Wakefield. It was to fall to his nineteen-year-old son Edward to seize the crown from Henry with his victory over the Lancastrian forces at the Battle of Towton near York on Palm Sunday in 1461.

England had a new king and Ireland a new coinage.

5. THE HOLLOW CROWN
The coinage of Edward IV (1460–70)

Although the Battle of Towton had dealt a decisive blow to the Lancastrians, the political position in England still remained uncertain. The Lancastrian Henry VI and his family had escaped the Yorkists and fled to Scotland, and in parts of the north of England Lancastrian forces still held sway. The early years of the young Yorkist king's reign were to be spent seeking out and defeating these last remaining pockets of Lancastrian resistance whilst Henry VI bided his time in Scotland waiting for the right moment to strike and regain his crown. The Anglo-Irish nobles took full advantage of the political uncertainty in England, and the weakness of the English king, to advance their own interests.

Having obtained the right to strike a distinctive coinage for Ireland from the new king's father, the Anglo-Irish lords had moved quickly. On 8 December 1460 Thomas Barby, a merchant, was appointed master of the mint and was instructed to proceed with the production of the new coinage. On 15 March 1461 Barby's appointment as master of the Irish mint was confirmed by a patent issued by the earl of Kildare in the name of the new king.

Edward IV, however, had his own plans for his mint in Dublin and had some six weeks earlier granted to Germyn Lynch, an Irish goldsmith living in London, the right to mint coins in Ireland. This grant was confirmed by the king on 6 August 1461, appointing Lynch as master of the Irish mint for life with the promise of virtually all the profits from the mint.

These two conflicting appointments were to be the opening shots in a wider 'battle of wills', which was to last 20 years, between the Anglo-Irish nobility and the English king for control of the Irish lordship.

The reign of Edward IV is of particular numismatic interest in that it was to see the widest range of coins, just under 150 different types or varieties, to be issued in Ireland's thousand-year numismatic history. At another level these silver and copper coins can be seen as representing a very real and tangible legacy of the struggle between the king and his lords for the mastery of Ireland in the fifteenth century.

The first coinage of Edward IV was struck in Dublin in early 1461 and consisted of a new coin, the groat (fourpence), and pennies. This issue was to

Fig. 31—Groat, Edward IV, 'Anonymous Issue', 1460–3. *SNC,* February 1998, No. 59

become known as the 'Anonymous Issue' because it bore no reference to the king — perhaps an astute move on the part of the Anglo-Irish nobles still uncertain of the final outcome of the dynastic struggles in England. The design of the coins followed closely the descriptions set out in the legislation passed in 1460 by the parliament at Drogheda.

The obverse design of the groat featured a large crown within a tressure of nine or eight arcs with no obverse legend. A number of varieties exist with minor variations in design, including fleurs, suns or rosettes, being incorporated into the tressure.

The reverse design featured a long cross with three pellets in each quarter and annulets between the pellets in two of the quarters, with the legend 'CIVITAS DUBLINIE' (city of Dublin) around the border of the coin.

The penny similarly featured a large crown within a tressure of nine or eight arcs, with the long cross and three pellets and annulet design on the reverse. Again, pennies exist with minor variations in design, including crosses in the angles of the tressure and a saltire (X) below the crown. One variety of penny features a crown on the obverse design without a tressure. All of the pennies of this first issue are very rare. An example of a Dublin penny without tressure sold at the Whyte's Millennial Collection Sale for £IR1,200.

An 'anonymous' penny has also been attributed to the Waterford mint; it features a crown within a tressure of fleured arcs on the obverse and the cross and pellets design on the reverse with the legend 'CIVITAS WATER' (city of Waterford). This penny is extremely rare.

These first coins of this issue were struck to a high standard on good-sized blanks. It is believed that the nine-arc coins were struck in early 1461, with the eight-arc coins, which were not struck to the same standard, being produced later in 1461 or 1462.

In 1461 further legislation was passed by the Irish parliament in Dublin allowing for the introduction of 'le maille of silver (a halfpenny), and Quadrant (a farthing), and that the said coyne bear the same writing and crown as the new Denier, and that the said coyne be made in the castle of Dublin, and that the said Maille and Quadrant be taken and received in said Land' (Simon 1749, 80).

Despite an act being passed to strike silver halfpennies and farthings, it is not believed that either of these coins were struck. The absence of these coins might in part be explained by the patent or contract that was granted to Thomas Barby by the Anglo-Irish parliament. Barby's income under his patent was based on the number of ounces of silver he turned into coin rather than the number of coins he produced from each ounce of silver. Under the terms of this contract he received just over sixpence for every ounce of silver he coined, of which fourpence was paid to the Treasury, leaving him with a profit of twopence. As a consequence, it was more profitable for Barby to strike just nine groats from an ounce of silver, rather than 36 pennies or 72 halfpennies or 144 farthings with the higher production costs involved. Barby in his two years in office was to convert over 12,000 ounces of silver into coin, most of it into groats. It is estimated that during this period up to 100,000 groats were produced, with a much smaller number of pennies.

In the absence of a silver halfpenny and silver farthing, the need for 'small coyne for change' was to be met by 'a coyne of copper mixed with silver (to) be made within the castle of Dublin, having on one side the print of a cross, and on the other part a crown of which four shall be taken for a penny; and that the said coyne shall have graven, within the circumference of the said cross, the name of the place where it is made, and on the other parts suns and roses in the circumference of the said crown, and that no sum shall be struck exceeding an hundred marks' (Simon 1749, 80).

The billon farthing that was struck essentially follows the design set out in the legislation. The obverse features a large crown in the centre, with suns and roses alternating around the border instead of a legend. The reverse design features a cross within a beaded circle with the legend 'CIVITAS DUBLINIE' (city of Dublin), with a rose between the two words in the legend.

Alongside the billon farthing a copper half-farthing was also introduced; this coin is the smallest in terms of monetary value in the Irish series. The obverse of this tiny coin features a small crown within a beaded circle and the legend around the border 'PATRIK' (Patrick) within a branch or wreath of leaves breaking up the letters of the legend. The reverse design of the coin simply features a cross. A second variety has the letters of the obverse legend in retrograde, whilst an extremely rare third variety has a 'P' in one angle of the cross on the reverse of the coin. It is thought that all the copper half-farthings were struck in Dublin. This coin is extremely rare and an exceptional example was sold at the Whyte's Millennial Collection Sale for £IR2,400.

Fig. 32—Half-farthing or 'Patrick', Edward IV, c. 1461. Whyte's Millennial Sale, April 2000, No. 113

The 1461 legislation also made reference to the patent granted to Germyn Lynch by Edward IV, which the Anglo-Irish parliament now acknowledged, although it was to be another two years before Lynch took up his right to strike coins in Ireland. Thomas Barby was to be responsible for the production of the billon farthing and, it is assumed, the copper half-farthing, although, like the pennies, only a very small number of these coins seem to have been produced, with Barby's profits from the production of the billon farthings amounting to £16 12s 1d.

The acknowledgement of Lynch's appointment and the inclusion of the sun and rose in the design of the farthing, both heraldic devices associated with Edward IV, could perhaps be seen as the first steps in the king's assertion of his authority over his Irish lordship.

The first issue of silver coins of Edward IV were struck to a standard which was three-quarters that of English coins; the Irish groat, whilst having a notional value of fourpence, weighed only 45 grains (the equivalent of threepence in silver), compared to an English groat of the period which weighed 60 grains. The penny was similarly struck to this three-quarter standard. The principal purpose for reducing the weight of the new Irish coins was to act as a disincentive for the coins to leave Ireland. It also, in effect, devalued the Irish coinage by 25% and was to prove the spur for an increase in the export of cheaper Irish goods to England.

By 1462 it seemed that everyone was content: the Anglo-Irish lords had asserted their independence from the Crown with a distinctive Irish coinage, and Irish merchants and traders had a ready supply of good money and into the bargain were making good profits with a flourishing export trade.

In England, with the last elements of Lancastrian resistance being hunted down, it seemed as if the new king was at last secure on his throne. But in Ireland the Yorkist supremacy was about to be challenged when the head of the Butler family rose up in revolt against Edward IV, aided by a force of English Lancastrians, and declared for the deposed Henry VI. After some initial Lancastrian successes, Thomas fitz James Fitzgerald, the earl of Desmond, took the field with a force of 20,000 men and put down the Butler revolt at the Battle of Pilltown.

The Butler insurrection and the threat it had posed to his crown were to be instrumental in making Edward IV turn his attention to his Irish lordship and the political ambitions and dubious loyalties of his Anglo-Irish lords.

In 1463 Edward IV appointed the earl of Desmond as his new deputy, recognising the pivotal role the earl had played in defeating this latest challenge to his crown. The king, however, had misgivings about Desmond's loyalty and his personal ambition. Too many people talked of Desmond as a future king of Ireland. It is possible that part of the price for the earl's appointment was the acknowledgement of Edward's earlier patent awarding the mastership of the mint to Germyn Lynch. In February 1463 Thomas Barby's patent was suspended, although it is possible that he had ceased to strike coins five months earlier in October 1462.

A parliament held on 6 August 1463 in Wexford confirmed the patent made to 'Germyn Lynch of London, goldsmith, warden and master-worker of our moneys and coyness within our castle of Dublin, and within our castle of Trymme, and graver of the punsions of the said money and coynes to occupy by himself or deputy during his life, giving him and them authority to make all our said moneys and coines'. Lynch was further required to 'make a privy sign on every piece of silver money' and was given 'power to take at all times as many labourers yearly as shall be necessary, and if any labourer refuses to work at the said mints, that the master or his deputy shall arrest such, and put them in prison, till he labours as desired' (Simon 1749, 80–2).

In addition to confirming his rights to strike coins at Dublin and Trim, Lynch was given the right to mint coins in Waterford, Limerick and Galway. The granting of this right was perhaps an attempt by the Anglo-Irish parliament to avoid the centralisation of all coin production within the Pale by creating a new mint beyond immediate royal control.

The same act also defined the coins to be produced: 'a piece of silver running at and of the value of four deniers … another piece of silver coine, of the value of two deniers … and another piece of silver coyne to the value of one denier'.

The act further authorised the striking of 'four pieces of brass or copper running at one penny of our said silver to be imprinted with the figure of a bishop's head and a scripture of this work "Patrick" about the same had on the one side and with a cross with this word "Salvator" then about on the other side, and to make as much or as little of every sort of the said moneys or coyness of brass or copper'.

Fig. 33—Farthing, Edward IV, 1463. *SNC*, February 1997, No. 258

The act authorised Lynch to also strike 'eight pieces of brass running at and of the value of one penny of our sound silver'. No distinctive half-farthings are attributed to this second coinage, possibly because none were produced or because Lynch simply continued to strike half-farthings to the old crown and cross design of 1461–2.

The most important element of the 1463 legislation for the king came towards the end of the act, where it was stated that Germyn Lynch should 'make such scripture on the said coyne of silver … on the side of the crown, Edwardus Dei

Gratia Dominus Hibernie'. The young king had won this first game in high politics with the Anglo-Irish lords by having his name and title restored to the coinage.

This second issue of coins, because of the inclusion of the royal titles, is known as the 'Titled Coinage'.

Fig. 34—Groat, Edward IV, 'Titled Coinage', 1463–5. Seaby and Purvey 1984, No. 6282

The second coinage was to be struck to the same standard as the earlier Anonymous Coinage, although there is some suggestion that there may have been some minor reduction in weight, perhaps necessitated by fluctuations in the price of bullion.

As with the previous issue, the groat tended to predominate and only small numbers of half-groats (twopence) and pennies were produced. Despite the authorisation to strike coins in five Irish mint towns, production was limited to just two mints.

The Dublin groat featured a large crown in a tressure with annulets in the spandrel or borders of the tressure, with Germyn Lynch's 'privy sign' or mint mark of a rose for Dublin and a cross pattée for Waterford at the start of the obverse legend, which read 'EDWARDUS DI GRA DNS HYBERNIE' (Edward by the grace of God lord of Ireland). The reverse design featured a large cross with three pellets in each quarter with two concentric borders, the outer border including the legend 'POSUI DEUM ADIUTOREM MEUM' ('I have made God my helper') with the mint signature 'CIVITAS DUBLINIE' forming the inner legend.

The half-groat follows the same design as the groat and was only struck in Dublin.

The obverse of the penny featured the crown within a circle and the abbreviated legend 'EDWARD DI G DNS HYB' (Edward by the grace of God lord of Ireland). The reverse featured the cross with three pellets in each quarter design, with the mint signature 'CIVITAS DUBLIN' (city of Dublin) forming the legend.

The act also authorised 'small coynes to be struck at Waterford in a place called Dondory, alias Raynold's Tower'. Groats and pennies were to be struck in Waterford. The groats essentially follow the same design as the Dublin groats but have pellets incorporated into the spandrels or border design of the tressure on the obverse of the coin and a cross as the mint mark at the start of the legend. Another Waterford variety has annulets in the spandrels and saltires by the crown on the obverse of the coin.

The Waterford penny similarly follows the design of the Dublin penny and both coins are distinguished by the Waterford mint signature 'CIVITAS WATERFORD' (city of Waterford) on the groat and 'CIVITAS WATERFOR' on the penny.

All the silver coins of this second issue are scarce and the first half-groat was not identified until 1964. A Waterford 'Titled' groat in very fine condition was sold at the Whyte's Millennial Collection Sale for £IR3,800.

The brass farthing issued under the 1463 legislation featured on the obverse a facing portrait wearing a mitre with the legend 'PATRICIVS' (Patrick), with a sun and rose incorporated into the legend. The reverse design featured a long cross with a sun and rose in alternate angles with the legend around the border 'SALVATOR' (Saviour). A number of varieties of this coin are known.

It is believed that this second issue of Edward IV was limited to 1463 and possibly the early part of the following year. Silver prices across Europe had begun to rise. The response of European rulers and the English king was to reduce the standard of their coins. In England the groat was reduced in weight from 60 grains to 48 grains; this reduction had immediate consequences for Ireland. The Irish groat was now almost at parity with the English groat, and many lightweight clipped English groats which had circulated in Ireland were now found to be close enough to the new official weight to be acceptable once again in England. Coupled with this drain of coins to England, the Irish mint could not afford — or, more likely, Germyn Lynch and his associates were not prepared — to pay the higher price for bullion which would adversely affect their profits.

The economic prosperity of the last few years seemed threatened as Ireland once again found itself 'drained' of good coin. Whereas Edward's father's response to a similar crisis four years earlier had been to sanction a distinctive Irish coinage, Edward's response was to centralise coinage production and introduce a uniform coinage throughout his English, Irish and French territories. In 1464 he appointed Lord Hastings 'Master of the Moneys' for England, Ireland and Calais, with central control over the production of punches and dies to be used in the manufacture of coins throughout the king's territories. Germyn Lynch's authority to produce his own puncheons and dies in Ireland was ended. All puncheons and dies were in future to be produced in London.

The following year the Irish parliament in Dublin authorised the introduction of a new or third coinage. This coinage, which is known as the 'First English Coinage' or 'Heavy Cross and Pellets', followed essentially the same design as the king's coins in England.

This third coinage was to consist of groats, half-groats, pennies and halfpennies.

Fig. 35—Groat, Edward IV, Dublin
'Heavy Cross and Pellets', 1465–7. *SNC*,
May 1995, No. 2787

The groats of this issue featured on the obverse a crowned facing portrait of the king within a tressure with the legend around the border 'EDWARDUS DEI GRA DNS HIBERNIE' (Edward by the grace of God lord of Ireland). The reverse featured the long cross with three pellets in each quarter with the two concentric borders, with the outer legend reading 'POSUI DEUM ADIUTOREM MEUM' (I have made God my helper). The mint signature 'CIVITAS DUBLINIE' (city of Dublin) formed the inner legend on the reverse.

A number of varieties of the Dublin coin exist with pellets and stars incorporated into the design. One variety includes the letter 'G' on the king's breast, which is thought to be the mark of the mint master Germyn Lynch.

A half-groat similar in design was also struck at the Dublin mint with two annulets on either side of the king's portrait. Again, varieties of this coin are known with minor variations to the design.

Fig. 36—Penny, Edward IV, Dublin 'Heavy Cross
and Pellets', 1465–7. *SNC*, February 1998, No. 64

The penny similarly featured a crowned facing portrait of the king with the abbreviated legend 'EDWARD DI GR DNS HYBE' (Edward by the grace of God lord of Ireland). The reverse featured a long cross with three pellets in each quarter. The mint signature of Dublin formed the reverse legend. As with the groat and half-groat, varieties with minor variations in the design exist. A tiny halfpenny similar in design to the penny was also minted in Dublin. This coin is extremely rare; a cracked and clipped example was sold at the Whyte's Millennial Collection Sale for £IR550.

Alongside the mint in Dublin the old mint towns of Cork, Limerick and Waterford were to produce 'Heavy Issue' coins from 1465.

The Cork mint produced two types or varieties of groat similar in design to the Dublin groat with the reverse legend 'CIVITAS CORCAIGIE' (city of Cork). Both types of groat are extremely rare. The Waterford mint produced four types of groat and at least one type of penny, again similar in design to the Dublin coins, with the mint signature 'CIVITAS WATERFORD' (city of Waterford) on the groat and 'WATERFOR' or 'WATFOR' on the penny. One variety of Waterford groat features an unusual sideways 'W' mark on the king's breast on the obverse of the coin.

One type of groat and penny similar in design to the two Dublin coins were produced at the Limerick mint with the mint signature 'CIVITAS LIMIRICI' or 'LIMERICI' (city of Limerick).

Three new mints were also to be involved in the issuing of the 1465 'Heavy Issue' coins: Drogheda, Galway and Trim.

Four distinct types of groat were to be struck at the Drogheda mint with the mint signature 'VILLA DE DROGHEDA' (town of Drogheda). The mint in Galway was to produce a half-groat with the legend 'VILLA GALWEY' (town of Galway) and a single variety of penny with the reverse legend 'VILLA DE GALWAY'. Finally, one type of groat and half-groat were to be struck at Trim during this period with the mint signature 'VILLA DE TRIM' (town of Trim). The half-groats of Galway and Trim, like those of Dublin, are extremely rare.

The weight of the groat was set at 45 grains, although most surviving examples seem to be about 42 grains, with the half-groat and penny in proportion. The halfpenny was struck to a slightly debased silver standard in recognition of the more expensive production costs associated with the manufacturing of smaller coins. It was because of their good weight that this series of coins is referred to as the 'Heavy Cross and Pellets' issue.

The reign of Edward IV saw significant amounts of silver leaving Ireland. In the past it had been to meet the needs of English kings' military campaigns, but by the fifteenth century most of the silver was not going in taxes to the treasury but as rent from Irish estates owned by the English nobles. The constant draining of silver from Ireland inevitably had serious consequences for the Irish economy. The early distinctive Irish coinage struck to a lower weight standard had in part halted the flow of silver coin, but the introduction of the new 'Heavy' coins with a more acceptable English design saw a resumption in the flow of silver coin out of Ireland. This flow was to be aided and abetted by some of the more unscrupulous elements of fifteenth-century Irish society.

Whilst the new 'Heavy' coins were heavier than previous issues, they were still slightly lighter (42–45 grains) than their English equivalents (48 grains) but to all other intents and purposes they looked the same. It was not long before there was a thriving 'black market' trade in 'light' Irish groats crossing the Irish Sea to be passed off to a mainly illiterate population as heavier English groats.

Edward's policy of centralisation had proved disastrous. By the autumn of 1467 most of the silver coin in Ireland had found its way to England; the Irish economy was almost devoid of coin and this in turn was leading to political disquiet. In England, merchants were up in arms over the 'light' Irish coins masquerading as

English coins. Edward IV now faced the dilemma of finding a way to keep Irish coins in Ireland and out of England.

In the years following the Butler insurrection Edward had consolidated his position in England. In May 1464 Lancastrian forces were decisively defeated at the Battle of Hexham, and a year later the deposed Henry VI was captured by Edward's forces and imprisoned in the Tower of London. Edward IV, however, continued to have misgivings about the earl of Desmond's rule in Ireland, and in 1467 he finally moved against his father's Anglo-Irish supporters. In late 1467 Sir John Tiptoft, later the earl of Worcester, was appointed as the new lieutenant deputy of Ireland. On 4 February 1468 Tiptoft arrested the two great Anglo-Irish lords, the earl of Desmond and the earl of Kildare, and charged them with 'horrible treasons'. Desmond was executed eleven days later and the earl's home province of Munster erupted in rebellion. Tiptoft, who had earned the nickname 'the butcher' because of his military exploits in England, moved swiftly and brutally put down the Munster rebellion with his army of 500 archers. In a couple of months he had effectively broken the power of the most important Anglo-Irish families in Ireland.

His solution to the economic problems of the lordship and the lack of good coins was to be just as drastic as his dealings with the Anglo-Irish lords.

In the preamble to Tiptoft's 1467 legislation, Ireland was described as 'destitute of silver, and the silver there made of late is daily carried away into divers countries, and so the people of this land continually take clipped money, contrary to statute' (Simon 1749, 82–3).

The deputy's solution to the shortage of coin in the lordship was to introduce a new coinage, the fourth issue of Edward IV's reign. The act of 11 December 1467 described the new coinage, 'that there be a piece of silver coined called a Double, having the print of a crown on one side, with this writing, Edwardus Dei Gratia Dominus Hibernie, and on the other part a sun with a rose, with this inscription about it, Civitas Dublinie, which shall pass in Ireland for eight deniers, and ten such pieces shall make an ounce'. The act also authorised the issuing of a half-groat, a denier, a half-denier and a farthing.

Tiptoft's solution to Ireland's problem was to create a new coin, a double-groat or eightpence, but containing just over fourpence worth of silver. The other coins named in the act similarly were to contain only half of their nominal value in silver.

In an age when a coin was meant to be worth the silver it contained, Tiptoft effectively devalued Ireland's currency in one stroke by 100%. His solution would certainly ensure that the new 'Doubles' remained in Ireland, but it was questionable whether the Irish themselves would accept the new coin. The deputy ensured that they would: the act introducing the new coinage concluded by stating 'that nobody shall after Easter next receive or pay any manner of silver coyne or money, but the coyne or money aforesaid, and that all other silver coynes or money in Ireland be from the feast of Easter next damned and annulled, and if any person or persons receives or pays otherwise, that such payment shall be adjudged felony in the payer as in the receiver'.

The act further set out 'that the said moneys and coyness be made in the castles of Dublin and Trym, the cities of Waterford and Limerick and the towns of Drogheda, Galway and Carlingford'. In the event the 'Doubles' were only to be struck in Dublin, Drogheda and Trim.

Fig. 37—Double-groat, Edward IV, Dublin 'Rose on Sun Coinage', 1467–70. Seaby and Purvey 1984, No. 6290

The double-groat or eightpence featured a crowned portrait of the king within a fleured tressure with the legend 'EDWARDUS DEI GRA DNS HYBERN' (Edward by the grace of God lord of Ireland). A rose mint mark was placed at the start of the obverse legend. The reverse design was a major departure from previous Irish coins and featured the king's badge, a large radiant sun with 24 rays with a rose at the centre; the mint signature of Dublin 'CIVITAS DUBLINIE' (city of Dublin) formed the reverse legend, with the words being divided by roses. A further variety of the Dublin double-groat has a tressure without the fleur designs on the obverse.

The smaller groat, or fourpence, broadly followed the same design with the crowned portrait within a plain tressure. The reverse featured the radiant sun and rose design with the same legends and use of rose mint marks as on the double-groat.

The half-groat, which was the size of a 'Heavy Issue' penny, followed the same design as the two previous coins. The obverse legend was abbreviated to read 'EDWARD D.G.D. HYBER' and the reverse legend 'CIVITAS DUBLIN'. A variety of Dublin half-groat features crosses by the neck of the king on the obverse. The penny again featured the crowned portrait of the king on the obverse with the contracted legend 'EDWARD D.G.DN. HYBER'. The reverse featured the rose and radiant sun device with the mint signature 'CIVITAS DUBLINI'.

Double-groats and groats were struck at Drogheda to a similar design with the reverse legend 'VILLA DE DROGHEDA' (town of Drogheda). Pennies were also struck at the Drogheda mint with the contracted reverse legend 'VILLA DE DROGH'.

Double-groats were also struck in Trim. These coins again followed the same design as the Dublin and Drogheda coins but incorporate two pellets over the king's crown and two pellets below the bust on the obverse. The reverse design featured the radiant sun and rose design with the legend 'VILLA DE TRIM' (town of Trim). The groat similarly followed the same design with additional pellets incorporated into the obverse design. Two varieties of half-groat were to be struck at Trim; one followed the same design as the Dublin penny, whilst the second incorporated two pellets over the crown on the obverse.

All of the 'Double' issue coins are very rare and some, particularly those from Drogheda and Trim, are extremely rare. An example of a Dublin double-groat in very fine condition sold at the Whyte's Millennial Collection Sale in April 2000 for £IR6,000.

The 1467 legislation also allowed for 'half-deniers and farthings to be made according to the same proportions, with like provisions: and that the print of the denier, with a scriptive as long as the master and workmen can make them'.

A copper farthing is associated with the 'Doubles' series. The obverse of the coin featured a shield with three crowns with three pellets around the shield and the legend 'EDWARDUS DNS HYBER' or 'HYBERNI' (Edward, lord of Ireland). The reverse featured a long cross over a radiant sun with sixteen rays with a rose in the centre, and the legend 'CIVITAS DUBLINI' (city of Dublin). These farthings, like the rest of the 'Doubles' coins, are rare and an example of this type of farthing sold for £IR1,900 at the Whyte's Millennial Collection Sale.

Despite being mentioned in the act, no 'Doubles' were to be struck at the old mint towns of Galway, Limerick and Waterford. Carlingford, which was named for the first and only time as a mint town in this legislation, is one of the best-preserved medieval towered towns in Europe and does boast a fifteenth-century mint tower. Despite its mention in the act, no coins at any point in Ireland's numismatic history are associated with this town. It is possible that the mint building may have acted as a *cambium* or point of exchange, rather than a factory, for the new 'Doubles'.

Whilst the new 'Doubles' did remain in Ireland, Tiptoft's devaluation of the Irish currency was to prove disastrous. The issue of the new currency inevitably fuelled inflation, with prices and wages doubling. In response, the Anglo-Irish parliament found themselves having to regulate the prices of foodstuffs and basic commodities to avoid economic crisis and social unrest. The new coinage was also unpopular for political reasons amongst the populace. The revenue or profit accrued by Tiptoft from the minting of these new coins also doubled, with the additional revenue being directed towards maintaining Tiptoft's increasingly unpopular administration and his standing army in Ireland.

In March 1470 Tiptoft was created deputy of Ireland in his own right by Edward IV, but his new powers were to be short-lived. In September 1470 a Lancastrian army invaded England with French support. Edward IV, faced with a much larger force than he could muster and the desertion of many of his key supporters, fled England on 2 October 1470 to take refuge in Burgundy. On 3 October Henry VI was released from the Tower of London and restored as king. Tiptoft chose this moment to return to England, possibly to rally support for Edward IV's cause. The deputy was, however, to find himself caught up in the violence and lust for revenge of the Lancastrian restoration, and was publicly executed before a baying mob in London on 14 October 1470.

The political confusion in England, as it had ten years earlier, presented the Anglo-Irish nobles and their parliament with the opportunity once again to advance their own political interests and to reassert their control over the lordship of Ireland.

6. A NOTABLE DIFFERENCE
The coinage of the second reign of Edward IV
(1470–83)

The Anglo-Irish parliament, working to the old maxim that England's difficulty is Ireland's opportunity, took advantage of the political confusion to reassert their rights. In the absence of a deputy, the Anglo-Irish parliament elected Thomas Fitzgerald, the seventh earl of Kildare, as justiciar or governor of Ireland. Despite the flight of Edward IV, the Anglo-Irish parliament were to remain loyal to the king and continued to pass laws in his name.

In November 1470 the earl of Kildare presided over a meeting of the Anglo-Irish parliament in Dublin which abolished Tiptoft's 'Doubles' coinage. In the preamble to the act it was noted that the 'Doubles' had left the Irish people 'so greatly impoverished, that many of them have given up their houses and avoided the land, and all merchandises, and especially victuals that have grown excessive dear, from which many people are like to perish through want'.

The act went on to declare 'that the master or masters of the coinage shall have the power to make and strike within the castles of Dublin and Trym, and the town of Drogheda, five sorts of silver coynes according to the fyness of the coynes struck in the tower of London, i.e. One Grosse, the Demy-Grosse, the Denier, the Demy-Denier, and the Quadrant'. The act then described the coins to be struck as having 'at one side the print of a head crowned with this writing, Edwardus Dei Gratia Rex Angliae, Dominus Hiberniae, or the name of any other King for the time being, and on the other part the print of a cross with the pellets according to the gros made in Caleys, bearing in the circumference of the cross in writing the place where the said gros is made and coined, and in the borders of the gross this writing Posui Deum adjutorem meum'.

To avoid the preponderance of groats, as in previous coinages, the act stipulated that 'the fifth part of every pound (of silver) be struck in small pieces, that is to say, Two-Denier, Deniers, Half-deniers and Quadrants. And as the said half-denier and quadrant require more labour and costs, in poising every pound, than the gross, the demy-gross and denier, it is enacted that the master or masters for the time being may allay (debase) every ounce of the said demi-deniers and quadrants according to a statute made in a parliament held at Trym, before Thomas Earl of Desmond, the fifth (regnal year 1465) of this King'.

The act finally demonetised the 'Doubles' coinage, 'that from this time to the feast of the Purification next, the Double shall be taken and pass for four deniers, the demy-double for two deniers, the demy-gross for one denier, and the denier for half a denier; and that after the said feast, the said double, demy-double, demy-gross, denier and demy-denier to be damned and not taken for coyne, and whoever pays or receives in payment any clipped money after Christmas next, that he shall be adjudged and taken as an attainted traitor' (Simon 1749, 83–4).

Kildare's loyalty to Edward IV was to prove a shrewd move. In spring 1471 Edward IV invaded England, supported by an army from Burgundy. The army of Henry VI was defeated at the Battle of Tewkesbury on 4 May 1471 and Henry himself was captured by Edward's forces. Edward was now determined that Henry should never again be a threat to his throne, and on 21 May 1471 the deposed king was stabbed to death on Edward's orders. In Ireland Kildare was confirmed as Edward's deputy.

The new coinage — the fifth coinage of Edward IV's reign — is known as the 'Second English Coinage' or 'Light Cross and Pellets Coinage' (1473–8). The initial weight of these new English-type coins was the same as the earlier English-type issue of 1465, weighing between 40 and 42 grains compared to the English groat weight of 48 grains. On average the early coins of this issue, struck between 1470 and 1473, were about $\frac{5}{6}$ the weight of their English equivalents. The coins were, however, to become increasingly 'lighter' during the early 1470s.

Some numismatists have sought to divide this fifth coinage into two distinct issues: the heavier coins issued between 1470 and 1473 forming the fifth coinage, and the second 'Heavy Cross and Pellets' coinage and the lighter coins issued between 1473 and 1478 forming a sixth distinct coinage.

The introduction of the new coinage struck to the old 1465 weight saw a significant reduction in profits, with just twopence to be shared between the treasury and the master or deputy master of the mint. It was, perhaps, in response to this reduction in profits that the mint masters began to strike 'light' coins rather than this being an official policy on the part of the Anglo-Irish parliament. Official records of the time note under-masters of the Irish mints, including Germyn Lynch, being indicted for striking lightweight coins. The situation was further complicated by a lack of central control. Despite the 1470 legislation limiting coin production to Dublin, Trim and Drogheda, coins were being struck in Cork, Limerick, Waterford and Wexford.

In 1472 the parliament was to pass legislation against 'divers coiners in the city of Cork, the towns of Yoghil (Youghal), Kinsale and Kilmallock, viz John Fannin, John Crone, Patrick Martel, William Synnot, Mortagh O Haurighon, Nicholas Rewy, and others, who make false coines without authority' (Simon 1749, 85).

The lack of effective control over minting operations was not assisted by the confusion regarding the position of master of the mint. On 18 October 1470

Thomas Barby had been reappointed master of the coinage in Dublin, Trim and Drogheda, a position he was to share with another merchant, William Crumpe; Germyn Lynch remained as under-master. In 1472 Barby died and Crumpe took over as master, although he seems to have had little interest in the day-to-day workings of the mints or the supervision of his under-masters. One such under-master was Patrick Keyn, a Dublin goldsmith who had been approved as under-master of the coyne to Barby and Crumpe and 'receiver of the money called the Doubles' in December 1470. In 1472 Keyn was found to have 'struck much of the coyne not of weight, nor of good alloy, of his own authority, and against the will of the said William Crump' (Simon 1749, 84). Whilst the fate of Keyn is unknown, Crumpe was pardoned and resigned his position in return for an official pension.

In 1473 the Anglo-Irish parliament moved to address the problems of the increasingly 'light' coinage and control of the mints. Its response was to limit the production of coins to 'within the castle of Dublin only, and in no other place within the four counties of Dublin, Meath, Kildare and Uriel, and in no other place in Ireland' (Simon 1749, 85). The act went on to address the problem of 'light' coinage by officially sanctioning the lower standard, allowing for thirteen groats to be made from an ounce of silver, 28 half-groats, 56 pennies and 112 farthings from an ounce. The groat was reduced in weight to 32 grains, about threepence worth of silver, the same standard as Edward IV's first coinage in 1460.

Finally, the Anglo-Irish parliament moved to strengthen the management and control of the mint by reappointing Germyn Lynch as 'master of the said mint during good behaviour, he answering for all manner of workmen he shall bring into the mint'. The act further stipulated that 'Philip Brentwood be one of the principal workmen under the said master, if he may be had at reasonable wages — that Christopher Fox be one of the principal deputy comptrollers of the said mint, if he may be had at reasonable wages, by the assent of the chief comptroller'.

The 1473 act seemingly reconciled two opposing views in the struggle between the king and his Anglo-Irish lords. There was now effective control over the Irish mint and the king had his English-type coinage complete with royal titles, whilst the Irish had their lower weight standard, which it was hoped once again would stop the drain of silver out of the lordship.

This sixth coinage of Edward IV was to consist of groats, half-groats and pennies, and is the most varied in terms of types or varieties of coins issued and also in the number of mints that produced coins. The coins essentially followed the same design as those issued between 1465 and 1467.

The groat featured a crowned facing portrait of the king within a tressure with the legend 'EDWARDUS DEI GRA DNS HYBERNIE' (Edward by the grace of God lord of Ireland). Some of the coins have a 'G' below the bust of the king which is believed to be a reference to Germyn Lynch. The reverse of the coin

Fig. 38—Groat, Edward IV, Dublin 'Light Cross and Pellets with 'G' below bust', 1473–8. *SNC,* May 1994, No. 3427

features a long cross with three pellets in each quarter or three pellets in two of the quarters and two pellets and a rosette in the other two quarters. The reverse, like the coins of the previous issue, includes two concentric borders, the outer border featuring the legend 'POSUI DEUM ADIUTOREM MEUM' (I have made God my helper) and the inner reverse legend 'CIVITAS DUBLINIE' (city of Dublin).

A number of mint marks are associated with this issue. They include a pierced cross, sun, rose, rosette, plain cross, crown and trefoil which are incorporated into the legends of the coins.

At least five other major varieties of the light Dublin groat exist with minor variations such as the placing of pellets and annulets in the spandrels of the tressure design or the placing of crosses by the king's neck. One variety has the initial 'I' on the king's breast.

Two varieties of half-groat are associated with the Dublin mint. The coins follow the same design as the groat. One variety has the standard crowned facing portrait of the king whilst the other features an annulet on either side of the king's neck.

The Dublin half-groat, along with the half-groats produced by other mints, is extremely rare.

The pennies of this issue provide the widest range of varieties — over 30 different types were to be struck by six mints, including Dublin. The coins found today are mostly clipped, almost to the central design, and often the mint town can only be identified by looking carefully at the traces or the bases of the letters that form the mint signature. Even where a coin is found which has escaped the clipper's shears the pennies seem to have been struck on blanks which were much smaller than the original die, resulting in coins which at best only have partial legends.

The pennies, unlike the groats and half-groats, are relatively common, although unclipped coins or coins struck on full flans are rare. At least nine varieties of penny are attributed to the Dublin mint. The coins tend to feature a crude crowned facing portrait of the king within a border with the abbreviated legend 'EDWAR DI GR DNS HYBE' or 'EDWARD DI GR DNS IBERNIE' (Edward by the grace of God lord of Ireland). In keeping with the instructions in the 1470 act some of these coins, possibly the earlier heavier coins dating from 1470–2, have the king's royal titles 'EDWARD REX ANG Z FR' (Edward, king of England and France).

The reverse of the penny features the cross and pellets design with the mint signature 'CIVITAS DUBLIN' forming the border of the coin. The varieties attributed to the Dublin mint have minor variations to either the obverse or reverse design. On the obverse crosses, saltires, pellets and stars are placed as distinguishing marks on either side of the king's neck, or in one case on either side of the crown. On the reverse of some of the Dublin pennies a quatrefoil is placed in the centre of the long cross, a feature which is to be found on the reverse designs of pennies from other mints. One unusual Dublin variety features the initial 'D' in the centre of the cross rather than a quatrefoil.

The mint at Drogheda similarly issued groats, half-groats and pennies. The Drogheda groat follows the same design as the Dublin groat, including the initial 'G' for Germyn Lynch incorporated into the obverse design. The inner legend on the reverse reads 'VILLA DE DROGHEDA' (town of Drogheda). Again a number of varieties are known, which include an annulet placed on either side of the king's neck, a trefoil mint mark on the king's breast, and an extra pellet in two of the quarters on the reverse.

The Drogheda mint was also to issue a half-groat which followed the same design as the groat.

Eight varieties of penny are associated with the Drogheda mint; as with the Dublin coins, there are a number of varieties which incorporate crosses, pellets, rosettes and saltires into the obverse design. Again the reverse design of some of the Drogheda pennies incorporates a quatrefoil into the central part of the cross, and on two varieties a small rose is placed at the centre of the cross.

The mint at Limerick also produced groats, half-groats and pennies. Two varieties of groat are known from the Limerick mint. Again, they follow essentially the same design as the Dublin groat. On one variety the obverse portrait of the king has an 'L' on his breast and crosses or quatrefoils on either side of his neck, whilst the other also has the 'L' mark but a rosette or cinquefoil on either side of the king's neck. The reverse of the coin features the normal cross and pellet design with the inner legend 'CIVITAS LIMIRICI' or 'LIMERICI' (city of Limerick).

Fig. 39—Groat Edward IV, Limerick 'Light Cross and Pellets' 1473–8 *SNC*, February 1998, No. 66

The Limerick mint also produced two varieties of half-groat, one featuring a facing portrait of the king with the initial 'L' on his breast and a rosette on either side of his neck, and another which does not have the initial 'L' incorporated into the obverse design. The reverse design was slightly different to that of the groat in that it featured a long cross with three pellets in two quarters and two pellets and a rosette in the remaining two quarters.

Two varieties of penny are associated with the Limerick mint, the first with a rosette or cinquefoil on either side of the king's neck on the obverse, and the other with crosses on either side of the king's neck on the obverse.

The Trim mint was only to produce groats and pennies during this period. Again, the groats followed the same design as the Dublin groats. At least four main varieties of Trim groat are known, with minor variations in the obverse design, including pellets being incorporated into the design of the tressure, a pellet on either side of the king's neck and an initial 'B' placed on the king's breast. The reverse design featured the cross and pellets with the inner legend 'VILLA DE TRIM' (town of Trim).

Four varieties of penny are associated with the Trim mint. The coins followed essentially the same design as the other mints, with varieties incorporating pellets into the obverse design and a quatrefoil featuring on the reverse design of some examples. The pennies of the Trim mint tend to be scarcer than those of the older and more established mints.

Waterford, like Dublin, Drogheda and Limerick, was to produce all three coins. The Waterford groat again followed the same design as the other mints. Four varieties are known with minor variations in the obverse design of the coin. They include a rosette being placed on either side of the king's neck, the initial 'V' on the king's breast and the initial 'G' on the king's breast.

A heavy-issue type of groat is also attributed to the Waterford mint, and is thought to belong to this second English issue. It features annulets at the king's neck, with the mint mark of a crowned leopard's head forming part of the obverse legend. The reverse of the coin features the standard cross and pellets design with the mint signature 'CIVITAS WATERFORD' (city of Waterford).

A half-groat is also associated with the Waterford mint. It follows the same design as the Waterford groat and the half-groat of other mints, although the mint signature on this smaller coin is abbreviated to 'CIVITAS WATERFO'.

Fig. 40—Penny, Edward IV, Waterford 'Light Cross and Pellets', 1473–8. *SNC*, May 1994, No. 3429

At least six varieties of penny are associated with the Waterford mint during this period. As with other mint issues, the variations principally relate to the incorporation of annulets, pellets and crosses into the obverse design and the inclusion of the quatrefoil in the reverse design.

Coins of the last two remaining mints, Cork and Wexford, are rare and it is assumed that only small numbers of coins were produced. The Cork mint was only to produce groats and pennies.

The Cork groat follows the same design as the other groats but is much cruder in design. Two varieties exist, one which features a crowned facing portrait of the king within a tressure, and another which includes a pellet on either side of the king's neck. The reverse features the cross and pellet design with the inner legend 'CIVITAS CORCAGIE' (city of Cork). It is believed that as few as twelve Cork light groats exist, of which seven are in museum collections. A Cork groat sold for £IR1,000 at the Whyte's Millennial Collection Sale.

Two varieties of penny are associated with the Cork mint — the standard crowned facing portrait of the king on the obverse and the long cross with three pellets on the reverse, and a second variety which features a larger portrait of the king than that found on other pennies. As with the groat, the pennies of the Cork mint are extremely rare.

The Wexford mint was to produce groats and half-groats and was the only mint not to produce pennies during this period. The Wexford groat is again crude in style. One type is known with the crowned facing portrait of the king within a tressure. The reverse features the standard cross and pellets design with the distinguishing inner legend 'VILLA WEISFOR' or 'VILLA WEIXFOR' (town of Wexford).

The half-groat associated with the Wexford mint follows the same design as the groat and is similarly crude in style, with the wording of the obverse and reverse legends often blundered.

Despite the Dublin parliament's attempts to ensure effective control of the Irish mint, the king still remained anxious about the management of his mint in Dublin and in August 1474 Germyn Lynch was replaced by Richard Heron, a London merchant, who was placed in charge of the mints of Dublin, Drogheda, Trim, Waterford, Cork and Limerick.

In 1475 the Dublin parliament once again moved to control the mints in Ireland and insisted 'that all the mints in Ireland shall cease, except those of Dublin, Drogheda and Waterford', and that in these mints strict controls should be introduced regarding the melting down of bullion and other silver.

The same legislation also set the exchange rates for English coins circulating in Ireland: 'the coins called the gross made in the reigns of Edward III, Richard II, Henry IV and Henry VI not clipped shall be the value of six deniers, the demy-gross not clipped of the value of three deniers, and the denier not clipped of the value of three half-deniers. The gross made in England in the time of the present king, not clipped, shall pass for five deniers, the demy-gross for two deniers and a half, and the denier for one denier and a quadrant, and all the moneys struck in Ireland to be of the same value as they new are' (Simon 1749, 85).

A year later the Anglo-Irish parliament, sitting in Drogheda, once again found themselves legislating against illegal mints: 'The silver lately made in Cork, Youghill, Limerick and other places in Munster, except Waterford, being neither lawful in itself, nor of lawful weight and allay, it is enacted that the same be utterly damned and taken in no payment' (Simon 1749, 85).

Despite the problems of the illegal mints, or possibly because of them and their illicit output, official records from about 1475 talk of the 'grande habundance of coynes' (Ellis 1978, 25). This abundance of coins is reflected in legislation from 1476 which set the local exchange rate for a range of English gold coins, including the ryal, the demi-ryal, the angel, the demi-angel and the noble. The act further sets rates for 'the currency of foreign coyne imported into Ireland, it is enacted that the Rider fine and good shall pass for five shillings of Irish silver, the Ducat five shillings, the Leo five shillings, the Crown five shillings, the Crusado five shillings, the Burgoin Noble ten shillings, the Half and Quarter in proportion, the Salute five shillings, and if any of the said gold want in weight of the rightful standard, so much to be abated in payment as it wants' (Simon 1749, 86).

The year 1476 saw further changes in the running of the Irish mints, with the appointment of Philip Brentwood as master of the Dublin Castle mint under Richard Heron. Within a year Germyn Lynch was back again as master of the mint in Dublin, in association with a London goldsmith, William Hateclyff, with Heron still in overall control of the Irish mints.

Whilst the 'Second English Coinage' with its 'lighter' weight had successfully met the needs of the Anglo-Irish nobles and the merchants and traders of the lordship, its similarity in design to English coins raised problems in England, where the 'light' Irish coins were once again being passed off as full-weight English coins. Merchants in England were increasingly voicing their concerns about the large numbers of Irish coins finding their way across the Irish Sea and demands were made that the Irish should adopt a more distinctive design for their lower-weight coinage.

It was against this background that Edward IV again took a direct interest in Irish affairs. In February 1478 he had consolidated his position in England with the imprisonment and murder of his brother George, the duke of Clarence, who had emerged as Edward's principal rival for the crown. Within a month the earl of Kildare, the king's deputy, was also dead. Edward, always wary of the ambitions of the Anglo-Irish lords, appointed an Englishman, Lord Henry Grey, as his new deputy. The Anglo-Irish parliament, however, had a different view on who should govern Ireland and elected Kildare's son, Gerald Fitzgerald, the eighth earl of

Kildare, as justiciar. Ireland found itself with two governors, one appointed by the king and the other elected by parliament.

The situation worsened when Grey arrived in the autumn of 1478 to assume the reins of government. He was refused admission to Dublin Castle and the chancellor refused to hand over the great seal of Ireland. Grey, in a bid to assert his own authority, dismissed the old parliament that had elected Kildare and summoned a new parliament. The old parliament refused to acknowledge Grey's command and continued to sit and pass its own legislation. Grey's new parliament also met and passed its own laws. Ireland, along with two governors, now had two parliaments. Faced with a worsening political situation, Edward IV compromised in this battle of wills; in May 1479 he confirmed Kildare as deputy but with one of the king's loyal supporters, Viscount Gormanstown, as lieutenant deputy. As part of the political 'horse-trading' which led to the compromise the king insisted that it was his man, Gormanstown, who would have responsibility for the regulation of the mint and the appointment of its officials.

In October 1479 Gormanstown appointed Germyn Lynch once again as master of the mint. By this stage, Edward IV was wary not only of his Anglo-Irish lords but also of his mint masters, convinced that much of the debasement of Irish coinage in recent years had been of their doing in an attempt to increase their own income at the expense of the Crown. Lynch's activities were to be closely monitored. He was required to strike coins to a new distinctive design set out in legislation passed the previous year. To ensure more effective control over the manufacture and standard of coins, the king further insisted that the new coins were only to be struck in Dublin.

The 1478 legislation authorising the issuing of a new coinage, the sixth (or seventh) issue of Edward IV, was passed in response to the problems associated with the importing of 'light' Irish coins into England. The legislation required the new coins to 'bear a notable difference in eyther side ... easy to be known to everybody'. The dies for the new coins were to be made in accordance with 'suche printes as been delivered unto the maister of the mynt here', and 'touching the fineness it be according to the standard of England' (Ellis 1978, 27).

The legislation required that the new coins should have on one side a cross and a rose, and as a consequence this series is known as the 'Cross and Rose' issue.

The dating of this particular issue of coins has been the subject of conjecture for a number of years. Until recently the accepted view was that the Cross and Rose coins had been issued some time between 1463 and 1467. Recent research by the numismatist John Stafford-Langan, based on a closer reading of official records and a process of elimination, now suggests that these coins should be placed at about 1478–9. This issue was to be limited to groats and pennies.

The groat features on the obverse a large rose with a small cross in the centre with the legend 'EDWARDUS DEI GRA DNS HYBERNI' or 'HYBERNIE'

(Edward by the grace of God lord of Ireland). The reverse features a radiant sun with sixteen rays with the two legends within concentric borders, the outer legend reading 'POSUI DEUM ADIUTOREM MEU' or 'MEUM' (I have made God my helper) and the inner legend 'CIVITAS DUBLINIE' (city of Dublin).

The penny similarly featured on the obverse the large rose with small cross design and the abbreviated legend 'EDW D.G. DNS HYBERN' (Edward by the grace of God lord of Ireland). The reverse featured a radiant sun with a pellet within an annulet at the centre of the sun with the legend 'CIVITAS DUBLINIE' (city of Dublin).

Both of these coins are extremely rare and it is thought that as few as twelve groats, with eight in the museum collections of the National Museum in Dublin and the Ulster Museum, and about 30 pennies may have survived from this issue. A magnificent example of a cross on rose groat fetched £3,500 (sterling) at a Glendining's sale in London on 19 July 2000, whilst a poorly struck and clipped cross on rose and sun penny sold for £IR1,100 at the Whyte's Millennial Collection Sale. The scarcity of surviving coins would suggest that the cross on rose issue was small. It has been proposed that Germyn Lynch may have interpreted the 1478 legislation too freely and that the replacement of the royal portrait by a radiant sun, which certainly was a 'significant difference' to the previous issue of coins, may have incurred the disapproval of the king and his officials. It is possible that the striking of these coins may be linked to his removal from the position of master of the Irish mint in May 1480.

Lynch was replaced as master by James Keyting, the prior of the Order of the Knights Hospitaller in Ireland. It seems unlikely that Keyting was directly involved in the day-to-day production of coins and more probable that his appointment, which may have been no more than a sinecure, was a further attempt by the king and his officials to exercise royal control over the activities of the mint and its officials.

The final issue of Edward's reign, the 'Sun and Rose' issue, also dates from this period. The 1478 legislation set out that the design of the coins should feature a cross and rose on one side and on the other a 'notable difference'. The cross and rose design was, perhaps, too distinctive a design for a king who had spent the best part of 20 years attempting to harmonise his coinage across his territories, and yet at the same time the lighter Irish coinage had to be sufficiently different to avoid confusion with his heavier English coinage. The resulting coinage, issued some time between 1479 and 1483, attempted to strike that balance.

The final coinage, as with the previous issue, was to consist of groats and pennies only.

The groat featured a crowned facing portrait of the king within a tressure, with the 'notable difference' being a sun and rose placed on either side of the crown and the neck. Two obverse legends are known on these coins, 'EDWARDUS DEI

GRA HIBERNA' (Edward by the grace of God lord of Ireland) and 'EDWARDUS DEI GRA REX AGL FRAE D' (Edward by the grace of God king of England and France). The 'D' may be an abbreviated reference to 'Dominus' (lord) of Ireland. The reverse design featured a long cross with a rose in the centre with two legends within concentric borders, 'POSUI DEUM ADIUTORE MEU' or 'ADIUTOREM MEUM' (I have made God my helper) and an inner legend 'CIVITAS DUBLINIE' (city of Dublin).

Fig. 41—Penny, Edward IV, 'Sun and Rose', 1478. *SNC*, May 1995, No. 2793

The penny featured the crowned facing portrait of the king with a sun and rose on either side of the neck and the legend 'EDWARD REX ANGL Z FRANC' (Edward, king of England and France). The reverse featured the long cross with a small rose in the centre and had a rose and two suns or one sun and two roses alternating in the angles of the cross; the mint signature 'CIVITAS DUBLIN' (city of Dublin) formed the reverse legend. A variety of penny exists where the sun and rose devices are slightly larger on the obverse.

Whilst this coinage might suggest some control over the activities of the Irish mint by the king's officials, royal instructions were still being flouted by the Irish. The king's instructions of 1478 had stipulated that coins were only to be produced in Dublin, but groats of this final issue were also to be struck at Drogheda, with the inner legend reading 'VILLA DE DROGHEDA' (town of Drogheda).

Again, this final coinage is rare and it has been suggested that these coins may only have been struck for less than a year, possibly between 1480 and 1481.

It was perhaps the increasing frustration of the king over his inability to effectively control his Irish mint that prompted a further round of changes in the running of the mint. In March 1483 Thomas Galmole (who had briefly held the office of master in 1478) was appointed master of the mint to oversee the production of a new issue of silver pennies and halfpennies to the English standard. This was to be Edward's last attempt to exercise any control over the Irish mint, its recalcitrant officials and its coins. Within weeks, however, the king was dead.

7. THE THREE CROWNS
The coinage of Richard III, Lambert Simnel and Henry VII (1483–1505)

As heralds and messengers travelled the country announcing the accession of King Richard III, the workmen at the Drogheda mint turned their hands to re-engraving the obverse dies of the dead king to produce coins for the new king. The 'EDW' of Edwardus was recut to read 'RIC' for Ricardus, although the faint traces of the 'EDW' were to linger like a ghost beneath the 'Ricardus' on the coins of the new king.

In Dublin, Deputy Kildare and his Anglo-Irish parliament soon found themselves at odds with the new king as he moved to establish his authority in his Irish lordship with the appointment of a new chancellor. Kildare, ever the pragmatist, eventually bowed to Richard's wishes. He remained as deputy but the king was determined to remove him.

The first coins of Richard III's reign were struck at the Drogheda mint, and consisted of a groat and a penny.

Two varieties of groat exist, one in which the traces of 'EDW' can be seen under 'RIC' in the obverse legend, and another which was struck from a newly engraved obverse die. The obverse of the coin features a crowned facing portrait of the king, essentially no different from the portrait of Edward IV, within a tressure with an alternating sun and rose device at the side of the neck and the crown. The legend 'RICARDUS DEI GRA DNS HYB (HYBE)' (Richard by the grace of God lord of Ireland) forms the border of the coin, with a rose mint mark incorporated into it. The reverse design was the long cross with a rose in the centre of the previous reign, with the outer legend 'POSUI DEUM ADIUTOREM MEU (MEUM)' (I have made God my helper) and the inner legend 'VILLA DROGHEDA' (town of Drogheda).

Both varieties of groat are extremely rare. An example of a Drogheda groat in very fine condition sold at the Whyte's Millennial Collection Sale for £IR2,000.

Fig. 42—Groat, Richard III, Drogheda 'Bust with Suns and Roses with Rose on Cross Reverse', 1483. *SNC,* February 1998, No. 71

The penny struck at Drogheda in 1483 again followed the same design as the last pennies of the previous reign, with a crowned facing portrait of the king and the sun and rose devices about the crown and neck on the obverse with the legend 'RICARDUS DEI GRA DNS HYB' (Richard by the grace of God lord of Ireland). The reverse of the penny featured the long cross with a rose at the centre with the legend 'VILLA DROGHEDA' (town of Drogheda) forming the border.

It is thought that these coins may have been struck by Germyn Lynch, who originally came from Drogheda, in an attempt to gain favour with the new king with a view to being restored to the mastership of the Irish mint. If this was indeed Lynch's plan, it was to come to nothing.

Pennies were also struck in these early months of Richard's reign at Dublin and Waterford. Unlike the Drogheda penny, the workers in the other two mints were to use the reverse dies of the old 'Cross and Pellets' issue of 1473–8.

The obverse of both coins featured a crowned facing portrait of the king with an annulet on either side of his neck and the shorter legend 'RICARD DNS HYB' (Richard, lord of Ireland). The reverse of both coins featured the long cross design with a quatrefoil in the centre and three pellets in each quarter. The mint signature 'CIVITAS DUBLIN' (city of Dublin) and 'CIVITAS WATERFORD' (city of Waterford) formed the legend around the border.

Like the Drogheda coins, the Dublin and Waterford pennies are extremely rare, with the Waterford coin being the scarcer. A Dublin penny was to sell for £IR2,200 at the Whyte's Millennial Collection Sale, and was believed to be the only example of a Dublin penny outside the National Museum and the Ulster Museum's collections.

Possibly in response to the continued minting of these English-style coins, Richard III wrote on 18 July 1483 to the council of the Irish lordship concerning 'the grete clamor, grugge and complaints' against the light Irish coins circulating in England and the problems they were presenting 'for lak of expresse difference that shud have be graved upon the same' (Ellis 1978, 28).

Two days earlier the king, in a bid to exercise control over the Irish mint, had confirmed Galmole's appointment as master, empowering him to strike groats and half-groats alongside pennies and halfpennies to the English standard and a new design.

In his instructions to the council Richard set out the 'expresse difference' for his new coinage: 'unto the time we have otherwise or deigned', all Irish coins should bear 'a clere and express difference fro that sylver that is coined here within this our royalme, that is to say, on the one side the armes of England, and on the other side iij corones' (Ellis 1978, 28). The king went on to order that 'the silver coignes of that ar land had hiderto be made and stryken at any place or tyme' should in future only be struck in Dublin and Waterford.

The three crowns design on the coins of Richard III was based on the coat of arms of the Irish lordship which had first been used in 1386. Originally the arrangement of the crowns had been similar to that of the arms of the province of Munster, but on Richard's coins the crowns were to appear on top of each other, reminiscent of the three crowns of a papal tiara.

The Anglo-Irish parliament meeting in Dublin and later in Naas in the following year passed the necessary legislation to authorise the production of the new coinage as set out in the king's instruction. But in the ongoing battle of wills between parliament and the king, the king's instructions were not to be followed to the letter, with the parliament insisting that the new coinage be struck to the lower standard authorised in 1471 and not to the English standard as Richard desired.

The act's preamble, as with previous legislation, was to set out the problems the Irish people and the economy of the lordship had experienced in the absence of a sound coinage: 'As the weal publique has been for these three years past greatly damaged, for that the kings mint for striking of silver coyn have not been ordered for the profit of the subject, by which all foreigners, as Portugals, Spaniards, Bretons, Frenchmen and Flemings, practising merchandise, have used to bring in the coins of their countries and other bullion, to be coined in the king's mint here, to the great profit of the said foreigners in exchange, and damage of the king's subjects. And as it hath happened thereby, that the common people cannot have small coins for buying and selling to paying small sums to servants, labourers and artificers, by which many of the inhabitants have and are about departing the land, and leaving their habitations desolate and waste' (Simon 1749, 88–9).

The act went on to set out the coins to be struck and the standard to which the coins were to be struck: 'It is therefore enacted, that it shall be lawful for the master of the mint for the time being, to strike and make four manner of coyness or money i.e. Grosses, Demy-grosses, deniers and Demy-deniers, in such a manner and in such places, as in ordained by a statute lately made in parliament held on Monday after the feast of St Catherine, the tenth of King Edward IV, and that the said manner of coins, so be struck, to be made of fineness and allay … as is ordered by a parliament in the twelfth of the said king'.

It continued with the design of the coins to be struck, following closely the king's instructions of the previous year: 'The Grosse, the Demy-gross, the Denier and Demy-denier, to have according to the king's commandment, the print on one side of the arms of England with a cross trefoile in every fine, with this inscription, Ricardus Dei Gratia Rex Angliae Dominus Hiberniae, and on the other side three crowns, one above the other, with a cross trefoil in every fine, bearing in the circumference of the same the name of the place, where in form aforesaid it shall be lawfully coined'.

The act set out the proportions to be struck: 'and for the ease of the common

Fig. 43—Groat, Richard III, Dublin 'Three Crowns Coinage', 1483–5. *SNC,* May 1995, No. 2795

people, the fifth part of such coin to be struck in small pieces, i.e. in Demy-grosses, deniers and demy-deniers. That the master, in presence of the controuler, may receive their stuff and all lawful bullion brought to the mint in cups, spoons and other waste, the merchant to receive back for every ounce of bullion four shillings and sixpence, the master two deniers and the residue of every ounce to go to the king'.

And finally, the act set out the penalties for people who might refuse to accept the new coin: 'That the coin struck within the Castle of Dublin, or elsewhere in Ireland, by the king's officers, according to the print described, shall pass and be current and among all the subjects, and that the refuser shall forfeit twelve deniers for every half-denier refused, one half to the king and the other half to the prosecuter'. Alongside this legislation, 'An Act for breaking all counterfeit money, and that all letters patent and acts, made in behalf of Germyn Lynch to be the master of the said mint, shall be void' was also to be passed.

Germyn Lynch's career was at an end; in all likelihood his unauthorised Drogheda coinage had led not to his restoration to the mastership but to his downfall.

The parliament further stipulated that the profits from coin production at the Dublin and other mints should go to the earl of Kildare rather than directly to the Crown to meet the cost of administering and defending the lordship.

It is thought that Galmole took up office in September 1484, although the day-to-day supervision of the mint was left to a local man, Richard Tailer, also known as Newall of Dublin. Coin production is believed to have commenced in January 1485. Despite the requirement in the 1484 legislation to produce half-groats, pennies and halfpennies, it seems that only groats were produced. This initial issue was to be short-lived and it is possible that production of coins ceased some three months later, in March 1485. Galmole's profits as master from this production run totalled £95 15s 9½d.

In the summer of 1485 it is thought that a second issue of 'three crown' groats took place. The two 1485 issues of groats can be distinguished: the earlier coins have a plain border to the shield with large fleurs-de-lis in the quarters of the royal arms, whilst the coins issued in the summer of 1485 have shields with a hatched border and smaller, neater fleurs-de-lis.

In another departure from the legislation, the Dublin groats did not include the city's mint signature.

The groats struck at Dublin featured the royal arms of England over a long cross with three pellets forming a trefoil at the end of each arm of the cross. The obverse legend, which forms the border of the coin, reads 'RICAR REX ANGL FRAN (FRANC)' (Richard, king of England and France). The reverse design featured the three crowns in pale or above each other within a circle over a long cross with trefoils of pellets at each end; the legend reads 'DOMINUS HYBERNIE' (lord of Ireland).

Groats, in line with the king's letter, were also struck at the Waterford mint. These coins follow essentially the same design as the Dublin groat, but with the royal arms within a tressure of four arcs rather than a circle over a long cross with trefoil pellet endings. The obverse legend, however, reads 'RICARDUS DEI GRAIA REX' (Richard by the grace of God king). The reverse design similarly places the three crowns within a tressure over a long cross with trefoil pellet endings, but instead of the king's Irish titles the legend, in line with the king's instructions, reads 'CIVITAS WATERFOORD' (city of Waterford). A number of varieties exist with slightly different spellings of the mint signature.

Again, both coins are rare, with the Waterford groat considered extremely rare.

Richard III was determined to wrest control of Ireland from the earl of Kildare. In a series of secret negotiations he began to bring together a coalition of Anglo-Irish nobles and native Irish leaders determined to remove the deputy. His scheming was, however, to come to nothing. On 22 August 1485 Richard III was killed at the Battle of Bosworth and the Lancastrian claimant, Henry Tudor, ascended the English throne as Henry VII. The change of dynasty marked the beginning of a period of uncertainty for the Yorkist Kildare and his supporters in the Anglo-Irish parliament, who continued to legislate in the name of the dead king until October 1485.

The first coins of Henry VII to be struck at Dublin reflect the Anglo-Irish parliament's ambivalence towards the change in royal dynasties and were to make no direct reference to the name of the new king. In an echo of the Anonymous Crown coinage of 1460, the obverse legend simply reads 'REX ANGLIE FRANCIE' (king of England and France). The Dublin mint was to issue groats, half-groats, pennies and halfpennies during the first two years of Henry's reign, all with the same anonymous legend.

Fig. 44—Groat, Henry VII, 'Three Crowns Coinage', 1485–7. *SNC*, February 1998, No. 72

The groat essentially followed the same design as that of Richard III, with the royal arms within a circle over a long cross with trefoil pellet endings. The obverse legend, which formed the border of the coin, read 'REX ANGLIE FRANC (FRANCIE)' (king of England and France). The reverse design featured the three crowns within a circle over the long cross with trefoil pellet endings. As with the Dublin groats of Richard III, the reverse legend read 'DOMINUS HYBERNIE' (lord of Ireland). Two other varieties are known, the products of mistakes in engraving. One variety features the legend 'DOMINUS HYBERNIE' on both sides of the coin, whilst the other features the reverse legend 'ET REX HYBERNIE' (and king of Ireland).

The Dublin half-groat followed the same design, with royal arms on the obverse and the anonymous royal legend. The reverse again featured the three crowns device but with the legend 'DOMINUS HIBERNIE' (lord of Ireland). The penny was to follow the same design as the half-groat but with the misspelled reverse legend 'DOMINUS VRERNIE'.

Fig. 45—Half-groat, Henry VII, Dublin 'Three Crowns Coinage', 1485–7. *SNC,* February 1998, No. 74

The tiny halfpenny was a test of the engraver's skill and similarly featured the royal arms design with the contracted legend 'REX ANGLIE' (king of England). The reverse design with the three coins device, like the penny, had a misspelled legend 'DOMINUS YRERNI' (lord of Ireland).

The Dublin penny is rare and the halfpenny extremely rare.

Whilst Kildare and his supporters in Dublin tried to ignore the change in kings, the Butlers in Waterford revelled in the triumph of the Lancastrians, and this Butler stronghold was to use its coinage to proclaim its loyalty to the new king.

Waterford's production of coin was to be limited to the groat. The obverse of the coin featured the royal arms within a quatrefoil over a long cross with trefoil pellet endings. The obverse legend, which formed the border, read 'HENRICUS DI GRACIA REX' (Henry by the grace of God king). The reverse design again featured the three crowns device within a tressure over a cross with trefoil pellet endings, with the royal cipher of a 'h' placed below the crown, yet again proclaiming the city's loyalty to the new king. Two fleurs-de-lis were incorporated into the reverse design on either side of the middle crown. The mint signature 'CIVITAS WATERFOR' or 'WATERFORD' forms the reverse legend.

Four other varieties of Waterford groat are known with minor variations in design, with the fleurs-de-lis omitted from the reverse design, annulets forming the trefoil instead of pellets, and stars incorporated into the reverse design next to the lower crown. An extremely rare variety has the royal arms with no framing quatrefoil and the three crowns on the reverse without their tressure border.

In November 1485 Henry VII moved again to assert his authority over the Irish mint. Robert Bowley was appointed master for life, with instructions to strike coins to the English standard in line with Galmole's warrant of 1483. This move to bring the Irish mint under royal control was reinforced by the appointment of Nicholas Flynt as controller and assayer of the king's moneys throughout his territories. Bowley's appointment, however, seems to have had little impact on the Irish mint. During the period of his appointment the Dublin mint continued to produce its anonymous coinage with no reference to Henry.

In March 1487 Bowley was replaced by John Estrele as master of the Irish mint, although it is thought that this appointment, which paid £20 a year, was no more than a sinecure or gift of the king to a loyal official.

Within two months of Estrele's appointment, one of the most extraordinary events in the War of the Roses was to occur on 24 May 1487 with the coronation of Lambert Simnel, the ten-year-old son of an Oxford joiner, who was proclaimed as the Yorkist 'King Edward VI' in Dublin's Christchurch Cathedral. Kildare publicly acknowledged this unlikely pretender as king, and ordered the striking of a coinage for the newly crowned Edward VI, with the obverse legend 'EDWARDVS REX'. Only groats were to be struck, with one variety having Simnel styled as 'REX HIBERNIE' (king of Ireland).

Fig. 46—Groat, Lambert Simnel as Edward VI, 'Three Crowns Coinage', 1487. *SNC,* February 1998, No. 75

All of Lambert Simnel's groats are rare. A poorly struck Dublin groat with the 'Rex Hybernie' legend fetched £IR1,800 at the Whyte's Millennial Collection Sale, and a muled Waterford groat with Henry's royal titles on the obverse and a reversed 'E' cypher engraved over a 'h' cypher fetched £IR2,000 at the same sale.

The attribution of coins of a Yorkist pretender to Waterford, a town held by the Lancastrian Butlers, has long been the subject of numismatic debate. One suggestion is that the Butler holding Waterford was a son-in-law of the earl of Kildare and that he may have struck the coins in deference to his father-in-law's wishes.

An alternative view is that, whilst these coins bear the mint signature of Waterford, they were not struck in Waterford but from dies prepared by an itinerant moneyer or engraver who was 'licensed' to work from the Waterford mint but may have been residing elsewhere. In the late 1470s moneyers were required to move from mint to mint. In 1478 Germyn Lynch was instructed that he could not 'continually dwell in one place'. Consequently it is thought that dies bearing a mint signature of a major mint may have been routinely used by moneyers in other parts of the country — hence the reference in the 1472 legislation to moneyers making false coin in Youghal, Kinsale and Kilmallock, although coins with mint signatures from these towns do not exist.

Yet another suggestion is that these coins were propaganda pieces, produced possibly in Dublin but with a Waterford mint signature to suggest that support for the new 'boy king' extended even to Lancastrian strongholds such as Waterford!

Lambert Simnel's coinage was to be short-lived. On 4 June 1487 his army of 2,000 German, Flemish and Swiss mercenaries and 4,000 Irish soldiers left Ireland. Twelve days later Simnel's army was defeated at the Battle of Stoke. The 'boy king' was captured by Henry VII and sent to London to work as a scullion in the royal kitchens.

With the defeat of Simnel, the Dublin mint reverted to striking 'anonymous' coins with no reference to the name of the king in the royal titles. These coins were, however, different from the earlier anonymous three crowns issue in that the deputy incorporated his own personal arms, the saltire of the Fitzgeralds, into the obverse design.

The reasoning behind the incorporation of his personal heraldic arms alongside the royal arms on these coins is unclear. In an age of symbolism it could be interpreted as an act of reconciliation, a demonstration of loyalty to the victorious king following the Simnel débâcle, or it may have been a challenge to the king's authority — a symbolic message that the king could not rule Ireland without him. Irrespective of whether it was a challenge or not, the king was to bide his time; with other Yorkist pretenders in the wings, now was not the time to challenge Kildare's supremacy in Ireland.

The 'Geraldine groats', as they are known, essentially followed the same design as the previous 'three crowns' coins, with the royal arms within a circle over a long cross with trefoil annulet endings. On either side of the royal arms is a small shield with the Fitzgerald arms. The obverse legend reads 'REX ANGLIE Z FRAN' (king of England and France). Whilst the obverse of the coin made no reference to Henry, the reverse design featured the king's 'h' cipher below the three crowns; Kildare was definitely hedging his bets. However, another variety of Dublin groat did not include the 'h' cipher. The reverse legend of the Geraldine groat, as with previous Dublin issues, read 'DOMINUS YBERNIE' (lord of Ireland).

Fig. 47—Groat, Geraldine Issue. Reverse without 'h' below three crowns, 1487. *SNC*, May 1995, No. 2799

The half-groat similarly features the royal arms with the smaller Fitzgerald shield on either side. Again, the obverse features the anonymous royal legend 'REX ANGLIE FRANCIE' (king of England and France). The reverse features the three crowns over the long cross with the legend 'DOMINOS VRERNIE' (lord of Ireland). Another variety of half-groat features the 'DOMINUS VRERNIE' legend on both sides of the coin. The half-groats of the Geraldine issue are extremely rare.

As with the Lambert Simnel groats, a Geraldine issue groat is also associated with the Lancastrian stronghold of Waterford. The coin features the standard anonymous obverse legend of a Dublin groat muled with one of the earlier Henry VII Waterford reverses, with the legend 'CIVITAS WATERFORD'. Again the question has been raised as to whether these coins were minted in Waterford at the time or are the result of a muling of two incorrect dies, possibly in Dublin, following the closure of the Waterford mint in 1488.

Kildare was to remain as deputy despite his treason, and was pardoned for his involvement in the Yorkist plot a year and a day after the bizarre events he had stage-managed at Christchurch Cathedral. Nevertheless, Henry was understandably wary of Kildare's loyalty. In July 1488 Sir Richard Edgecombe was sent to Ireland to receive Kildare's formal submission to the king. The king's fears were well founded; despite his pardon Kildare refused to submit to Edgecombe, and it was to be another year, including a brief spell for Kildare in the Tower of London, before the king and his deputy were finally reconciled.

In a bid to ensure more effective control over the Irish mint, the king authorised the closure of the Waterford mint in 1488; all minting activities in Ireland were to be concentrated in Dublin.

The final issue of 'three crowns' coins took place between 1488 and 1490 and consisted of groats, half-groats and pennies. All the coins of this final issue were struck in Dublin and can be distinguished from those struck between 1485 and 1487 by the trefoil annulet endings of the long cross on either side of the coin.

The groats followed the same design as the previous three crowns coins with the royal arms within a circle upon a long cross. The obverse legend saw the king's name restored and read 'HENRICUS REX AN' (Henry, king of England). The reverse featured the three crowns device with a 'h' below the lower crown and the legend 'DOMINUS VBERNIE' (lord of Ireland). Three other variations of groat are associated with this last issue. With two the difference is in the obverse legend, with one reverting to the anonymous legend 'REX ANGLIE Z FRANC' and the other with the legend 'DOMINUS VBERNIE' on both sides of the coin. The fourth variety has a significantly different reverse design in that the top crown is arched or closed rather than open and the legend reads 'CIVITAS DUBLIN' or 'DUBLINI' (city of Dublin).

Again the half-groats follow a similar design. Seven varieties of half-groat are known with minor variations, including the use of pellets and annulets in the cross endings and the presence or absence of the 'h' cypher. Again there are two varieties which have the 'DOMINUS' or 'DOMINOS VBERNIE' legend on both sides and a further two varieties with the 'CIVITAS DUBLINIE' reverse legend. On some of these coins Dublin is rendered as 'DEBLIN' or 'DEBLI'. One of the 'Civitas Dublinie' coins has a blundered obverse legend reading 'HENRICUS DI ORAE' (possibly 'Henry by the grace of God') and others reading 'HENRIC DOM OBAR (possibly 'Henry lord').

One variety of half-groat features the curious legend 'DOMINE KERIE'. Whilst it might be interpreted as a very poor rendering of the 'lord of Ireland' title, the general view is that it is a rendering of the title 'Lord', or 'O Lord', into Latin (*Dominus*) and Greek (*Kyrie*). If this is the case, it is the only coin in the Irish series which includes a Greek legend!

A very fine example of a 'Domine Kerie' half-groat was sold at the Whyte's Millennial Collection Sale for £IR1,200.

Three varieties of penny were to be struck at the Dublin mint. Again the varieties follow a similar pattern to the other coins, with one having the anonymous royal titles legend, a second featuring the 'DOMINOS VRERNIE' legend on both sides, and the third having the 'CIVITAS DUBLINIE' legend on the reverse without a royal cypher.

The blundering of legends and the muling of the obverse and reverse dies which is a feature of the 'three crowns' series is perhaps a reflection of the standards of workmanship and supervision at the Dublin mint. The poor quality and standard of workmanship was to become increasingly evident in the final coinage of Henry VII from 1496 to 1505.

In a bid to further exercise royal control, and possibly as a response to the poor standard of workmanship at the Dublin mint, Robert Bowley was reappointed master in place of Galmole, with a John Coton as joint master, working under the direction of Flynt, who continued as controller of the king's mints. The Irish mint was now in the hands of the king's men. This assertion of royal control was to prove timely. In November 1491 Perkin Warbeck, yet another Yorkist pretender, arrived in Cork, supported by the earl of Desmond. This time, however, no coins were to be struck for 'Richard IV'!

The arrival of another Yorkist pretender in Ireland and the active involvement of Kildare's relatives in support of his bid for Henry's crown finally prompted the king to act against Kildare. In June 1492 Kildare was removed as deputy. In the wake of his removal, widespread disorder and near civil war broke out between the earl's supporters and his long-standing Butler foes. In response to the worsening political and military situation in Ireland, Henry VII dispatched Sir Edward Poynings as the new deputy with an army of 400 men. Kildare was arrested and sent to London. In July 1495 a further Yorkist invasion of Ireland took place which was defeated by Poynings. The new deputy was charged with restoring order, reforming the administration of the lordship and limiting the power of the Anglo-Irish parliament. Poynings restored order at a cost of £23,000 to Henry VII's treasury. He also, however, managed to put the lordship on a firmer financial footing with revenues of over £3,000 being raised, but his most important legacy was to be 'Poynings' Law'.

In December 1494 the Anglo-Irish parliament at Drogheda passed an act stating that no Irish parliament could be summoned without the king's prior consent and no bill could be introduced except for those already approved by the king and his council in England. The act effectively broke the power the Anglo-Irish parliament had wrested from the Crown over the last three centuries.

One effect of Poynings' Law was that no legislation to introduce a new coinage could be moved without the consent of the king. In order to increase royal control over the lordship's coinage, the powers of the deputy in relation to monetary matters were further curtailed, including the right to pardon counterfeiters. During this period of direct rule the king entrusted the mastership of the mint to Thomas Garth, the military governor of Dublin Castle, but even military governors were not beyond reproach when it came to the stewardship of the Irish mint. A later governor and master, Richard White, was to be charged for withholding profits of £125 5s 1d from the king!

In July 1495 minting operations began again at Dublin Castle. The new coins were, however, all to be struck to an English design. It is thought that the first run of these new coins were struck between July 1495 and September 1496.

The king, the shrewdest businessman to sit on the English throne, in authorising this new issue of coins probably wanted to ensure that there was sufficient coin available for people to pay their taxes to the Crown. He was also not averse to taking his share of the profits from the production of the very same coins that were required to pay his taxes!

Fig. 48—Groat, Henry VII, clipped late portrait issue, 1496–1505. *SNC,* February 1998, No. 81

The coins issued between 1496 and 1505 are known as the 'Late Portrait' issues and consisted of groats, half-groats and pennies. All the coins of this latest issue were struck in Dublin.

The earliest coins of this last issue were struck to a standard of 32 grains, about 80% of that of their English equivalents. The decision to strike a distinctive English-style coin again raised concern about light Irish coins finding their way to England where they might pass as full-weight English coins. It is possible that the poor quality of the workmanship of these coins may have been an attempt by the Irish mint to differentiate these coins from English coins and keep them within the lordship, working on the assumption that the English would be wary of coins of such poor quality and standard.

The groat featured a crowned facing portrait of the king within a fleured tressure with the legend 'HENRICUS DI GRA DNS HYBERNIE' (Henry by the grace of God lord of Ireland). The reverse design featured a long cross pattée with three pellets in each quarter. The reverse also contained two legends within concentric borders, the outer legend reading 'POSUI DEUM ADIVTOREM MEU' (I have made God my helper) and the inner legend reading 'CIVITAS DUBLINIE' (city of Dublin). About five variations of the 32-grain groat exist with minor variations in design, mainly relating to the size of the king's portrait and whether he is wearing an open or closed arched crown. One has a different reverse legend reading 'PROVERBO ADIVTORIUM' ('I will provide help' or 'I will furnish God my help').

Fig. 49—Half-groat, Henry VII, Dublin, 1496–1505. *SNC*, February 1998, No. 82

Half-groats were also struck to this basic design with the crowned facing portrait of the king, although on all the half-groats the king has an arched rather than an open crown. The obverse legend is also different, reading 'HENRIC DEI GR REX ANGL FR' (Henry by the grace of God king of England and France). The reverse design features the long cross with three pellets in each quarter with the outer 'POSUI DEUM ADIVTOR MEU' legend and the inner Dublin mint signature legend, although on some Dublin is spelt with an 'x' — 'DUXLIN'.

Two other varieties of the half-groats are known, with the main difference being the addition of a 'v' or inverted 'v' on the king's breast. All three varieties of half-groat are extremely rare and a groat with the inverted 'v' was sold for £IR1,200 at the Whyte's Millennial Collection Sale.

Two distinctive types of penny belong to the early years of this last issue of Henry VII. The first type features a large arched crown over a 'h'. The coins are struck on a very small flan and there are traces of an obverse legend which is not decipherable. The reverse legend features a long cross and three pellets; because of the small flan used, the pellets and cross device takes up almost all of the space on the coin, although it is possible to discern the legend 'CIVITAS DUBLIN' (city of Dublin) forming the border of the coin.

A second variety of penny features a crowned facing portrait of the king; again, because of the small size of the flan or clipping, the obverse legend is difficult to determine. The reverse features a long cross with split ends and three pellets in each quarter with the legend 'CIVITAS DUBLINIE' forming the border. A variety of this type of penny has a pellet placed on either side of the king's portrait.

The pennies of this coinage are all extremely rare. A penny with the pellet on either side of the king's portrait realised £IR1,500 at the Whyte's Millennial Collection Sale.

During 1496, Henry's direct rule of Ireland through Poynings came to an end. The earl of Kildare, now married to a cousin of the king, was restored to the position of deputy. However, Henry, always wary of Kildare, insisted that he leave his son in London as a hostage for his good behaviour. Whilst Kildare was to rule Ireland for nearly another twenty years, his wings, and those of the Anglo-Irish parliament, had been effectively clipped.

The coinage of this period is characterised by a marked reduction in the standard of workmanship and the quality of the coin. It has already been suggested that the poor workmanship was a deliberate policy to keep silver coin within Ireland and make it unacceptable in England. Despite the poor workmanship, 'light' Irish coin still managed to find its way to England. In 1497 and 1499 proclamations were issued against the importing of Irish coin into England.

In 1497 a second issue of English-type coins was authorised; the coins were, however, to be struck to a lighter standard of 29 grains, three grains lighter than the 1495 issue, about 75% the weight of their English equivalents.

These later English-style portrait coins can be divided into two sub-issues or groups. The earlier, dating from about 1497, retained the tressure design on the obverse combined with the cross and pellets design on the reverse, the cross having split ends. About seven varieties of groat can be attributed to this earlier sub-issue with minor variations in design, including the use of both open and arched crowns, heraldic devices such as saltires, annulets, rosettes on either side of the crown or the king's neck, and the presence of a 'h' or rosette in the centre of the cross on some coins.

The final group of coins issued, possibly in about 1506, consists of groats and pennies. They show a slightly more realistic facing portrait of the king wearing a low flat crown within a circle with the legend 'HENRICUS DI GRA DNS HYBERNIE' (Henry by the grace of God lord of Ireland). The groat reverse features an indented cross with split ends and the three pellets in each quarter, with the two concentric legends as on the earlier portrait coins. The mint signature on some of these groats reads 'SIVITAS' instead of 'CIVITAS DUBLIN'.

The penny features a similar facing portrait of the king with a flat open crown, although the portrait is much cruder. Again, because of the small size of the flan the obverse legend is difficult to determine. The reverse features an indented cross with three pellets in each quarter and the Dublin mint signature.

Alongside the reduction in weight, the legends on these later coins were to become increasingly blundered and the quality of engraving and striking poorer. It is thought that this much lighter issue may have been driven by the desire to increase profits rather than the earlier deliberate policy to try and keep coin in the country. It has been suggested that there may indeed have been some royal connivance from as early as 1494 in debasing or lowering the standard of Ireland's coinage to maximise royal profits and to ensure that the coins were unacceptable not only in England but also in Ireland!

As English landlords and merchants increasingly refused to accept the 'lighter' Irish coins in payment, the Irish found themselves calling for good English silver rather than a distinctive Irish coinage. An official in Waterford in 1501 was to write: 'the mints have uterly undoon this land, and it shall be never wele ordred while any mynte shall be kept here' (Ellis 1978, 32). Other records talk of 'now half oure silver is copir and tyn' and 'that ye coynhe of Irland should be as gode silver as the coyne of England, but not of so grete peise and value' (ibid.).

In 1506 Thomas Galmole was reappointed to supervise the third issue of portrait coins, but the rot had set in. Coin production was driven by the profits to be made from producing light substandard coins. The policy of centralised control had left the day-to-day running of the mints to English officials who did not wish to remain in Ireland and quickly deputised their responsibilities to local men looking to make a quick profit or to military men with more interest in campaigning than coining.

By the turn of the sixteenth century it could be said that few in Ireland, from the king and deputy down, had any interest in making coins, but all were keen to make money!

The production of lighter and lighter coins was to further Henry's centralising ambitions. As distinctive Irish coins became unacceptable to the Irish, the void was filled by English coins. Some 45 years after the Anglo-Irish parliament had won the right to strike their own distinctive coins, the Irish abandoned their coinage in favour of English coins. The Dublin mint was closed down in 1506. For nearly 50 years king and parliament had struggled for control of Ireland's coinage: it seemed that the king had finally won.

8. USE IT AS SILVER
The great Tudor debasement (1536–51)

It was to be almost 30 years after Henry VII's closure of the Dublin mint before a coinage was once again struck specifically for use in Ireland, and this time it was to be at the king's behest rather than that of his Anglo-Irish parliament.

During the last years of Henry VII's reign and the first 25 years of his son Henry VIII's reign, the Anglo-Irish colonists were to use the coins of England in their day-to-day transactions, supplemented by some Scottish coins and gold and silver coins from the Continent. Henry VII, towards the end of his reign, had embarked on a major reform of his English coinage. A new gold pound piece (20 shillings) was introduced in 1489, and a new testoon or shilling coin (12 pence) in 1504. Pounds and shillings were no longer simply units of account but coins circulating alongside pennies. Henry VII's reign also saw the abandonment of the old stylised medieval facing portrait of the king in favour of a new realistic Renaissance profile of the monarch.

A sound coinage enabled the development of a healthy Irish trade in fish, meat and hides, iron, salt and wine and other commodities from the Continent in the early sixteenth century. The Irish economy prospered. This prosperity had an impact not only on the lives of the Anglo-Irish colonists in the Pale and the great eastern port towns but also on the lives of the native Irish. The flourishing economy saw money increasingly used throughout the island, and this growing familiarity was reflected in the nicknames the Irish gave the coins they used in their day-to-day transactions. The three crowns coins of Richard III and Henry VII were known as 'croise caoile' (narrow cross), a reference to the cross under the royal arms, and the handsome profile coins of Henry VII and Henry VIII were called 'salfas' or half-faces.

Henry VIII on his accession left the government of his Irish lordship to Gearoid Mór, the Great Earl of Kildare. The Great Earl died in 1513, and his son, the ninth earl of Kildare, was appointed as deputy. Whilst the end of the War of the Roses had brought prosperity and political stability in England, the old rivalries between the Butlers and the Fitzgeralds continued in Ireland. These came to a head in 1519, and in 1520 Henry was forced to send a new lieutenant, the earl of Surrey, to restore order and bring his Anglo-Irish nobles and the Irish chieftains 'to further obedience'. Henry instructed Surrey 'to spend as much money (as necessary) for the reduction of that land'. He balked, however, at the cost of Surrey's proposed campaign and turned to the Anglo-Irish lords, first the Butlers and then the Fitzgeralds, to restore order. This uneasy accommodation broke down in 1534 when 'Silken Thomas', the son of the ninth earl of Kildare, rose in revolt against Henry. The rebellion quickly spread, supported by Anglo-Irish lords and Irish chieftains. It seemed as if Ireland might be lost, but in the autumn of 1534 Thomas Skeffington arrived in Ireland with 2,300 troops. Over the winter months the rebellion faltered and finally 'Silken Thomas' surrendered to Skeffington in August 1535. Six months later the young earl and his five uncles were executed at Tyburn.

A year before the Geraldine Rebellion, Henry had divorced Katherine of Aragon, married Anne Boleyn and broken with Rome. He was now anxious to consolidate his position in Ireland, fearful that it might be used as a base for invasion by rival European powers. The near success of the Geraldine Rebellion reinforced this view. Royal authority was to be re-established, with an English administration in Dublin backed by a standing army. The maintenance of a civil administration and a military force were to have significant revenue consequences for a king who had frittered away his father's inheritance on a series of military campaigns against France and the building and extravagant embellishment of a string of palaces. It was estimated that the suppression of the Geraldine revolt had cost £40,000. Henry had to find a way of making sure his money in Ireland went further.

In March 1536 a commission or instruction was issued authorising the introduction of a new Irish coinage, 'coins of the harp', which was to consist of 'harps' and 'half-harps', groats and half-groats, although it is thought that Henry's first coins were struck earlier, possibly as early as 1534 or 1535.

The name of the coin derives from the crowned harp featured on the reverse. Whilst there is a tradition of the harp being associated with Ireland as a heraldic device since the fourteenth century, this was the first time it appeared as a national symbol on Ireland's coins. Henry's replacement of the three crowns device with the harp is said to be due to the fact that the three crowns as presented on the Irish badge looked too similar to the papal tiara: the abandonment of the three crowns badge was symbolic of Henry's break from Rome and from any suggestion that the lordship of Ireland was held in gift from the pope. If this is the case, then there is a certain irony in the fact that the harp represented on Henry's coins is believed to have been a gift from Pope Leo X and is possibly the Brian Boru harp displayed in Trinity College, which in time was to become the model for the harp used on modern Ireland's coinage.

Henry's way of ensuring that his money went further was to reduce the silver content of his Irish coinage. This was not without risk in an era when the acceptance of coin was based on the simple premise that the value of the coin was determined by its silver or gold content: a groat was expected to contain four pennies' worth of silver.

In order to conceal this initial debasement, Henry's new Irish coins were to be struck not in Dublin but at the Tower mint in London and shipped to Ireland. The new Irish harps and half-harps were also to be struck to a lighter weight than their English equivalents, the groat and half-groat. It is estimated that the Crown was to make a profit of 12–13% on every pound of silver turned into coin. Following a further debasement in 1540, the king received profits of 23% on every pound of silver, and with his last debasement in 1546 the profits were even greater!

Henry's first coins were struck to .842 fineness, whilst his English coins continued to be struck to the sterling standard of .925 fineness.

The groats of Henry VIII's first coinage featured a crowned shield with the royal arms over a cross on the obverse with the legend 'HENRIC VIII D.G.R. AGL Z' (Henry VIII by the grace of God king of England and), with a crown mint mark incorporated into the design at the start of the legend. The reverse featured a crowned harp dividing the royal cyphers 'H' for Henry and 'A' for Anne Boleyn, with the reverse legend a continuation of the obverse legend, reading 'FRANCE DOMINUS HIBERNIE' (France, lord of Ireland). Again a crown mint mark was placed at the start of the legend.

The half-groats of this first issue essentially followed the same design but with the Roman numerals of 'VIII' sometimes replaced by an '8'.

The inclusion of the queen's personal cypher on coins was not unusual. Katharine of Aragon's cypher appeared on some of Henry's gold coins, as later did the cyphers of Anne Boleyn and Jane Seymour. It is thought that the inclusion of Anne's 'A' cypher on an Irish coin may have carried a subtle political message. As the granddaughter of a Butler it may have signified the fall of the Fitzgeralds and the triumph of their arch-enemies, the Butlers of Ormonde. Whatever the reason,

Fig. 50—Groat, Henry VIII, first harp coinage, Anne Boleyn, 1534–6. *SNC*, February 1998, No. 83

Anne's triumph was short-lived. Within three months of the letter of commission of March 1536 she was beheaded on Tower Green. Anne's downfall can be further traced in the hastily re-engraved dies where the 'A' was etched out to be replaced by the 'I' of the new queen.

Fig. 51— Groat, Henry VIII, first harp coinage, Jane Seymour, 1536–7. *SNC*, February 1998, No. 84

The groats and half-groats issued between 1536 and 1540 follow the same design but with the 'A' on the obverse being replaced by the 'I' of Jane Seymour from August 1536 to June 1537, and from August 1540 to February 1542 by the 'K' of Katherine Howard. It has been suggested by some historians that the 'HK' coins were struck and stockpiled whilst Katherine was still Henry's mistress, ready to be issued on their marriage!

Fig. 52—Groat, Henry VIII, first harp coinage, Katherine Howard, 1540. Whyte's Millennial Collection Sale, No. 141

Whilst the groats of three of Henry's queens are relatively common, with those of Katherine Howard the scarcest, all the half-groats are extremely rare. It is estimated that as few as 30 examples may still exist. An Anne Boleyn half-groat was to fetch £IR1,000 at the Whyte's Millennial Collection Sale in April 2000.

A fourth type of groat is also attributed to this first coinage, and it is believed to have been struck possibly between 1537 and 1540, following the death of Jane Seymour but before Henry's six-month marriage to Anne of Cleves in 1540. The obverse follows the same design as the 'Anne' and 'Jane' groats, but the reverse features only Henry's cypher of 'H' and the 'R' for 'Rex' on either side of the harp.

On 19 July 1540 Henry took another step to try and cover his deliberate policy of debasement by prohibiting the import of Irish 'harps' into England with the threat of forfeiture of three times the value of the coins, as well as a fine and imprisonment.

The late 1530s and early 1540s were to see a further consolidation of English rule, as Henry's forces moved out of the Pale and across the Shannon to Galway, and into Munster and Ulster. These military campaigns sought to establish Henry's authority over the native Irish chiefs through his policy of 'surrender and regrant', by which Irish kings and chieftains acknowledged Henry's supremacy, surrendering their old native titles for English peerages and confirmation in their territories. This policy of conciliation was to draw the native Irish into the English sphere of influence, with Irish chiefs taking their seats in the Anglo-Irish parliament. On 18 June 1541 the Irish parliament was to offer Henry the title of 'king of Ireland', although the king, perhaps piqued by the idea of a parliament making him king, did not formally use his title until 23 January 1542, and not in Ireland until April 1542!

Henry's second coinage, which was issued between 1540 and 1542, was to consist entirely of groats struck in .758 fineness. The design of the groat followed that of the 'HR' version of his first coinage, with the crowned royal arms on the obverse and the crowned harp with the 'HR' cipher on the reverse. These coins include a trefoil mint mark incorporated into the obverse and reverse legends. Three varieties of this groat were struck; the first two have minor variations in the obverse legend, including or omitting the 'VIII' in Henry's title. The third variety of groat, issued in about 1542, is more significant in that the reverse legend includes Henry's new title of 'HIBERNIE REX' (king of Ireland) for the first time.

Fig. 53—Groat, Henry VIII, second harp coinage with title 'Hibernie Rex', 1542. *SNC*, February 1998, No. 87

Henry's third coinage was issued from about May 1542 to September 1543. In contrast to the last two debasements, this coinage saw a restoration to .835 fineness. Again, this coinage consisted entirely of groats which followed the same crowned shield and crowned harp design of his second coinage. This issue is, however, distinguished from earlier issues by a rose mint mark at the start of the obverse and reverse legends. This issue was to be short-lived, and in truth was a subterfuge for a far worse debasement in the coinage that almost paralleled it. It is thought that Henry's fourth coinage, which saw a reduction to .666 fineness, may have been issued at almost the same time as his finer third coinage and it continued to be issued until 1544. This coinage was distinguished by a fleur-de-lis mint mark at the start of the obverse and reverse legends.

The same technique of issuing a finer coinage alongside a baser coinage was also to be used in England. Henry, who by now was once more engaged in wars with the French king, began a process of rapid debasement of England's coinage in 1544 with an initial debasement to .758 fineness, followed a year later to .500 fineness and by 1546 to about .300 fineness, earning Henry the nickname of 'Old Copper Knob' in England, his nose being the first point of the coin to wear thin to reveal the copper!

A fifth issue of groats was to take place between 1544 and 1545, again bearing the fleur-de-lis mint mark of 1544. These coins saw a further debasement to .500 fineness, and whilst the same weight and size as earlier groats, it was declared that they should pass for six Irish pennies. Two varieties of 'sixpenny groats' can be attributed to this fifth coinage of Henry VIII, one of which has the king's titles in the reverse legend followed by an 'S'. Some numismatists have suggested that the 'S' may refer to the Southwark mint in London, although it is generally thought that the Southwark mint was not open at the time this coin was struck. The second type has a reverse legend reading 'FRANCE ET HIBERNIE REX 37'. This sixpenny groat is the first dated Irish coin, with the '37' referring to Henry's regnal year, the 37th year of his reign, 1545.

Fig. 54—Sixpenny groat, Henry VIII, fifth harp coinage, 'Hibernie Rex S', 1544–5. *SNC*, February 1998, No. 88

The final coinage of Henry VIII's reign was struck in Bristol in 1546–7. It was to see the coin finally debased to .250 fineness. Again these groat-sized coins were to pass for sixpence. The coins follow the same design as the five earlier issues, with the crowned shield on the obverse and the legend 'HENRIC 8 DG ANGL FRANC' (Henry VIII by the grace of God England, France). The reverse features the crowned harp flanked by the royal cipher and the legend 'WS ET HIBERNIE REX 38' (WS and Ireland king 38), the '38' referring to the king's regnal year of 1546. The 'WS' are the initials of the Bristol mint master, William Sharrington, who was contracted to issue the most debased silver coinage the Irish had seen. The issue of this coinage was recorded in the Annals of the Four Masters with an entry for 1546 which reads: 'New coin was introduced into Ireland, i.e. copper, and the men of Ireland were obliged to use it as silver'.

Fig. 55—Sixpenny groat, Henry VIII, Bristol, sixth harp coinage, 'WS', 1546–7. *SNC*, February 1998, No. 89

A variety of the sixpenny groat exists that does not include the '38' in the reverse legend. In some senses this coin does not belong to Henry VIII's coinage but to that of his son, Edward VI. The omission of the '38' was not an error on the part of a careless engraver, but marked the passing of a king. These dies were prepared after 28 January 1547, the regnal year no longer mattering as the long reign of 'Old Copper Knob' was at an end.

Fig. 56—Sixpenny groat, Henry VIII, counter-marked fourth harp coinage with four pellets. *SNC*, February 1998, No. 90

A variety of these last harp coins with a four-pellet countermark is known. It is thought that these four pellets may signify a later reduction in the value of the coin from a 'sixpenny groat' to fourpence during the reign of Edward VI.

By the time of Henry's death, his policy of conciliation had broken down. The withdrawal of his troops to fight his war in France offered an opportunity for the Irish chiefs to rebel against the king's authority. It was for his successor, the boy King Edward VI, to restore order. Economically the country was also ruined. The debasement of the coinage had led to inflation. Inevitably Crown officials and soldiers, who were initially paid in these base coins, found that their pay was not sufficient to meet their needs and found themselves being drawn into corrupt practices or simple extortion.

As the coinage became increasingly and obviously debased, the intrinsic value of a coin, the actual amount of silver it contained, became more important than its notional fourpence or sixpence value. The Irish now looked for payment in 'croise caoile' or 'salfas' or in 'dominick grotes', the early harp groats of Henry which bore his title of 'Dominus' rather than 'Rex' and had been struck in .842 fineness or .758 fineness. The later base coins were to become known as 'white money' because of their grey-white colour and their porous or pitted surface. The earliest reference to white money is to be found in the Annals of the Four Masters, where in 1545 it is recorded: 'Great dearth in this year so that sixpence of the old money were given for a cake of bread in Connaught and six white pence in Meath'.

Whilst Sharrington's last sixpenny groats might be considered the first coins of Edward VI's reign, Edward's first coins were not to appear until 1547. The king's uncle, Edward Seymour, the Protector of the Realm, and the young king's other advisers were anxious to improve the standard of coinage in England and Ireland, but decided to issue coins initially in the same .250 fineness as Sharrington's last issue with the aim of restoring the coinage at a later date.

In order not to associate the new king with the continuing issue of debased coins, it was decided to issue coins featuring the late king's portrait and titles in the hope that a finer coinage might be issued at a later date in the new king's name. It is thought that the fineness of this first coinage was to improve in time, and its silver content varies from .250 fineness to .388 fineness.

Edward's first coinage was issued between 1548 and 1550 and consisted of groat-sized coins which were to circulate for sixpence, half-groats which were to circulate for threepence, pennies which circulated for three-halfpence and halfpennies which were to pass for three farthings. In a departure from the centralising policies of Henry VII and Henry VIII, the young king authorised the reopening of the Dublin mint on 10 February 1548 to strike this new issue of coins.

Fig. 57—Sixpence, Edward VI, 'Posthumous issue of Henry VIII' Late Tower style portrait, 1547–50. *SNC,* February 1998, No. 91

All the coins of this first issue followed the same design. The 'sixpenny groats' featured a crowned facing portrait of Henry VIII with the legend 'HENRIC 8 DG AGL FR Z HIB REX' (Henry VIII by the grace of God king of England, France and Ireland). Variations of this obverse legend are to be found on these coins. The reverse design featured the royal arms over a cross with the reverse legend 'CIVITAS DUBLINIE' (city of Dublin) forming the border. Three mint marks are associated with this first coinage: a harp, the letter 'P' and a boar's head, which are incorporated into the reverse legend.

At least four varieties of these Dublin 'sixpenny groats' are known. Two would seem to have been struck with dies prepared in London, and these are known as the 'Tower Mint style' coins. One variety has a crowned facing portrait of the king, the early Tower Mint bust, whilst the other has a smaller, neater bust of the king facing half-right on the obverse and is known as the later Tower Mint bust.

The other varieties seem to have been produced using cruder locally prepared dies and feature a large crowned facing portrait of the king and a smaller crowned facing portrait of the dead king.

The posthumous 'threepenny half-groats' of 1547–50 follow the same design as the groat coins. Three varieties are known, one featuring a crowned facing portrait of the king either struck from or based on the early Tower Mint style portrait of the king, and the second with a right-facing portrait of the monarch, again probably struck from dies engraved in London. The third variety features much cruder obverse and reverse designs and was in all likelihood struck from locally engraved dies. Four mint marks — the boar's head, the harp, a sun and the letter 'P' — are associated with this group of coins.

Two varieties of 'three-halfpences' were to be struck. The obverse featured a crowned facing portrait of the king with the legend 'HDG ROSA SINE SPINE' (Henry by the grace of God; a rose without a thorn). It is thought that the obverse of this coin, which features an early Tower Mint bust, was struck from a die for an English penny. The reverse featured the crowned arms over a cross with the legend

'CIVITAS DUBLIN' or 'DUBLINIE' (city of Dublin). The other variety of this coin features a smaller portrait of the king facing right, the Tower Mint bust.

Fig. 58—Three-halfpence, Edward VI, 'Posthumous issue of Henry VIII' Early Tower style portrait, 1547–50. *SNC*, February 1998, No. 94

The final coin in this first coinage of Edward VI was the tiny 'three farthings' or halfpenny. This coin again featured a crowned facing portrait of the king with the abbreviated legend 'HDG ROSE SINE SP' (Henry by the grace of God; a rose without a thorn). Again, the die of an English halfpenny was used for the obverse. The reverse echoed the coins of Edward IV and Henry VII, with a long cross with three pellets in each quarter design within a circle with the legend 'CIVITAS DUBLIN' or 'DUBLINIE' (city of Dublin).

The reopening of a mint in Dublin was a curious decision, as it was generally accepted that it was cheaper to mint coins in London and to ship them to Ireland rather than to establish a mint in Dublin. A comparison of production costs in the 1550s would suggest 5% on-costs for minting coins in London and shipping to Ireland rather than the 16% on-costs associated with establishing and running a mint in Dublin. The costs of running the Dublin mint in Edward VI's reign were to be in the region of £2,377 a year.

The first master of the new Irish mint was a Crown official, Thomas Agard, who was charged with the production of 5,000lb. of silver into £14,032 of new coin between March 1548 and August 1549. Thomas Agard's mark, the boar's head, was to appear on the coins struck under his mastership. In about 1549 Agard died and his post was taken up by Martin Pirry, who had been appointed comptroller and surveyor of the Dublin mint in 1548. Pirry's appointment was extraordinary for a man who had fled England seven years earlier for unofficially coining and clipping coins!

Coins issued under Pirry's tenure of office were to bear a 'P' mint mark. The dies for the earlier coins up to March 1549 are believed to have been engraved by the Tower engraver, Coldwell. Production under Pirry commenced on 9 August 1550 under an arrangement whereby the king was guaranteed a profit of 13s 4d on every pound of silver coined. The king from October 1550 to July 1551 is believed to have received profits of £13,273 16s 5½d from over £47,785 worth of coin produced by Pirry. The success of the Dublin mint, as in previous reigns, was, however, dependent upon the amount of bullion available to be turned into coin. It is thought that coin production associated with this first issue ended sometime in 1551.

Edward's reign was to see further military intervention in Ireland under Edward Bellingham, who restored order in Leinster in 1548. Bellingham consolidated royal authority by building a series of forts in Leix and Offaly and establishing English settlers or 'planters' in these former rebel territories. Between 1547 and 1553 the English Crown was to spend £250,000 on subjugating the Irish and restoring order. Inevitably the cost of these campaigns exhausted Crown revenues and placed an increased burden on the king's Irish and English taxpayers. In England attempts had been made to restore the fineness of the coinage in 1549; this policy was reversed in 1551 with the introduction briefly of a debased coinage struck to .250 fineness. In Ireland the added expense of these military campaigns left the king and his advisers with no other option but to continue the policy of debasement.

On 27 June 1552 Martin Pirry was commissioned to strike a new coinage for the king. Between June and November 1552 Pirry was to supervise the processing of 4,500lb. of silver into £32,400 of shillings. A further £8,000 worth of coin was to be produced between December 1552 and the early months of 1553. It is believed that Pirry died in November 1552. Local bullion supplies were drying up and it is thought that the Dublin mint was closed shortly after Pirry's death. Over £95,000 worth of coin was to be produced at the Dublin mint during Edward's reign, with profits of over £16,500 for the Crown.

This second issue of coins was to have consisted entirely of debased billon (.250 fineness) shillings, the first time that this denomination was struck for Ireland. The coin was based on English shillings issued during this period which were also struck to .250 fineness. These coins were to be the last official regal 'silver' coins struck at the Dublin mint.

The obverse features a crowned profile portrait of the young king looking right, with the legend 'EDWARD VI DG AGL FRAN Z HB REX' (Edward by the grace of God king of England, France and Ireland). The reverse featured the royal arms set in an oval garnished shield with the cipher 'E' and 'R' on either side of the shield and the legend 'TIMOR DOMINI FONS VITE MDLII' (The fear of God is the fountain of life MDLII). This shilling was to be the first Irish coin to bear a calendar date, the Roman numerals MDLII standing for 1552. The Irish shilling of Edward VI can be distinguished from Edward's more common English shillings of the same design by the harp mint mark at the start of the obverse legend. The copper or brass content of these coins, like his father's coins, quickly showed through once they were in circulation, and it is possible that they earned the nickname 'brown-backs' from their browny-coppery appearance. An example of a 1552 shilling in very fine condition was sold at the Whyte's Millennial Collection Sale for £IR1,300.

These handsome coins were in turn to be copied in brass and copper and 'silvered over' by counterfeiters. Once the silver had worn off, the brass or copper was revealed. Despite the fact that they were forgeries these brass 'bungals' (from the Irish 'bonn geal', white groat) had some unofficial approval and were to circulate in the west of Ireland as penny pieces.

Fig. 59—Bungal, Edward VI, brass copy of Edward VI shilling, 1552. *SNC*, February 1998, No. 96

Alongside the silver shillings it is thought that base English Rose pennies of Edward VI, struck at the York mint, may have also been shipped to Ireland to meet the small denomination needs of the Irish.

Edward's ambition to restore the standard of coinage was to be achieved in England in 1551 with the issuing of a new silver coinage consisting of crowns, half-crowns, shillings and sixpences. In November 1551 consideration had also been given to improving Ireland's coinage with the issue of an Irish crown, half-crown, shilling and sixpence and to restoring the standard of Ireland's coinage to a .758 fineness, but military and financial imperatives resulted in the debased 1552 coinage a year later.

In January 1552 the lord deputy of Ireland called for Ireland's coinage to be restored to a 'lyke valuation waight and fyness only, but in waight of suche rate that vid may way the grote sterling'. It was, however, Edward's sister, Mary Tudor, who was to restore the fineness of Ireland's coinage.

9. 'NEW COYN'D WITH HER OWN FACE'
The coinage of Mary Tudor and Elizabeth I
(1554–1602)

The accession of Mary in 1553 saw the Dublin mint remain closed. Irish coins were from now on to be produced in the Irish mint within the Tower of London. Mary continued her brother's policy of restoring the fineness of England's gold and silver coins, and during her reign began the process of recalling the debased silver coins issued by her father and brother. In England work was put in hand for the introduction of a new Irish coinage. Mary's accession to the throne had not been without problems, and it was to be thirteen days after the death of her brother before she was secure on the throne. The accession of the first woman monarch and a devout Catholic presented problems for the mint's engravers. How would the queen be represented on her new coins? Would she rule as queen of Ireland, a title awarded to her father by a schismatic Irish parliament, or as a dutiful daughter of the church would she settle for the older title of lord of Ireland?

In 1861 the British Museum acquired a pattern coin which had previously been attributed to Lady Jane Grey, a Protestant cousin of Mary, who briefly ruled England for nine days following the death of Edward VI. The pattern coin, which was obviously Tudor, featured on the obverse a Tudor rose (based on Mary's English ryal design) within a wreath of heraldic devices with the legend 'SI DEUS NOBISCUM QUIS CONTRA NOS' (If God is with us who [can be] against us). The reverse of the coin featured the old three crowns device of the lordship within a tressure with the legend 'JUSTITIA VIRTUTUM REGINA' (Justice queen of virtues). The generally accepted view is that the pattern was an Irish pattern shilling produced in the early days of Mary's reign, possibly August 1553, when the queen's position with regard to the appropriate Irish title she was to use remained unclear. The uncertainty was to be short-lived. Mary retained her father's title, and her earliest English and Irish coins issued later in 1553 were to proclaim her as 'Queen of Ireland'.

On 20 August 1553 Mary authorised the issuing of a new Irish and English coinage. The Irish mint was established in September, and by 7 October 1553 new 'harp' coins bearing Mary's portrait had been introduced.

Mary's commitment to improving the standard of her coins was to extend to Ireland as well as England. Her first issue of Irish coins saw the silver content double from the .250 fineness of her father and brother's reigns to .583 fineness. These first coins of her reign were struck between 1553 and 1554 and consisted of a shilling, groat, half-groat and penny.

Fig. 60—Shilling, Mary, MDLIII, 1553. Davissons, 12 March 2002, No. 381

All of Mary's coins were struck at the Irish mint in London and shipped to Ireland. The four coins followed essentially the same design. The obverse featured an attractive crowned portrait of the queen with flowing hair, facing left within a circle, and the legend 'MARIA DG ANG FRA Z HIB REGINA' (Mary by the grace of God queen of England, France and Ireland). The reverse saw a return to the crowned harp of Henry VIII, with a small crowned 'M' on one side of the harp and a crowned 'R' on the other side within a circle with the legend 'VERITAS TEMPORIS FILIA MDLIII' (Truth the daughter of time 1553). This coin was to be issued in two years, and the other coins bear the Roman date 'MDLIIII' (1554). The 1553 shilling is rare, whilst the 1554 shilling is extremely rare. An example was sold at a Whyte's sale in February 1998 for £IR1,900. The coin featured a fleur-de-lis mint mark incorporated into the obverse and reverse legends.

The groat followed the same design as the shilling, although the Roman date MDLIII was omitted from the reverse legend. Examples are known of groats with the dates 'MDLIII' and 'MDLIIII', although it is thought that these two varieties are forgeries. The genuine groat is extremely rare.

The half-groat again follows the same design and is extremely rare. A version of this coin with an uncrowned harp was at one stage considered genuine but is now thought to be a forgery.

The penny, whilst following the same design, features the abbreviated obverse legend to be found on the posthumous 'three halfpennies' and 'three farthings' of Henry VIII, 'M DG ROSA SINE SPIN' (Mary by the grace of God a rose without a thorn). The reverse follows the same design as the other first issue coins. The Roman date is again omitted from the reverse legend of these tiny coins. As with the other denominations, the penny is extremely rare.

It is a measure of the rarity of this particular issue that all of these coins were to be forged in Victorian times to be foisted on unfortunate collectors.

It is generally thought that the engraving of Mary's two coinages was the work of Derrick Anthony and John Lawrence, the under-graver at the mint.

The accession of Mary was to see little change in the policy of coercion and plantation in the Irish midlands which had been initiated in Edward VI's reign. As a devout Catholic Mary was, however, to reverse many of the reforms to the Irish church that Henry VIII and Edward VI had brought about as part of the English Reformation. On 25 July 1554, Mary married her cousin, Philip of Spain, the son of the Holy Roman Emperor, Charles V. Philip, who had been created king of Naples and Jerusalem by his father before his marriage to Mary, was to reign alongside Mary as king-consort. The use of the schismatic title 'Queen of Ireland' continued, however, to trouble the queen. In 1555 the queen's cousin, Cardinal Pole, petitioned the pope to confer the title on Mary, and on 7 June 1555 Pope Paul IV issued a papal bull creating the kingdom of Ireland and recognising Mary and Philip as queen and king of Ireland.

Mary's second coinage of 1554–8 was to see a return to the baser standard of .250 fineness of her father and brother, although some attempt to compensate was made in terms of silver content by increasing the weight of these coins by about a third from her earlier 1553–4 issue. This second coinage was limited to two coins, the shilling and the groat.

As was the case with Edward VI, this debasement was driven by military and economic necessity, with royal revenues having to be raised to finance a campaign against the Ulster chieftain Shane O'Neill and incursions by Scottish mercenaries along the north-east coast of Ireland.

The shilling featured two facing portraits of Philip of Spain and Mary with a crown above and the date 1555 in an exergue below the portraits within a circle. This coin was the first Irish coin to bear the calendar year in Arabic numerals. The obverse legend interestingly made no reference to Mary's Irish titles and reads 'PHILIP ET MARIA DG REX ET REGINA ANG' or 'ANGL' (Philip and Mary by the grace of God king and queen of England). The queen may not have wanted to anticipate the outcome of her petition to the pope on her use of the title 'Queen of Ireland'.

The reverse of the coin featured the crowned harp of the earlier coinage but with Mary's royal cypher of the crowned 'M' and 'R' replaced with a crowned 'P' and 'M' on either side of the harp.

Fig. 61—Shilling, Mary and Philip, 1555. *SNC*, May 1996, No. 2207

The reverse saw a return to the coins of Edward IV and Henry VII, with the legend reading 'POSIVIMUS DEUM ADIUTOREM NOSTRUM' (We have made God our helper). A portcullis mint mark was incorporated into the legend.

Groats were also struck to a similar design in 1555. The obverse, however, featured the two facing portraits with a crown above which divides the date into '15' and '55'. Again, the obverse legend makes no reference to Mary's Irish titles. At least five varieties of groats are known with different dates, covering the four years from 1555 to 1558. Portcullis and rose mint marks differentiate these coins as well, although the only significant variety is a 1557 groat which replaces the 'ET' in the obverse legend with the abbreviated 'Z'.

Fig. 62—Groat, Mary and Philip, 1555. *SNC*, May 1996, No. 2208

Both of Mary's Irish issues were struck from debased silver coins which were being withdrawn in England. Between March 1555 and June 1559 it is believed that eleven commissions or orders for coin were made, totalling about £138,000 in coin. This was produced in London from withdrawn English base coin worth about £69,000, ensuring profits for the Crown of about 100% for every coin produced! It has also been suggested that King Philip may have brought with him supplies of debased or billon coin from Spain as part of his marriage settlement which was also to be turned into Irish coin at a profit for the Spanish king.

The second issue coins of Mary were not struck to the same standard as her finer English coins and her earlier Irish coins, and in many cases these later coins were weakly struck, giving the appearance of worn or partial portraits.

On 19 September 1556 base rose pennies struck in the reign of Henry VIII and Edward VI were prohibited in England, and it is believed that large quantities of these coins were shipped over to meet the small currency needs of Mary's Irish subjects, as they had been in her brother's reign. It is also thought that additional supplies of base pennies were produced in York during Mary's reign solely for use in Ireland. These featured the royal arms on the obverse with the abbreviated names and titles of Mary and Philip forming the legend, whilst the reverse featured a rose and the mint signature 'CIVITAS EBORACE' (city of York).

Mary Tudor died on 17 November 1558, her husband — now King Philip II of Spain — having left England a year earlier. Besides their numismatic legacy of debased shillings and groats, the more significant and lasting legacy of this royal marriage was to be the renaming of Leix and Offaly as Queen's County and King's County.

The accession of Elizabeth I brought no change in the condition and standard of Ireland's coinage. Three commissions for base coin to be supplied to Ireland were made on 17 February, 1 May and 16 June 1559. Elizabeth's efforts, like those of her sister, were directed towards maintaining the fineness of England's coinage and withdrawing the base coinage of her father and brother. As in Mary's reign, Irish coins were produced from base English coins at twice their face value. The commissions of 1559 were to see £20,000 worth of English base coin transformed into £40,000 worth of Irish coins. It is thought that the striking of Elizabeth's first coinage was completed by August 1559. In all, it is estimated that 400,000 shillings and 1,200,000 groats were struck and shipped to Ireland.

The practice of converting English base coin into Irish coin was so widely known that James Simon (1749) in his essay on Irish coins refers to an Elizabethan ballad celebrating the fact:

'Let bone-fires shine in every place,
Sing and ring the bells a-pace,
And pray that long may live her grace,
To be the good Queen of Ireland.
The gold and silver which was so base,
That no man could endure its scarce,
Is now new-coyn'd with her own face,
And made go current in Ireland'.

The first coinage of Elizabeth I, issued in 1559, continued the standard established by her three predecessors. Shillings and groats were struck with a silver content of .250 fineness.

The obverse of both coins features a crowned portrait of the queen facing left, with the legend 'ELIZABETH DG ANG FRA Z HIB REGINA' (Elizabeth by the grace of God queen of England, France and Ireland). The reverse features a crowned harp with crowned royal cypher 'E' and 'R' on either side of the harp and the legend 'POSUI DEUM ADIUTOREM MEUM' (I have made God my helper). A rose mint mark is incorporated into the start of the legends on both sides of the coin. In some cases the 'REGINA' on the obverse legend of the groat is contracted to 'REG'.

Fig. 63—Shilling, Elizabeth I, first base coinage, 1558. *SNC*, May 1996, No. 2829

Elizabeth's first attempt to regulate Ireland's coinage took place in December 1560 when a proclamation referring to base English coins of Edward VI circulating in Ireland declared that 'the shilling countermarked with the portcullis [should be valued at] 7d Irish, and that with the greyhound 3½d' (Morrieson 1923–4, 237).

On 26 March 1561 a commission for a new fine coinage for Ireland was issued. This was to be struck to .916 fineness, the same standard as English coins, but to a lighter weight, about a quarter less than the English equivalents. This new issue was to be limited to shillings and groats, which were to pass in England for ninepence and threepence. In April 1561 the Tower mint produced about £11,988 worth of fine coins consisting of approximately 215,000 shillings and 72,000 groats.

Fig. 64—Shilling, Elizabeth I, 'Fine Coinage', 1561. *SNC*, May 1996, No. 2211

This second issue of Elizabeth's coins was struck to a much higher standard than those of her Tudor predecessors and probably rank amongst the most handsome ever struck for Ireland. The obverse features a beautifully detailed crowned portrait of the queen facing left and a border with the legend 'ELIZABETH DG AF ET HIBERNIE REGI', with the emphasis on her Irish title (Elizabeth by the grace of God queen of England, France and Ireland). Variations of the obverse legend occur with 'REG' and 'RGI' rather than 'REGI'. The reverse design is a departure from previous coins, with three small harps featuring on a crowned shield with the date '15' on one side and '61' on the other. This curious rendering of the Irish harp is thought to be a throw-back to the three crowns of the old lordship of Ireland.

The quality of the engraving, which is thought to have been undertaken by Derrick Anthony, is evident from the detail of the queen's portrait. It is thought that the central motif of the three crowns on the shield was engraved onto one puncheon and then sunk into the die rather than being prepared from a series of

Fig. 65—Groat, Elizabeth I, 'Fine Coinage', 1561. *SNC*, May 1995, No. 2833

smaller puncheons with elements of the design. A harp mint mark is incorporated into the legends on both sides of the coin.

The groat follows the same design as the shilling, with the title on the obverse contracted to 'REGI' or 'RE'.

With the introduction of this new coinage a dual monetary system operated in Ireland, made up of the new fine silver coins and a mixture of coins issued under four monarchs with varying silver content. The complexity of the monetary system facing the early Elizabethan Irish is perhaps best captured in the accounts of the Merchant Tailors Guild of St John the Baptist of Dublin. An entry of 1561 records:

'Recd d John Roche, Shepe St, fine due 12 white groats

John Kene, fine for an income as a brother, 8 white testers

Jeffery Mysell, income as apprentice, 6 testers 2 groats, 3ob

Henry Small, income as journeyman, 2 white groats

Recd of John Desmond, Wicklow, rent. Mich-term

Walter Byrford for loft over the poor house, 9 brown backs' (Morrieson
1923–4, 236).

On 14 July 1561 the English authorities took steps to further regulate the dual monetary system with a proclamation that set out the value of a range of coins, including 'the harp shilling of Mary, at 8d Irish', 'the harp shilling of Philip and Mary and that of 1558–9, 5¼ Irish', 'the harp groats of the same stamp and standard, 1¾ or three 5¼d', 'the harp groat of Henry VIII, 1¼ Irish', 'the rose penny 3/2 farthings, Irish, or four for 1½ d' (ibid., 237).

This proclamation, and the earlier December 1560 proclamation, were to prove an accounting nightmare for clerks and merchants. A shilling, depending on its silver content, had five different values, 12d, 8d, 7d, 5¼ d or 3½ d, and groats had three possible values, 4d, 1¾ d or 1¼d.

The 1561 fine silver issue was to be short-lived, and any attempt to further improve the standard of Ireland's coinage was abandoned. From 1561 through to 1564 base coins which had been gathered in and demonetised in England were simply shipped over to Ireland to meet the coinage needs of the Irish. It was to be another 40 years before a distinctive coinage was to be struck for Ireland again. The coinage needs of the Irish were met by fine English coins and from 1582 English coins struck to the new sterling standard, which circulated at a third over their notional value, and Continental and base Irish coins which circulated at their intrinsic bullion value.

Elizabeth's reign was to see further consolidation and extension of royal authority. For much of her reign, the efforts of the queen and her statesmen were directed against the O'Neills of Ulster and the Fitzgerald earls of Desmond in Munster. The first of the O'Neill rebellions was to end in 1565 with the death of Shane O'Neill, and it is likely that the decision not to improve Ireland's coinage in the early 1560s can be linked to the Crown's need to direct limited revenue towards putting down the O'Neill rebellion. It is ironic that when the head of the murdered O'Neill was brought to Dublin the Anglo-Irish colony was so short of good coin that the mayor of Dublin could only offer the messenger a clipped 'crusadoe' coin by way of reward.

As well as seeking to subjugate the north, Elizabeth's forces sought to establish royal authority in the west and south of the country with the establishment of the presidency councils in Connacht and Munster. This policy was to bring the Crown into conflict with Irish chieftains and Anglo-Irish nobles, most notably the earls of Desmond. The Desmond rebellion was to continue for over a decade, with the rebels receiving military and financial support from Philip II of Spain and the pope. It finally collapsed in 1583, leaving Munster devastated by famine and war.

The greatest challenge to Elizabeth's authority occurred in the 1590s when Hugh O'Neill, the earl of Tyrone, broke with the Crown and led a rebellion which was eventually to spread throughout Ireland. On 14 August 1598 O'Neill defeated Elizabeth's army of 4,000 soldiers at the Battle of the Yellow Ford. In the wake of this defeat, royal authority collapsed throughout Ireland. Some 10,000 soldiers were sent to Ireland to bolster royal control at significant costs to the Crown.

In March 1599 a force of 17,000 under Robert Devereux, the earl of Essex, arrived to subjugate O'Neill. Essex's expedition was to prove disastrous. Agreeing to a truce with the Irish chiefs, he returned to London to face a charge of treason and the block. O'Neill's position seemed unassailable and it was against this background that Elizabeth's final coinage was to be issued.

For 40 years the needs of the Irish had been met by a mixture of English and foreign coins, principally those of Spain, which was one of Ireland's major trading partners, even during the period of the Armada. Alongside these coins Irish base silver coins continued to circulate, some dating back nearly 70 years to the reign of Henry VIII. As late as 1600 proclamations were setting out the value of these debased coins. In December 1600 the values of a range of coins still circulating were set out: 'harp shillings 11oz fine were said to be testons coined at 12d, and now current for 4d (st); the white groat coined at 4d and now current at three for 4d (st); the red harp coined at 4d, and now current at 1d (st); and also dominic groats, Galway pence and other ancient coins' (Challis 1971, 115).

In the absence of a sound coinage, merchants and traders attempted to plug the gap by issuing their own coins or tokens. The first recorded unofficial token coin belongs to this period. It was issued by Adam Dulan of Kilkenny in 1578 and was a pewter coin, about the size of a modern two pence coin. It is thought that the design of the token was based on a French *écu d'or* with a cross fleury forming the central design on the obverse and the legend 'ADAM DVLAN 1578' forming the border. The reverse featured the crowned arms of France with the legend 'OF

KILKENE' forming the border. It is thought that Dulan was an importer of wines from France, hence his choice of design.

On 2 February 1601 an indenture was issued authorising the striking of a new coinage. The military campaign against O'Neill had cost Elizabeth nearly £2 million. An English official wrote in 1600 that 'these Irish wars do exhaust the treasure of England'. Debasement of the coinage had been used by Elizabeth's predecessors to fund military campaigns in the past to allow 'money to go further'. This debasement was, however, to be different as Elizabeth and her advisers introduce a debased coinage as a means of economic warfare against the Irish.

The new coin was struck to the old .250 fineness, 'according to that antient standard which was in use for this realme in the daies of her majesties father, brother and sister' (Simon 1749, 91). The aim of the policy was to replace all gold and silver coins circulating in Ireland with a debased coinage which would be unacceptable for international trade, in particular to those merchants and traders who were supplying arms and goods to O'Neill's rebel forces. On 24 May 1601 a proclamation was issued by the queen authorising the issuing of the new coinage and declaring from 10 June 1601 that 'all other monies current in this kingdom should be annulled, esteemed as bullion, and not as the lawful and current money of the said realm' (ibid., 92). All Irish money, irrespective of its silver content and intrinsic value, was to be replaced on a penny by penny basis with the new debased coin, with the exception of coins struck in sterling silver which were to attract a 5% premium. The importing of coins into Ireland was also banned, as was the exporting of the new coin except through a highly regulated system of official exchanges.

The production of this new coinage was granted to 'Richard Martyn of London, Knighte, and Richard Martin his sonne citizen and goldsmith of London, masters and workers of her highness moneys within the towere of London' in an indenture of 23 April 1601. Richard Martin and his son were contracted to 'making and coyning of five sorts of money: that is to say the Shillinge Irishe running and currante for twelve pence Irishe; the half-shilling Irishe running and currant for sixpence, the Quarter of the shilling running and current for three pence Irishe, the penny running and currant for one penny Irish; and the Half-penny running and currant for one half penny Irish' (Simon 1749, 90).

Fig. 66—Shilling, Elizabeth I, base issue, 1601–2. *SNC*, May 1996, No. 2213

The shilling, sixpence and threepence were to be struck in .250 fine silver, and the penny and halfpenny in copper. One pound of silver with an intrinsic value of 16s 1½d was to be coined into 62 shillings of coin and one pound of copper valued at 6½d into 16 shillings of pennies and halfpennies. The profits from this venture were to be 45s 10½d on every pound of silver processed and 15s 5¼d on every pound of copper turned into coin. The scheme overall was to produce £307,281 worth of coin with anticipated profits of £223,755. It is thought that in excess of ten million coins were to be produced, and from 2 February to 20 May 1601 some 26,307lb. of 'white money' were struck.

As set out in Richard Martin's indenture, the third and final coinage of Elizabeth was to consist of billon shillings, sixpences and threepences. Whilst Henry VIII had issued 'sixpenny groats' and Edward VI 'sixpenny groats' and 'threepenny half-groats', this was the first time that the denominations of sixpence and threepence were struck for Ireland.

Fig. 67—Sixpence, Elizabeth I, base issue, 1598–1602. *SNC*, May 1996, No. 2215

The coins all followed essentially the same design. The obverse featured the royal arms within a circle with the legend 'ELIZABETH DG ANG FR ET HIBER RE' (Elizabeth by the grace of God queen of England, France and Ireland) forming the border. The reverse featured a much cruder crowned harp than earlier coins within a circle with the legend 'POSUI DEUM ADIUTOREM MEU' (I have made God my helper). The mint marks of a trefoil, a star and a martlet (a tiny bird) can be found at the start of the legends on both sides of the coin. These coins were in many cases struck on poorly prepared flans or blanks which cracked under the pressure from the hammer blow. Inevitably parts of the design and the legend are difficult to determine or missing because of the poor production techniques.

Alongside the debased silver coins the Martins oversaw the introduction of two new copper coins, the penny and the halfpenny. These essentially followed the same design as the 'silver' coins and were struck in 1601 and 1602. The obverse includes the royal arms, but on the copper coins the 'E' and the 'R' of the royal cypher are placed on either side of the shield whilst the reverse features the date '16' '01' or '16' '02' on either side of the crowned harp. It seems likely that these additional devices were included to differentiate the small copper coins from the smaller 'silver' coins and to prevent the more unscrupulous from dipping them in silver wash and passing them off as threepences.

Fig. 68—Halfpenny, Elizabeth I, 1602. *SNC,* May 1995, No. 2842

One variety of penny exists where the obverse is clearly struck with the die for a threepence, and an extremely rare variety of penny also exists featuring a star mint mark from 1601 but with no date on the reverse, apparently struck using the reverse die for a threepence. Rather than these coins being accidental 'mules' it has been suggested that consideration might have been given to striking the threepence in copper and that these might be trial pieces.

As with the 'silver' coins, trefoil, star and martlet mint marks are incorporated into the design at the start of the obverse and reverse legends. Whilst Charles Anthony was the chief engraver at the mint at that time, the engraving of this third coinage was probably the work of the under-engraver John Rutlinger.

The coinage proved unpopular, not only with O'Neill's rebels but also with the queen's soldiers and officials. The Irish refused to accept the new base money and were reluctant to change whatever little sterling or other coin they had for the new base coins. In June 1602 the authorities were driven to increase the exchange rates for the new base coin, offering a 10% premium on sterling coins and a 5% premium on old Irish money, but people were reluctant to give up the old coin. Within a short period of time old Irish base coins and sterling silver coins were attracting a premium of between 50% to 100% over their intrinsic value in day-to-day transactions. Inevitably prices increased, in some cases threefold. This in turn prompted further regulation by the authorities. The June 1602 proclamation, besides increasing exchange rates, instructed mayors and the chief officers of corporations to stop 'merchants, retailers and victuallers and such like (who) do by colour of this new standard money, inhance the prices both of victuals and other necessaries' (Simon 1749, 99). Six months later a further proclamation was to threaten people with imprisonment for refusing to accept the new money or if they continued to 'trafficque or trade with any of the decried monies or bullion' (*ibid.,* 102).

In rebel-held areas, supplies of Spanish coin circulated. Between 1601 and 1604 O'Neill was sent 40,000 Spanish crowns' worth of coin, possibly as many as 500,000 coins, and he ordered that these should circulate as Irish coin under pain of death! It is thought that these Spanish coins (*reales*) entered the Irish national consciousness as 'reul', the origin of the Irish word for a sixpence, and 'leat reul' or half-sixpence, the Irish for threepence. In 1590 the small Spanish silver coin, the *reale*, was worth about sixpence.

Whilst Elizabeth's great debasement may well have contributed to the military success of bringing about the end of the O'Neill rebellion, it was to prove an economic disaster for the Crown.

At the outset a commitment had been made to 'honour' the base money in sterling outside of Ireland. This was to ensure that necessary trade was not adversely affected by the introduction of the new coin. Exchanges were established in Dublin, Cork, Galway and Carrickfergus where 'base' coin could be exchanged for sterling bills of exchange which could then be cashed for sterling coin in London, Bristol and West Chester. Inevitably speculators took advantage of the situation by accepting the new base coin at discounted rates and then presenting the coins at the exchanges at the official rate for sterling bills, which were then cashed in England. It is estimated that in time one in three of the new coins were to find their way into the exchanges to be exchanged for sterling bills. In all, £231,046 15s 5½d was to be paid out by the English exchanges in London, Bristol and Chester against bills of exchange issued in Ireland. It seems very likely that the anticipated profits from this scheme were eaten up in 'honouring' sterling bills of exchange.

Whilst the base silver coins proved unpopular, the copper coins did meet a real need for small denomination coins which merchants' tokens had begun to fill. The base silver coins, despite their unpopularity, inevitably did circulate and were accepted. Josias Bodley, visiting Lecale in County Down in 1602–3, describes festivities he attended where 'one of the maskers carried a dirty pocket handkerchief with ten pounds in it, not of bullion but of the new money lately coined, which has a harp on one side and the royal arms on the other' (Foster 1989, 27).

As the maskers performed in Lecale, O'Neill's rebellion was coming to an end. A Spanish invasion force arrived too late to assist him. O'Neill and his forces were driven back to Ulster by the queen's deputy, Lord Mountjoy, where in October 1603 he was required to kneel for an hour before formally submitting to the deputy. Elizabeth was not, however, to savour this final victory: she had been dead for six months.

Don Philip O'Sullivan Beare, reflecting in exile some 20 years later on the O'Neill rebellion, wrote that 'brass money was, by order of the Queen, sent to Ireland in 1601, by which on the one hand the Queen replenished the exhausted resources of her army, and on the other withdrew Irish gold and silver. As soon as the war was finished this brass money became valueless, to the great injury of the Irish and the Queen's tax-payers, especially merchants' (MacCarthy 1996, 21).

On 11 October 1603 the new king, James VI of Scotland and first of England, devalued Elizabeth's base shillings from twelve pence to fourpence, and the other denominations proportionately. The Lecale masker's hoard of coins in his dirty pocket handkerchief was now worth just £3 6s 8d!

10. KINGDOMS UNITED
The coinage of the early Stuart monarchs (1603–41)

Within a few weeks of the Scottish king's accession to the English throne, James's officials in Dublin issued their first proclamation relating to Elizabeth's base coinage on 18 April 1603. The proclamation was in response to a growing concern that the population was being encouraged through a 'whispering campaign' by the 'worst affected persons' to refuse the base coin on the grounds that with the death of Elizabeth the requirement in her proclamation of 1601 to accept the new coinage no longer applied.

The proclamation set out that 'for as much sithence the decease of our said soveraigne lady and in the tyme of our most gracious soveraigne lord the king that now is, some ignorant and misconceiving persons (as we are informed) doe affirme, that by the decease of our said soveraigne lady the force and effect of the said proclamation is determined, some others covetous and greedy persons doe refuse to receive by way of payment, or commercinge, the said monies of the new standard, and others, the worst affected persons of all, doe very lewdly and seditiouslie give out a lawful libertie upon a supposed vacancy and interregnum' (Simon 1749, 105–6).

James's officials were adamant that the base coin, despite their own misgivings and its obvious unpopularity, should continue to be accepted and in the proclamation required and commanded that 'all manner of officers and subjects of this realme, of what name, dignitie, honour, stile or qualitie so ever they be, and everie of them, to be obedient, and well to performe the proclamation aforesaid of the new standard coyne in particular'.

James and his officials, however, recognised that there was a need to reform the coinage of Ireland. On 11 October 1603 a proclamation was issued by the lord deputy announcing the introduction of a new fine silver coinage and the devaluing of the base coinage of Elizabeth. The new coinage was to be struck to 'a new standard of nyne ounces fine silver, being the ancient standarde of kingdome'. The proclamation went on to announce the devaluation of 'the base mixt monyes of three ounces fine to their value in silver, and for the use of the poorer sort to allowe the moneyes of mere copper, as pence and halfpence, to have still their course amongst his majhasties subjects'. The proclamation set out to describe the new coins and their value: 'each peece of the said new standard of nine ounces fine, bearing the name of a shilling, shall goe current and be taken of all persons in this kingdome for twelve pence sterlinge and all other peeces of that new standard of silver rateablie, according to their proportion to the said twelve pence' (Simon 1749, 106–7). The rating of the new Irish shilling at twelve pence sterling was to cause confusion — or, in the official language of the time, 'did breed an error' — since it was smaller and lighter than its English equivalent and only contained ninepence sterling's worth of silver.

It was, however, to be three years before a proclamation was issued correcting the October 1603 proclamation and declaring 'that the said harpe shillings shall have and beare the name and value onlye of twelve pence Irishe, according to the old standarde of this realime, which in true value is but nyne pence English'. The proclamation further set the rate of the English shilling at sixteen Irish pence: 'sixteen pence of the said new harpe monies of nyne ounces fine silver, for every such twelve pence sterlinge, or twelve pence currant money of or in England' (Simon 1749, 109).

The October 1603 proclamation also began the process of devaluing Elizabeth's base silver coinage with 'the said mixt moneyes be called down to a third parte, the piece of twelve pence to be currante for foure pence of this new standard, and all other peeces of the said mixte coyne, after the same rate, and so to run currant and be taken by all his majesties subjects in this kingdome'. The proclamation further declared that 'we doe further straightelie chardge and command all manner of people within this kingdome, to observe all this his majesties will and commandment upon payne of fortie dayes imprisonment'.

A proclamation of 22 January 1604 was to further devalue Elizabeth's base coinage, with 'the peece formerlie beinge twelve pence, and sithence being so made four pence, is and shall be currant for three pence of the said new standard of silver, and all other peeces of the said mixt coyne after the same rate'. Again, failure to obey the royal will was punishable by 'payne of fortie dayes imprisonment'.

The copper pennies and halfpennies which it was felt met a genuine need among 'the poorer sort' of the king's subjects were to retain their value, but their use was to be limited to fourpence in any transaction.

The first of James's fine coins were issued between 1603 and 1604 and were to consist of an issue of shillings and sixpences. Both coins were struck to .758 fineness but were smaller and about three-quarters lighter than their English equivalents.

Fig. 69—Shilling, James I, first coinage, 1603–4. *SNC*, May 1995, No. 2853

The obverse of the shilling coin featured a crowned portrait of the king facing right. Two main types exist: one which features the king with a square-cut beard and a second which features a pointed beard. The obverse legend reads 'IACOBUS D G ANG SCO FRA A HIB REX' (James by the grace of God king of England, Scotland, France and Ireland). The reverse features a crowned harp with a griffin head within a circle and the legend 'EXURGAT DEUS DISSIPENTUR INIMICI' (Let God arise and his enemies be scattered) forming the border.

Three mint marks are associated with this first issue — a bell with the square-cut beard and a bell or marlet with the pointed beard obverse design. The mint marks are to be found at the start of the legends on both sides of the coin.

The sixpence followed essentially the same design as the shilling, with a crowned portrait of the king and the legend 'IACOBUS D G ANG SCO FRA ET HIB REX' (James by the grace of God king of England Scotland, France and Ireland). The reverse featured the crowned harp design of the shilling with the legend 'TUEATUR UNITA DEUS' (May God guard the united), a reference to the new united kingdoms, forming the border.

The bell and marlet mint marks again appear on the sixpences of this first issue.

Whilst James's original intentions may have been to harmonise the coinage

Fig. 70—Sixpence, James I, first coinage, 1603–4. *SNC*, May 1995, No. 2844

across his three kingdoms, his actions in Ireland in 1603 and 1604 seemed to work against this aim. Three monetary systems were to be established within his kingdom of Ireland, with the sterling English shilling valued at sixteen Irish pence, the Irish shilling valued at twelve Irish pence or nine English pence, and the 'mixt money' shilling valued initially at four Irish pence and later at three Irish pence.

Later in 1604 or 1605 a second coinage was to be issued in James's name with his new title as 'King of Great Britain'.

The second coinage of James I was issued between 1604 and 1607 and again consisted of a shilling and sixpence. The shilling featured a crowned portrait of the king facing right with a long pointed beard within a circle with the legend 'IACOBUS D G MAG BRIT FRA ET HIB REX' (James by the grace of God king of Great Britain, France and Ireland). The reverse features a crowned harp within a circle with the legend 'HENRICUS ROSAS REGNA IACOBUS' (Henry the Roses James the kingdoms), a reference to Henry VII uniting the

Fig. 71—Shilling, James I, second coinage, 1604–7. *SNC*, May 1995, No. 2850

warring houses of York and Lancaster and James uniting the kingdoms of England and Scotland, forming the border. Three mint marks are associated with this second coinage, a martlet, a rose and an escallop shell. A second type of shilling also exists in which the obverse portrait of the king's clothing is less ornate and the king sports a larger, bushier beard. The rose and escallop mint marks are associated with this second type of shilling, which is much scarcer than the first type.

The second issue sixpence followed the same design as the shilling with a crowned portrait of the king on the obverse and the legend 'IACOBUS D G MAG BRIT FRA ET HI REX' (James by the grace of God king of Great Britain, France and Ireland). The reverse features the crowned harp and the 'roses and kingdoms' legend of the shilling. The martlet, rose and escallop mint marks are also associated with this coin.

This was the last official silver regal issue of coins to be struck for Ireland. It seems that in 1607 James abandoned the idea of a separate silver coinage for Ireland and decided that the needs of the Irish for a silver coin would in future be met through English silver coins, which in time would circulate alongside his earlier fine silver shillings and sixpences, the devalued 'mixt money' of Elizabeth and the copper pennies and halfpennies. It is possible that James's abandonment of a distinct silver coinage for Ireland may have been the first step in an attempt to integrate the English and Irish currency systems, with the aim of establishing a single currency system across his three kingdoms.

A proclamation of 19 May 1607 announced the king's decision to cease the production of his fine Irish coins 'because the monies of the said new silver standard cannot be coyned in England, and sent over thither with such speed as his majestie's service doth many tymes require, nor in such quantitie as is sufficient and necessarie for his majesties subjects to use in commerce and traffique' (Simon 1749, 110). In their place the king authorised the use of English coins which had been prohibited since Elizabeth's proclamations of 1601.

The 1607 proclamation set out to 'revive the use of the said monies of England within this realme' at the now established rate of twelve pence sterling to sixteen Irish pence. It was, however, to be another six years before the next step to harmonise the coinages of the two countries was taken when a new copper farthing coin was introduced which was to be current in England and Ireland.

In 1613 James I granted a licence to produce farthings to John Harrington. The granting of these licences or patents was to be used by the Stuart kings as a way of rewarding favoured courtiers or as a means of raising money to supplement the royal income. In the case of Harrington, the king saw it as a means of raising some ready cash and in selling the monopoly to Harrington also insisted on half of the profits. Harrington was assured large profits from the venture as he had the sole right to produce farthing coins throughout the kingdom and was not required to produce coins which contained their intrinsic value in metal. Inevitably the light, tiny coins which were produced were to prove unpopular with the people and were soon being counterfeited.

The Harrington farthings were first issued in 1613 and whilst they were to circulate in Ireland almost immediately, it was not until 1622 that the Irish parliament formally approved their use.

To ensure their acceptability these tiny copper coins were dipped or washed in tin to give a silver appearance, although this was quick to wear off. Two types of Harrington farthing are known: the small type which measured about 12.5mm, and the later larger type which measured about 15mm.

The small coins featured on the obverse a crown superimposed upon two crossed sceptres with the legend 'IACO D G MAG BRIT' (James by the grace of God of Great Britain), whilst the reverse featured a crowned harp with the continuation of the obverse legend 'FRA ET HIB REX' (France and Ireland king). At least seeventeen mint marks, including letters of the alphabet and heraldic devices, are associated with the Harrington coins, being located between the sceptres or on the bands of the crown on the obverse or at the start of the legend on the reverse.

The larger Harrington farthing follows the same design as the smaller coin and again a number of mint marks are associated with this second issue. In contrast to the earlier and smaller farthings, these later coins were not dipped or washed in tin.

In 1614 Harrington died and his licence passed to his son and then his widow, who is believed to have sold the licence on to the duke of Lennox in about 1616.

Under the duke of Lennox the size of the farthing was again slightly increased, although the coin follows essentially the same design as the Harrington coins. These farthings, like the later Harrington farthings, were not dipped or washed in tin. At least 26 different mint marks are associated with the Lennox farthings.

A number of varieties exist with minor differences relating to the placing or absence of the mint mark on the obverse and reverse sides. There is also a variety which features larger crowns than those to be found on most of the Lennox coins.

One particular variety of the Lennox farthing is oval-shaped and features elongated sceptres on the obverse design. It is thought that this particular coin may have been intended for use solely in Ireland. A cross-pattée mint mark is associated with this coin.

James I died in 1625; his reign had been characterised by the further extension of English control in Ireland. An initial reconciliation with O'Neill and the other Ulster chieftains had been followed four years later by the 'Flight of the Earls' on 4 September 1607, which signalled the end of the old Gaelic order in Ireland. James moved quickly to seize Ulster for the Crown. A policy of plantation by English and Scottish Protestant settlers was initiated, with political and religious consequences which still resonate today. The plantation was to prove so successful that by 1613 a ban was placed on further planters moving to Ulster without the appropriate licence. The plantation of other parts of the midlands and Munster also continued, with land being seized from the native Irish.

James's reign was to see the beginning of the first significant shifts in the ownership of land from Catholic landowners to new Protestant settlers. Not only were the native Irish to suffer, but the old Anglo–Norman families, now known as the 'Old English' to distinguish them from the new English and Scottish settlers, also found their lands being seized by the Crown. The political power of the Old English was also to be broken with increased representation in the Irish parliament by the new settlers through the creation of 'rotten boroughs'.

Despite initial tolerance, the Irish and Old English found themselves penalised by the restrictions placed upon the Catholic church. In July 1605 the authorities ordered attendance at Protestant church services on pain of a fine of twelve pence for those who failed to obey.

Inevitably the loss of land, the diminution of political power and the restrictive penal laws were to distance the native Irish and the Old English from the Crown. These policies were to be continued into the reign of Charles I, ultimately with terrible consequences for Catholics and Protestants alike.

With the accession of Charles I, the practice of striking farthings under a royal licence for use in England and Ireland continued. The duchess of Richmond, in partnership with Sir Francis Crane, was granted the licence to issue farthings following the death of her husband, the duke of Lennox, who had become duke of Richmond in 1623. The first farthings to be issued under Charles I were a continuation of the Lennox farthings and are known as the 'Richmond' or 'Royal Issues'.

Some eight different varieties are associated with this first issue of Charles I; they follow the same design as those of his father, although it is evident from some of the coins that, rather than engraving new dies for the new king, the 'IACO' in the obverse legend was recut to read 'CARO' — 'CARO DG MAG BRI' (Charles by the grace of God of Great Britain), 'FRA ET HIB REX' (France and Ireland, king). The main differences in the varieties of Richmond farthings relate to the harp, with one example having an eagle's head whilst others have the harp beaded or bejewelled. Some 39 mint marks are associated with these coins, including a harp.

In 1634 Charles I issued another licence for the minting of farthings to Lord Maltravers, Henry Howard and Sir Francis Crane, who were to continue to produce farthings to essentially the same design as the previous licence-holders. The 'Maltravers' farthings are, however, better coins in terms of the quality of design and engraving compared to the earlier farthings, and are distinguished from the earlier coins by having the central devices on both sides within an inner circle.

A transitional variety with features from the older Richmond and the newer Maltravers coins is also known, with harp and quatrefoil mint marks.

Ten mint marks are associated with the Maltravers farthing. As with the Lennox farthing of James I, a number of oval farthings were also to be struck to the Maltravers design, and nine mint marks are associated with these coins. In this case the sceptres were once again lengthened on the obverse, and the inner circle characteristic of the Maltravers design was removed.

Despite the Irish parliament's endorsement of the farthing tokens in 1622, the tiny farthings were not necessarily popular and at times people were unwilling to accept them. In September 1634 the lord deputy issued an order in response to 'diverse complaints have been made unto us the lord deputy from several parts of this kingdome, concerning the stop and refusal of farthing tokens' (Simon 1749, 111–12). The refusal was in part prompted by concerns over the number of counterfeit farthings circulating in Ireland. The lord deputy sought to reassure the country, in particular 'any poore labourers or workmen', by limiting the number of farthings that could be accepted in payment and promising the 'losse of ears or other corporal punishment' on those found forging or bringing counterfeit farthings into Ireland!

The threats to counterfeiters' ears were not to prove a deterrent, and the number of forged farthings circulating in England and Ireland continued to increase. In a bid to restore confidence Lord Maltravers was instructed in 1636 to issue a new style of farthing which would be more difficult to counterfeit. The new farthings were to contain a small brass plug inserted into the centre of the coin, possibly one of the earliest attempts by monetary authorities to use a 'security device'.

This final issue of farthings to be struck in England under royal licence during the reign of Charles I are known as the 'Rose farthings' and are thought to have also circulated in Ireland. As with the earlier farthings, the obverse features the crown and crossed sceptres design, whilst the reverse features a crowned double rose within an inner circle rather than the crowned harp. These coins were to be struck on a smaller but thicker flan than the earlier farthings, and a brass plug or wedge was fitted into the coin to act as a much-needed deterrent against forgery.

Some seven varieties of this farthing are known, with minor differences in the detail of the design or in the wording of the legend, with one exception in which the crossed sceptres are to be found resting below the crown rather than cutting through the crown. Five mint marks, including fleur-de-lis, martlet, cross pattée, mullet and crescent, are associated with this final issue of farthings.

Charles I was to continue his father's policy of reliance on sterling silver coins to meet the monetary needs of the Irish. On 6 April 1637 a further step towards the harmonisation of English and Irish currencies was attempted when the lord justices and council of Ireland issued a proclamation instructing that, from 1 May 1637, all 'accounts, receipts, payments and issues of his majesties moneys ... all records to be made by, from and after the said time, of any of his majesties moneys or debts' should only be 'made up, reckoned and accounted in English money' rather than 'in Irish money, or harpes' (Simon 1749, 114). Despite this proclamation, accounts, including government accounts and other official records, continued to be reckoned in Irish money rather than in sterling.

It is questionable whether the policy of exporting English silver coins was sufficient to meet the coinage needs of the Irish. Records of the time talk of shortages of coin, a deficiency which was supplied by the importing of gold and silver coins from France, Spain and the Low Countries. But even this was not enough, and calls were increasingly made for the establishment of an Irish mint and the striking of an Irish coinage.

In July 1641 King Charles reversed the policy of reliance on English silver coins when he finally acceded to petitions from the Irish parliament and his lord deputy, and it was agreed that 'gold and silver money should be struck here, of the same standard of those of England for weight and assay, and of such species, and with impressions and stamps, as his majesty should direct, or as the lord deputy and council should think fit, so as they be of an impression clearly distinguishable from the monies of England' (Simon 1749, 45).

Despite royal approval an Irish mint was not to be re-established: within five months of the king's instruction Ireland was plunged into civil war — the Great Rebellion, or the Confederate War as it is known in Ireland.

11. A KINGDOM DIVIDED
The coinage of the Great Rebellion (1642–9)

The frustrations of the native Irish finally erupted into rebellion in October 1641. Irish Catholics, angered by land confiscations and religious restrictions, turned on the new Protestant settlers in Ulster. It is estimated that 4,000 English and Scottish planters were murdered in the autumn of 1641, and a further 8,000 died of exposure after being forced from their homes in the winter months. In the war of propaganda that followed, the number of victims killed in these Ulster atrocities quickly mounted. In August 1642 the English parliament condemned the murder of 154,000 planters, and by 1647 the supposed number of victims stood at 200,000. The rebellion spread through Ireland in a matter of weeks. Soon all but Dublin and the Southern Cities of Refuge, an enclave around the towns of Bandon, Cork, Kinsale and Youghal, was in rebel hands.

The Old English families soon joined forces with the native Irish leaders. By March 1642 the rebels had established a government and summoned a parliament, a general assembly, to meet in the Confederates' capital of Kilkenny. The Confederate Catholics in October 1642 declared their loyalty to Charles I but their opposition to his government in Dublin, which was headed by James Butler, twelfth earl of Ormonde. The outbreak of the Civil War in England in August 1642 saw three warring factions in Ireland: the Catholic Confederates in Kilkenny, who were loyal to the king but opposed his government; the Royalist government in Dublin led by Ormonde and in Munster by Murrough O'Brien, Lord Inchiquin; and the English Parliamentary forces who invaded Ulster in 1642, led by General Robert Munro.

Despite the initial success of the Confederates, Ormonde and his Royalist forces were to regain Drogheda and Kildare for the king, whilst Munro took Newry and other key towns in the north in the name of the English parliament. The increasingly desperate position of the Royalists in England in time forced King Charles to attempt to reach some accommodation with the Confederates. The arrival of the papal nuncio Rinuccini in 1645 and his demands for the re-establishment of the Catholic church were, however, to thwart the king's attempts to reach an accommodation. Rinuccini's malign influence was also to weaken the Confederate cause in time by exposing the splits between the Irish and the Old English factions.

Ormonde eventually reached an accommodation with the Irish leadership in 1646, with the promise of an independent Irish parliament in return for their military support. The price was, however, too high for the king, who was already at war with an independent English parliament, and Ormonde's carefully negotiated treaty fell. The civil war in Ireland was not simply a series of military campaigns but also a game of political manoeuvring amongst the leadership of the Confederate, Royalist and Parliamentary forces. The king's initial approaches to the Confederates were to split the Royalist leadership, with Lord Inchiquin changing allegiances and taking Munster over to the Parliamentary side rather than throw in his lot with the Confederate 'rebels', and in time Ormonde was to reach an accommodation with both the Confederate forces and the Parliamentary forces!

The first coinage of the Great Rebellion was issued by the Catholic Confederacy in the autumn of 1642 when the Confederate authorities turned their attention to monetary concerns in the areas under their control.

On 15 November 1642 the Confederates issued a proclamation referring to 'much scarcitie of money and coyne in this kingdome' and 'therefore declare that all money plate and coyne as well as silver as gold English and forraine shall be raised and inhanced … That peeces of 8 be raised to 6s, the peeces of 4 and 2 rateablie, the Portugal testing to 1s8d, the Cardique of France to 2s, the half-cardique to 1s, the Pistolet of 14s to 20s, the quarable and single rateably, the Rider of Scotland to 2s, the Jacobus of 22s to 29s and 4d sterling, the 20s of James and Carolus to 26s and 8d, the half and quarter rateablie. The Albertus raised to 13s and 6d, the half accordingly, the rose of 4s4½d to 5s and 6d' (Willson Yeates 1919–20, 191–2).

Having raised the value of all foreign coins, the Confederate authorities also raised the value of a range of Irish and English silver coins, including some dating back to the reign of Henry VIII, such as the dominick grote and Edward VI's 'copper' groat, as well as the white groats of Mary Tudor and Elizabeth I which were still continuing to circulate in Ireland, in some cases a century after they had first been issued: 'The 13½d is to be raised to one shilling 6d, the 1s sterling to 1s4d, the 6d to 8d, the 9d to 12d, the 4d to 5d, the 3d to 4d, the 4½d to 6d, the 2d to 3d and the dominick grote to 4d, the copper grote to 5d, the white grote of coper to 2d and that the 9d of the said severall coyness be henceforth reputed and doe pass for 1s and half a crown peece doe pass henceforth for 10 groates'.

The proclamation was finally to order the striking of a copper coinage: 'Wee do likewise publish and declare that there shall be 400L of red copper coyned to farthings and ½ pence with the Harp on one side and the Crowne and to septers on the other and that everie pound of copper be made to value of 2s 8d and that this coin shall be currant before as well payment'.

Two types of halfpenny are known. The first type, produced on crudely

Fig. 72—Halfpenny, Confederate Catholics, Kilkenny, 1642–3. *SNC*, May 1995, No. 2862

prepared flans, feature on the obverse a crown over two sceptres within a beaded circle with the legend 'CAROLUS D G MAG BRI' (Charles by the grace of God of Great Britain) within a second beaded circle. The reverse features a crowned harp with the cypher 'C' and 'R' on either side of the harp within a beaded circle, with the legend 'FRA ET HIB REX' (France and Ireland king) within a further beaded circle. The second type tend to be rounder in shape and follow essentially the same design as the first, the principal difference being that the harp is much more angular and cruder in design and the royal cypher 'CR' is omitted from the reverse design. Examples of Kilkenny halfpennies are known with two counter-marks, with a stamp with a castle over a 'K' or a rosette on either the obverse or reverse of the coin. It has been suggested that the counter-marks may have been a way of authenticating the coin and allowing wider circulation outside the immediate area of Kilkenny.

Only one type of farthing was produced. Like the halfpennies, the coin was crudely produced and featured a crown and sceptre device on the obverse and the legend 'CARO D G MAG BRI' (Charles by grace of God of Great Britain) forming the border. The reverse featured a crowned harp with a continuation of the obverse legend 'FRA ET HIB REX' (France and Ireland king). Despite the large numbers of these coins produced, all are now very rare. An example of the second type of halfpenny with the crude harp design was to sell for £IR870 at the Whyte's Millennial Collection Sale in April 2000.

Whilst the halfpennies and farthings can be dated to 1642 and 1643, there is less certainty about the other coins attributed to the Catholic Confederacy. The Confederates were also to be responsible for the striking of a silver half-crown, the so-called 'blacksmith's half-crown'. Some numismatists have attributed this coin to 1642, as the 'half a crown peece to pass henceforth for 10 groates' of the November proclamation. Others have suggested that it may have been struck by the Confederates in Kilkenny as late as 1649. The coin is based on an English half-crown of the time but is much cruder in terms of engraving and production. Its nickname derives from the observations of the nineteenth-century numismatist Snelling, who wrote of this particular coin that 'Amongst the great variety of this king's money, although we meet with many very rude of bad workmanship, yet

Fig. 73—Half-crown, Charles I, 'Blacksmith Issue'. *SNC*, May 1994, No. 3490

we think none of them comes up to the half crown, the barbarous work of which was certainly that of a smith and not an engraver' (Willson Yeates 1919–20, 215).

The obverse features the king on horseback with a cross on the horse's livery within a beaded circle with the legend 'CAROLUS D G MA BR FRA ET HI(B) REX' (Charles by the grace of God king of Great Britain, France and Ireland). A cross mint mark appears at the start of the obverse legend. The reverse features the royal coat of arms within an oval shield with the legend 'CHRISTO AUSPICE REGNO' (I reign under the auspices of Christ) forming the border. A harp mint mark is to be found at the start of the reverse legend.

A variety of the 'blacksmith's half-crown' was also produced without the cross design on the horse's livery.

The outbreak of the Civil War in England brought an end to regular supplies of sterling coins to the king's supporters in Dublin. In January 1643 the lord justices and the council in Dublin found themselves faced with similar problems to the Confederates in Kilkenny.

Their response was to order the people of Dublin and the County of Dublin to hand over to the authorities half or more of their plate 'for the relieve of the officers of the army'. The appeal was to raise a disappointing £1,200 worth of plate, which the lord justices observed 'can in no degree give any contentment to the officers of the army towards their great arrears' (Willson Yeates 1919–20, 200–1). The citizens of Dublin were promised compensation of five shillings per ounce for silver plate of sterling standard or 'plate as is true touch'. A pro rata payment was also to be made for lesser-quality plate. Arrangements were made for citizens donating their plate to receive 8% interest on the value of their plate pending final payment of their compensation.

The proclamation of 14 January 1643 required citizens to deliver their plate to Alderman William Bladen and Sheriff John Pue, who were then required to pass the plate to two Dublin goldsmiths, Peter Vaneyndhoven and Gilbert Tonges, who were 'to try the touch' and determine the quality of plate and the appropriate compensation. Vaneyndhoven and Tonges were both founder members of the Dublin Goldsmith's Company in 1637. Vaneyndhoven was warden of the Company in 1639–40 (and later in 1644–6). Gilbert Tonges was later to be a warden and master of the Company between 1646 and 1647.

The plate was to be cut into 'pledge pieces' between January and May 1643. These were irregularly shaped pieces of plate which were cut to set weights and stamped or counter-marked with the weight on both sides. They were known as pledge pieces since the stamp or counter-mark guaranteed the weight and intrinsic value of the piece.

Fig. 74—Half-crown, lord justices' issue, 1642–3. Davissons, 12 March 2002, 384

Six types of pledge pieces were issued initially under the authority of the lord justices; the largest piece, which was stamped with the weight '19 dwt 8 gr' within a circle, was to pass as a crown or five shillings; the second, with a stamp of '9 DW tt 16 gr' within a circle, passed as half a crown or two shillings and sixpence; and a third piece, with a stamp of '3 DWT 21 gr' within a circle, passed as a shilling. The fourth piece of cut plate had a weight of '2 DWT 20 gr' within a circle stamped on both sides and passed as ninepence. A smaller piece with the weight of '1 DWT 22 gr' within a circle stamped on both sides passed for sixpence, and a final piece with a weight of '1 DWT 6 gr' passed for fourpence.

A second issue of lord justices' pieces was also to be struck. These were rounder in shape and included the weight on one side as in the first issue, but a number of annulets on the reverse to indicate the monetary value of the piece. These are generally known as 'Annulets Coinage'. Four pieces were struck. The largest featured the weight '2 DWT 20 gr' within a circle on the obverse and nine annulets on the reverse, a reference to its value as ninepence. This is the only occasion that a ninepenny 'coin' was struck and circulated in Ireland. The remaining pieces were a sixpence with a weight of '1 DWT 22 gr' on the obverse and six annulets on the reverse, a fourpence or groat with a weight of '1 DWT 6 gr' on the obverse and four annulets on the reverse, and the smallest piece in the series, a threepence with '23 gr' on the obverse and three annulets on the reverse.

All of these lord justices' pieces are extremely rare. A 'half-crown' piece was sold by Whyte's in February 1998 for £IR1,600. At the Whyte's Millennial Collection Sale in April 2000 a first-issue 'crown' piece was to sell for £IR4,800, whilst an annulets groat in very fine condition fetched £IR6,500 and a clipped annulets threepence, one of only four known, fetched £IR6,000.

In 1643 the lord justices authorised the issue of a further set of counter-marked pieces of plate, known as 'Dublin Money', which gave each piece a monetary value rather than a weight. This third issue of 'coins' authorised by the lord justices consisted of a crown piece with 'V S' within a double circle stamped on the obverse and reverse, representing five shillings, and a half-crown with 'IIs VID' within a double circle on both sides.

These pieces are again extremely rare, and a crown piece sold for £IR2,400 and a half-crown piece for £IR1,900 at the Whyte's Millennial Collection Sale.

On 25 May 1643 Charles I authorised the issuing of a new Irish coinage to be struck in Dublin. From his headquarters in Oxford he wrote: 'Our subjects in Ireland are so reduced by Rebellion that they are desirous to coin a little money out of their own plate as a last remedy for their support. This sum is so small that it is not worth while to set up a Mint for the purpose in Ireland and this would take too much time. You shall therefore authorise such persons as you may think fit by commission to melt down the plate and make it into five shillings, half crowns, twelve pences and six pences. You shall receive these coins and stamp them with CR and a crown on one side and their value on the other. They shall be of the same value and allay as the currant money in England'. The king concluded: 'You shall give what allowances you think fit to the coiners, and take security against fraud from them' (Willson Yeates 1919–20, 203–4).

Following the king's instructions, some seven coins were issued. including a crown, half-crown, shilling, sixpence, groat, threepence and half-groat or twopence; the last three were in addition to the king's original letter. It is thought that along with his instructions Charles sent his Royalist forces in Dublin £100,000 in worn silver coin to supplement whatever plate the Dublin citizens might donate.

All seven coins follow essentially the design set out in the king's letter, with a crowned 'CR' cypher on the obverse, for *Carolus Rex* (King Charles), within a double circle with the outer circle normally beaded. The reverse features the value of the coin within a double circle with the outer circle normally beaded. In the case of the crown the value is represented as 'Vs' with the 's' above the 'V'; the half-crown 'IIsVID', with the letters 's' and 'D' above the numerals; the shilling 'XIID', with the 'D' above and to the right of the numeral 'X'; the sixpence with the value of 'VID', with the 'D' above and to the right of the 'V'; the groat or fourpence with 'IIII', with the 'D', in a departure from the other coins, either above or below the numerals; the threepence with 'III' with the 'D' above the numerals; and the half-groat or twopence with 'II', with a small 'D' above the numerals.

A proclamation was issued in Dublin on 8 July 1643 authorising the use of the new coins. It was signed by the earl of Ormonde along with Lancelot Bulkeley, archbishop of Dublin, and other members of the king's council. It is probably from his signature on this proclamation that this series of emergency coins is commonly known as 'Ormonde Money'. It is thought that as much as £120,000 worth of Ormonde Money was produced primarily for general circulation rather than to pay the army. On 13 October 1643 the coins were made legal tender in England.

Fig. 75—Half-crown, Charles I, 'Ormonde Money', 1643–4. *SNC*, May 1995, No. 2853

Fig. 76—Shilling, Charles I, 'Ormonde Money', 1643–4. *SNC*, May 1995, No. 2858

Fig. 77—Sixpence, Charles I, 'Ormonde Money', 1643–4. *SNC*, May 1995, No. 2859

The next major group of coins issued during the Great Rebellion are thought to have been struck in imitation of the Ormonde coins by the Catholic Confederates in Kilkenny in 1643–4, and are known as 'Rebel Money'. It may be an indication of the troubled times and the absence or destruction of records in times of war and rebellion that, whilst these coins are attributed to the Catholic Confederates, it has also been suggested that they could have been manufactured in Dublin by Parliamentary forces under the command of Colonel Michael Jones sometime after March 1647.

The Rebel Money series consists of two coins, a crown and a half-crown, both of which are extremely rare. At the Whyte's Millennial Collection Sale a Rebel Money crown was sold for £IR4,000, whilst a half-crown fetched £IR4,200.

Both coins follow essentially the same design with the central device of a large cross within a circle, with a pellet and star mark in the border between the circle and the edge of the coin on the crown, and a star in the case of the half-crown. It has been suggested that the cross was derived from the cross on the seal of the Confederates, although other commentators feel that the cross is more similar to that used by the Parliamentary forces on their banners and the later Commonwealth coinage.

Fig. 78—Half-crown, Confederate Catholics Rebel Money. DNW, 9 October 1999

The reverse of both coins features the value of the coin within a circle — in the case of the crown a large 'V' with a smaller 'S' above, and for the half-crown 'IIS VID' within a circle with the 'S' and 'D' above the numerals.

Whilst there may be some doubts about the origins of the Rebel Money and whether it was issued by the Catholic Confederates or the Parliamentarians, there are no doubts about a small group of coins issued in 1646–7 by Parliamentary forces in Cork and Youghal. The Southern Towns or Cities of Refuge included Bandon, Cork, Kinsale and Youghal. The enclaves around these four towns formed a safe haven for English planters following the atrocities in Ulster in the autumn of 1642. Initially these towns were loyal to the Crown, but with the desertion of Murrough O'Brien (Lord Inchiquin), president of Munster, to the Parliamentary side, these towns also switched their allegiances. The first emergency pieces produced by the Southern Towns of Refuge were authorised by Lord Broghill, the vice-president of Munster, on 20 March 1646 to alleviate a shortage of small coin in Youghal. The order set out that the vice-president 'thought fit that certain small pieces of copper and mixed metal be coined and stamped by Nicholas Stowe Gent and Marmaduke Deverox in manner following, namely: every such piece to be in value a farthing and pass in all exchanges within the English quarters and weigh one quarter of an ounce or with 12 ounces in each pound weight to be formed and cut square, having a ship stamped on one side and YT on the other charging all his majesty's subjects within the town of Youghal to receive the said peeces so stamped' (Willson Yeates 1919–20, 208–9).

Whilst emergency coins were attributed to all four towns, it is now thought that only Cork and Youghal issued emergency coins during the Great Rebellion and that the coins attributed to Bandon and Kinsale were issued in the 1650s.

The Youghal farthing, as set out in Broghill's orders, was produced on a small square piece of brass with the obverse design of the letters 'YT' (Youghal town) above the date '1646', with a small bird facing left above the 'YT'. The reverse featured a galley within two double circles. At least eight varieties of the Youghal farthing are known, with minor variations to the obverse and reverse designs. It is generally accepted that no more than £50 worth of Youghal farthings were issued.

Fig. 79—Farthing, Youghal, 'Southern Cities of Refuge', 1646. *SNC*, May 1995, No. 2865

It is thought that Lord Inchiquin as president of Munster may have been responsible for an issue of silver shillings and sixpences in Cork in May 1647. The two coins follow essentially the same design, with the word 'CORK' above the date '1647' within a toothed circle on the obverse, and the numerals 'XII' within a toothed circle for the shilling and a 'VI' within a toothed circle for the sixpence on the reverse. A halfpenny has in the past been attributed to Cork at this time, but it is now thought that this counter-marked coin might belong to the later civil war of the 1690s. Similarly, a Cork farthing which was attributed to this period is now thought to have been struck in the 1650s, like those of Bandon and Kinsale.

Fig. 80—Sixpence, Cork, 'Southern Cities of Refuge', 1647. *SNC*, May 1996, No. 2227

A Cork shilling was to sell for £IR3,600 and a Youghal farthing for £IR1,000 at the Whyte's Millennial Collection Sale in April 2000.

In the summer of 1646, Queen Henrietta Maria, the wife of Charles I, sent 10,000 pistoles' worth of gold coins (about £6,600) from France to the Royalist forces in Dublin. The Royalist authorities were again facing problems in paying their troops. At that time the total weekly cost of the Dublin garrison was about £263 9s 0d, with the 2,500 soldiers receiving twelve pence a week in payment.

On 27 July 1646 the earl of Ormonde and the lord justices issued a warrant authorising the issuing of a new gold coinage to be struck from the gold supplied by Henrietta Maria to pay the soldiers of the Dublin garrison. Ormonde's warrant stated that 'whereas the extreame necessity of the souldrs in the citty of Dublin other guarrisons neere adjacent is extraordinary great, and wee, willing to sustaine their present indigencyees, having taken into or tender comiserac'on their grievous distresses, and having in or custody some bullion of gould ... have thought it goode that it should be moulten downe ... to make thereof certaine pieces or pledges for the relief of the sd distresses of the souldrs' (O'Sullivan 1964, 142). The warrant went on to outline arrangements for the production of these pledges and commanded 'Peter Vaneyndhoven and Gilbert Tonges of the city of

Dublin, gouldsmiths, to take the said gould into their custody and the same to melt downe' and 'bring unto a standard of 19 carrots' and 'to cut one into pieces or pledges, the one sort weighting eight peny weight and fourteene graines and the other sort weighing for penny weight seven graineess'. The warrant further stated that Vaneyndhoven and Tonges were to 'receive for their labour twelve pence out of every twenty shill'worth of bullion of gould by them wrought'.

Fig. 81—Pistole, Charles I, Dublin, 1646.
Whyte's Millennial Sale, April 2000, No. 248

Whilst the pieces struck by Vaneyndhoven and Tonge were not strictly coins they were to become known as 'pistoles'. The Spanish two-escudo piece which weighed about 104 grains and was struck to a fineness of 21½ carats was generally known as the pistole. It is thought that the authorities sought to encourage the idea that these Irish pieces were the equivalent of the Spanish pistoles. The Irish pledge pieces struck in July 1646 were, however, lighter in weight and were struck in 19 carat gold (.790 fineness). The general view is that the term 'pistole' was applied to these pieces at a later date, possibly from the time of William III.

Two pledge pieces were to be struck with both pieces following the same design: the double-pistole, with the weight '8 dw tt 14 gr' in two lines on the obverse and the reverse, and the pistole, with the weight '4 dw tt 7 gr' again in two lines on both sides.

Both pieces are extremely rare, with possibly only two double-pistoles in existence and about twenty pistole coins, of which ten are in private hands. One of these ten private pieces, with a provenance stretching back to the seventeenth century, was auctioned at the Whyte's Millennial Collection Sale in April 2000, where it sold for £IR100,000.

It is thought that the double-pistole initially circulated at 25 shillings and the pistole at twelve shillings and sixpence.

It has been suggested that as many as 3,000 double-pistoles and 15,000 pistole pieces could have been struck to meet the needs of the Irish garrison in Dublin and other areas under Royalist control, which would have been well in excess of the gold sent by Henrietta Maria, even taking into account the lower gold content of these pieces.

In February 1647 a further issue of gold pledge pieces was authorised by the Dublin authorities in response to 'the extreme necessity of the inhabitants of this citty of Dublin and the guarrisons neare adjacent have been and are such as they have been forced to coin their plate now as their lost refuge are inforced to make away the gold rings, chains and broken gold they have left'. Again, Peter Vaneyndhoven and Gilbert Tonges were authorised to receive the citizens' gold and 'cutt and stampe itt into the like pledges as for the weight as they late made'. These pieces, however, were to be struck to a higher standard of between 20 and 22 carats (.830 –.920 fineness) and possibly circulated at a value of 13s 4d. This second issue was smaller than the earlier July issue.

It has been suggested that about 25,000 pledge pieces were produced in the summer of 1646 and the winter months of 1647 — £20,000 worth of gold, in all.

Within a few months of the issue of the last 'pistole' pieces Dublin was occupied by Parliamentary forces. Following the surrender of Charles I in England, Ormonde handed over the city of Dublin to the Parliamentary army under Colonel Michael Jones rather than let it fall to the Catholic Confederates. In 1648, faced with the news that the king was to be tried, Ormonde and his Royalist army agreed a treaty with the rebel Confederates to fight for the king, but it was too late. Within weeks the king was dead, executed on 30 January 1649.

The last coinage of the Great Rebellion was struck in the first months of 1649 by order of Ormonde in the name of the new king, Charles II. Ironically this coinage is believed to have been struck from silver supplied to the earl of Ormonde by the Parliamentary forces following the surrender of Dublin in 1647.

Fig. 82—Half-crown, Charles II, second Ormonde issue, 1649. DNW, 9 October 1999

It consisted of two coins, a crown and half-crown. Both followed the same design, with a large crown within a circle on the obverse with the legend 'CAR II D G MAG BRIT' (Charles II by the grace of God of Great Britain) forming the border. The reverse featured the value of the coin 'VS' within a circle for the crown and 'IIS VID' within a circle for the half-crown, with the obverse legend continued on the reverse 'FRA ET HYB REX FD' (France and Ireland king, defender of the faith). This coin, besides being the first Irish coin struck in Charles II's name, is also the first coin struck in Britain or Ireland which includes the letters FD for *Fidei Defensor* (defender of the faith) in the king's titles. This title, which was awarded to Henry VIII by Pope Leo X, was not to be used on a British coin until 1714 and never again on an Irish coin. Both these coins are extremely rare. A crown piece in very fine condition was to sell for £IR7,500 and a weakly struck half-crown in fine condition for £IR1,800 at the Whyte's Millennial Collection Sale in April 2000.

Following the death of Charles I, Ormonde gathered the Royalist and Confederate forces together in support of the new king. The Parliamentary forces, victorious in England, now turned their attention to Ireland and the rebel Royalists and Confederates. On 2 August 1649 Ormonde's 'Royalist' army was decisively defeated by Parliamentary forces, led by Colonel Jones, at the Battle of Rathmines. Two thousand Royalist prisoners were taken and possibly as many as 4,000 Irish killed, but worse was to follow. On 15 August 1649 the new lord lieutenant of Ireland, Oliver Cromwell, landed at Ringsend, near Dublin, with a force of 20,000 men to put down the 'Popish rebels' in Ireland.

12. A GREAT SCARCITY OF COIN
The coinage of the people and the king (1652–88)

Within weeks of Cromwell's arrival in Ireland, Drogheda and Wexford had been seized and the defending garrisons massacred. Over the winter months Cromwell's army advanced against other Royalist strongholds, with Kilkenny, the old Catholic Confederate capital, falling in March 1650. Officers, in the parlance of the day, were 'topped on the head' and ordinary soldiers chained and transported to the plantations of the West Indies. Cromwell's brutal military campaign came to an end on 26 May 1650 when he left Ireland to resume his role as leader of the new Commonwealth in England.

With the surrender of Kilkenny the Great Rebellion came to an end. An estimated 616,000 people had died over the eight years of its duration.

With the end of the military campaign, Cromwell's officials in Ireland turned their attention to the civilian population who had supported the Confederates or the king, in particular the Catholic landowners. Under the 1652 Act of Settlement, nearly half of the land in Ireland was taken from Irish Catholics and handed over to new English Protestant settlers. 'Innocent Papists' who had not been involved in the Rebellion were also forced to hand over their estates or properties and to migrate to new properties in the harsh lands of Clare and Connacht.

In 1653 the power of the old Irish parliament was also broken when Ireland was formally united with England in the new Commonwealth of England and Ireland. In 1654, 30 Irish representatives took their seats in the English parliament sitting at Westminster. The 1653 union of England and Ireland is perhaps best captured in the new English coinage of the Commonwealth, which featured on its reverse a shield with the St George's Cross of England and a shield with the Irish harp. The Irish harp was later to be incorporated into the arms of the lord protector, which featured on the reverse of gold and silver coins issued by Oliver Cromwell and bearing his portrait on the obverse from 1656 through to 1658.

During the Commonwealth no distinctive Irish coinage was to be struck. It was anticipated that the coinage needs of the Irish would be met through the new English Commonwealth gold and silver coins with their conjoined English and Irish shields. The reality was to be very different and very little good English coin was to make its way to Ireland throughout the 1650s. Instead the Irish found themselves once again relying upon supplies of foreign gold and silver coin, which often circulated at inflated values, and clipped and counterfeit English coins. The early 1650s were to see the importation of such large quantities of clipped and counterfeit coins that it was estimated that almost half of the silver coins circulating in Ireland were not worth more than twopence in silver content. In the absence of an officially sanctioned copper coinage, 'the great scarcity of small change' was to be met by copper and brass tokens issued by local traders and town corporations.

In December 1652 the authorities issued the first in a series of proclamations to deal with the deteriorating state of Ireland's coinage and 'prohibited English clip't money to be passed in payment, above the intrinsic value, which we have declared to be five shillings per ounce troy' (Simon 1749, 118). A year later the problem was no better and official correspondence between Dublin and London talks of 'very great quantities of clip't English money being sent over out of England, by merchants and others for the gains that was to be gotten thereby' (ibid., 119). In the same letter the Dublin authorities go on to report that 'the passing of clip't English money currant in pay in Ireland, and the uncertain rates that forein monies went at, hath been a very great prejudice to your service here, and tended much to the diminution of the English coin'.

The relative status and value of English coin in Ireland was, however, not the only concern of the Committee of Irish Affairs. There were increasing concerns that the success of Cromwell's policy of confiscation and plantation, coupled with the maintenance of a standing army in Ireland, might be seriously undermined in the absence of a sound monetary system. It was in response to these concerns that Secretary Thurloe and the Committee of Irish Affairs wrote to London requesting 'that power may be speedily sent hither for the stamping or coyning of twenty thousand pounds'.

The Irish Committee repeated their fears directly to the lord protector in a letter some two months later, in which they wrote: 'there will be in a short time noe money left to pay your forces, or for necessary exchange amongst the people, but counterfeit and bad money, and consequently your affairs here will unavoidably fall into disorder' (Simon 1749, 121).

It is possible that in response to these two desperate pleas tentative steps were taken by the Commonwealth government to remedy the problem, as a further letter from the Committee of Irish Affairs of 15 July 1653, while once again talking of the 'pressing necessities of a mint to be appointed in this country, by reason of the great want of small English money' (Simon 1749, 119), does acknowledge that the English parliament had approved an 'order for one hundred thousand pounds to be coyned in Ireland'. It seems that progress in establishing a mint was slow, with the authorities experiencing 'some difficulty about sending persons over out of England for it'. Needless to say, no mint was established in Dublin.

Three years later the Irish authorities were again making requests to London to remedy Ireland's monetary problems. In the absence of good English coin, foreign coin was increasingly being put into circulation, with some base and counterfeit foreign coins passing at rates significantly above their intrinsic value. The most notorious at the time was a coin known as the 'Peru Piece', which initially circulated at a rate of 4s 6d but in reality was worth no more than 2s 4d in silver content.

Official frustration with the state of Ireland's coinage continued to be a regular feature of correspondence between London and Dublin through the 1650s. A letter to the lord protector of 16 April 1656 talks of 'the miserable condition this nation is in, through that vast quantity of Peru and other base and counterfeit coyne, this poor nation hath of late bene burthened with'. In the same letter the officials go on to describe the base and counterfeit coin circulating in Ireland as 'more such trash' before their frustrations come to a head: 'for like a gangren this adulterate coyne spreads farr and near. It banishes hence the currant coyne of Spain and eats up the good English money which the merchants make it a secret trade to export into England'.

This appeal, like the early appeals, seemed to fall on deaf ears in London. No attempt was made by the authorities to remedy Ireland's coinage needs and no Irish mint was to be established during the Commonwealth. Instead it fell to town corporations, merchants and innkeepers — and indeed butchers, bakers and candlestick-makers — to remedy Ireland's need for small change.

The small lightweight farthings which had been issued under the royal patents of James I and Charles I had never been popular. In 1644 the English parliament finally revoked the patents granted by Charles I but no officially sanctioned farthing coin or other small denomination coin was authorised to be issued in their place. In Ireland, as in England, town corporations and individual merchants, shopkeepers and innkeepers had to manufacture and issue their own copper and brass coins to meet the needs of their businesses and their customers.

The earliest trade tokens issued about this time in Ireland date from 1653 and are in the main small penny pieces. In all, about 800 tokens from 170 cities and towns were to be issued between 1653 and 1679.

Whilst the 1653 Union had ended Ireland's political independence, the introduction of free trade between England and Ireland saw a flourishing of commerce, and the number of trade tokens issued during the Commonwealth and the early years of the Restoration is perhaps an indication of the economic prosperity that Ireland was to enjoy despite its lack of a sound coinage.

Most tokens were round in shape, but some square and heart-shaped examples were also to be issued. Tokens issued by towns or corporations normally incorporated the civic coat of arms into the design of the coin, whilst those issued by shopkeepers or merchants generally included a reference to their trade or business — a wheat sheaf for a baker, a sugar loaf for a grocer, a bottle for an innkeeper and a tankard for a pewterer. Tokens also normally bore the name and address of the issuer, and sometimes the issuer's initials formed part of the design. In the southern counties of Ireland the wife's initial was also often incorporated into the design along with those of her husband. In other cases the issuer's personal coat of arms was incorporated into the design, whilst some of the designs used on tokens were a 'play' on the issuer's name, such as in the inclusion of a harp on the tokens of John Harper of Ballymoney or the early Christian symbol of the fish on tokens issued by Abraham Christian of Galway.

Inevitably the greatest concentration of tokens was in the cities and larger towns. Dublin alone during this period saw 170 different tokens struck by 145 issuers. Similarly Belfast, Drogheda, Galway, Limerick, Waterford, Wexford and Youghal all saw significant issues of tokens, but even towns in the more remote parts of Ireland, such as Dingle in the south-west, Baltimore in the south, Enniscrone in the west and Rathmullen in the north, were able to boast tokens issued by local merchants. In all, tokens can be attributed to at least 30 of Ireland's counties during this period.

A listing of Dublin tokens identifies traders in 27 streets or localities within the city issuing tokens from the 1650s through to the 1670s. In St Thomas Street, or Thomas Street as it is known today, Christopher Bennet, merchant, John Dutton, Gilbert Johnson, Randal Lester, John Lovett and Richard Warren all issued tokens. Lester's tokens issued in 1655 were to feature an Indian smoking on the reverse.

In Kerry, merchants in four towns, Dingle, Glanerough, Killarney and Tralee, were to issue tokens. Perhaps the most intriguing is the Dingle Penny issued in 1679 which featured a Janus head on one side and Cupid pointing his arrow at a couple under a tree on the other side.

Under Cromwell's rule the Protestant Ascendancy was to be firmly established in control of the land and the political machinery of Ireland. The restoration of Charles II in May 1660 brought no change. On 30 November 1660 the new king issued a declaration essentially confirming the Cromwellian settlement of Ireland. This was to be enshrined in the Act of Settlement of 31 July 1662, with some belated attempts to return some land to 'innocent papists' who had supported the Royalist cause during the Great Rebellion. The Irish parliament was also re-established in 1660, but in a time of changing fortunes the new parliament was to have only one Catholic member. With the Protestant Ascendancy confirmed, there was some attempt in the late 1660s and 1670s to allow some religious toleration and the lifting of some penal laws against Catholics.

Within a few months of his restoration, the new king was to write to the lord justices of Ireland: 'We are informed that there is a great scarcity of coin in Ireland' (Simon 1749, 120). In 1661 the first in a series of measures was put in hand to deal with the country's desperate monetary position. Like his earlier Stuart forebears, the king's response was to grant a patent to 'Sir Thomas Armstrong, Knight, his heirs executors, administrators and assignes, full power during the terme of twenty one years from the date herof, to coyne such a quantitie of farthing tokens of copper, as may be conveniently issued during the said terme amongst our subjects of Ireland' (Powell 1978, 174). The new coins, in the words of the patent, were for 'the greate and generall use and benefits to our people of our realme of Ireland, as well as amongst tradesmen for exchange of moneys in the course of their severall trades, and especially of the poore and meaner sorte'. Armstrong was to pay the Crown £16 13s 4d each year for the privilege of minting these new farthing coins. The patent also set out the process of manufacture and the design of the new coins: 'they shall be made of copper by engines, and shall have on one side two sceptres crossing one diadem, and on the other side a harpe crowned with our title Carolus secondus magne Brittanie, Francie et Hibernie Rex, and to weigh twenty graines or more'.

Fig. 83—Farthing, Charles II, 'Armstrong Issue', 1660–1. *SNC*, May 1994, No. 3493

These first regal farthings of Charles II were to follow essentially the same design as the earlier Harrington and Lennox farthings of James I and Charles I. The obverse featured a crown with two crossed sceptres within a beaded circle with the legend 'CAROLUS II D G M B' (Charles II by the grace of God, of Great Britain). The letter 'R' is to be found incorporated into the design of the band of the crown and it is thought that this may be a reference to the engraver Thomas Rawlins. The reverse features a crowned harp partly within a beaded circle with the legend 'FRA ET HIB REX' (France and Ireland, king). A plume mint mark is incorporated into the reverse design.

Silver proof versions or special strikings of this farthing are also known.

The reference to the production of these new farthings 'by engines' reflects the changes in the manufacturing of coins that had taken place over the last century. The production of coins using machines instead of the traditional hammer blow had been developed in Renaissance Italy. In England machine-produced coins made a brief appearance in the 1560s during the reign of Elizabeth I and later again for short periods under James I and Charles I.

The Lennox and Harrington farthings which circulated in Ireland throughout the 1620s were produced using a mangle-like 'rolling-mill' in which the strips of copper were passed through rollers which had the design of the coin engraved on them. It was, however, during the reign of Charles II that machine-produced coins, or 'milled' coins as they became known, finally replaced hand-produced 'hammered' coins in England and in Ireland.

By the mid-seventeenth century rolling-mills had been largely replaced by the screw press, which, it is thought, was developed in Germany in the 1550s. The screw press employed the same principles as the hammer, with pressure being applied through a screw mechanism rather than a hammer blow. The machine or press was placed in a pit or well, with the lower die fixed to the base of the machine. The upper die, which moved up and down, was set into the lower part of the screw mechanism. Pressure was applied manually by four men swiftly turning the arms of the machine, which turned the screw in a sharp downward thrust.

The blanks for the coins were fed into the machine by an apprentice sitting in the pit below the machine. The boy had no more than split seconds to place the blank metal disc on the lower die, wait for the screw to come down and rebound upwards, and then flick away the finished coin and replace it with another blank. It is estimated that as many as 30 coins a minute could be produced on the screw press; inevitably fingertips, if not whole fingers, were lost in the process!

This and other developments in minting technology during the sixteenth and seventeenth centuries allowed the process of coin production to be speeded up and resulted in thicker and more regularly shaped coins, often with engraved, grained or 'milled' edges which brought an end to the widespread clipping of coin.

Eighteenth-century print of a screw press in operation

Further measures to reform Ireland's coinage were put in place on 13 October 1660 when steps were also taken to regulate the 'outlandish' or foreign coin circulating in Ireland, with a proclamation setting out the value of fourteen foreign gold coins and some 30 foreign silver coins which were declared 'currant coin of the kingdom' at officially set values.

Within a year steps were also taken to bring to an end the production of trade tokens. On 17 August 1661 the lord justices issued a proclamation 'forbidding any person or persons whatsoever, to make, or cause to be made, any brass, or copper money or tokens without special licence from his majesty' (Simon 1749, 124) under pain of forfeiture of coins, tools and engines.

The final measure initiated by the king was the establishment of a new distinctive Irish silver coinage through a patent issued to Sir Thomas Vyner, Robert Vyner and Daniel Bellingham of Dublin on 28 April 1662. The patent was to authorise the striking of five silver coins — a halfpenny, penny, twopence, threepence and fourpence — and the establishment of a mint in Dublin. As with previous patents, the patent document granted to Vyner set out the design of the five new coins: 'Whereas the minting, coining and uttering of small silver money hath been found to be of great and general use and benefit to our people of this our realme of Ireland, as well amongst tradesmen for the exchange of monies in the course of their several trades .... we conceive it requisite to erect and create a mint office in our city of Dublin, for minting an coining of all sortes of smalle silver money of the denominations of ... Halfe-penny pieces, having upon one side a crowne, and the other a harpe; Penny pieces having on one side the effigies of our selfe or our successors, with a figure to distinguishe and denominate the same, and the harpe on the other side; Two penny pieces having on one side the effigies of us, or our successors, with figures to distinguishe and denominate the same, and the harpe crowned on the other; Three penny pieces, having on the one side the effigies and title of us, and our successors with figures to denominate and distinguishe the same, and the harpe crowned with the motto, oblectat et reperat, on the other side; and Groats or Fower-penny pieces having on the one side the effigies of us, or our successors, with our title and figures to distinguish and denominate the same, on the one side, and the harpe crowned with the motto, oblectat et reperat, on the other side, or such stamps, impressions, mottos and inscriptions, as the lord lieutenant, deputy, justices or other chiefe governour or governours for the time being shall direct...' (Simon 1749, 126–7).

The king was to receive in payment from Vyner 'twelvepence of the said smale silver money out of every pound troy weight of sterling silver which shall be soe minted'.

With the exception of the regulation of 'outlandish' coins, all of the early monetary reforms of Charles II were to fail. Within six months of receiving it Vyner surrendered the patent to the king. It is generally thought that Vyner realised that there would not be sufficient profits from the venture, and the silver coins set out in the patent were never to be struck.

Armstrong proceeded with the striking of farthings under his patent, but was soon to run into difficulties. The lord justices' proclamation of 17 August 1661 which outlawed the issuing of tokens also technically outlawed his tokens, and a second proclamation had to be issued on 13 September 1661 which, whilst once again forbidding the production of tokens, did acknowledge his patent from the king. Armstrong's problems were not over: despite the granting of a royal patent and the issuing of a proclamation by the lord justices of Ireland, the lord lieutenant of Ireland, the duke of Ormonde, refused to authorise the coinage. In the official language of the time, Armstrong was not to 'obtayne allowance from the chiefe governor of Ireland to issue the said farthing tokens'. The more cynical suggest that Armstrong either failed to offer an appropriate 'backhander' to Ormonde to ensure his support for the new coinage or that the 'payment' offered was not sufficient for the newly created duke. Ormonde did not endorse the new farthings and Armstrong, after his investment in equipment and metal, found the patent to be worthless without the lord lieutenant's support.

A small quantity of farthings were, however, struck under the patent, and it is evident from the condition in which these coins are found that some of them must have circulated. It is thought that Armstrong, stuck with supplies of farthings which did not have official approval, sold them to agents who in turn sold them on to traders and merchants to circulate alongside the now-illegal base metal tokens.

With no officially sanctioned base metal coins, the lord justices' proclamation of 1661 outlawing trade tokens was ignored.

In the absence of an officially sanctioned silver and copper coinage, the monetary needs of the Irish for the next 20 years were to be met once again through supplies of foreign gold and silver coins and trade tokens. The 1670s were to be increasingly characterised by more proclamations forbidding the production and circulation of trade tokens, others regulating the value of foreign coin, and measures forbidding the exporting of gold and silver 'money, plate or bullion' out of Ireland. A proclamation of 1677 that sought to regulate the value of foreign coins included Portuguese crusadoes and Dutch 'New Lyon Dollars', which, like earlier foreign coins, were circulating at a significantly higher value than their real silver content.

Despite the threats of confiscation of coins and minting equipment, town corporations and individual merchants continued to issue their tokens through the 1660s and 1670s. Amongst the hundreds of tokens issued at this time one particular series is of special numismatic interest — St Patrick's Money, a series of private tokens including a halfpenny and farthing which were issued in about 1673. A number of explanations or theories have emerged over the years to account for the origin of these coins. Early numismatists seemed to think that they dated from the Civil War or Great Rebellion period, no doubt inspired by the obverse design of the coin, with some suggesting that they were minted in Oxford in 1643 by Charles I and shipped to Ireland to pay Irish troops. Other suggestions are that they were struck on the Continent and brought to Ireland by Nuncio Rinuccini, or that they were struck by the Catholic Confederates, along with silver shillings of the same design.

Putting these numismatic musings to one side, it is now generally acknowledged that these coins were struck in Ireland, probably in Dublin, in the early 1670s. The issuer of these handsome and intriguing halfpennies and farthings is, however, unknown. The reverse design featuring St Patrick is very similar to a token issued by Richard Grenwood of High Street in Dublin. Unfortunately, Grenwood's tokens are undated and it is not possible to determine whether the design on his token may have inspired the St Patrick's Money or whether Grenwood's token was simply a copy of the larger St Patrick coins.

The halfpenny and farthing were both struck in copper with a brass plug set into the coin. The obverse of the halfpenny features a kneeling king, thought to be the biblical King David but clearly based on Charles I, playing a harp with a crown above the harp, roughly at the point where the brass plug is placed. The legend on the obverse reads 'FLOREAT REX' (May the king flourish).

The reverse features St Patrick preaching to a crowd. The saint is variously described as holding a cross or a trefoil, which looks very much like a sprig of shamrock, in his right hand. If it is a shamrock, it is the first representation of this national symbol on an Irish coin. To the saint's right is a shield with the three castles coat of arms of the city of Dublin. The reverse legend 'ECCE GREX' (Behold his flock) is to be found on either side of the saint's mitre. Minor variations of this coin are known; in one type the obverse legend is broken up to read 'FLORE AT T REX' instead of 'Floreat Rex', whilst others incorporate a star design into the obverse legend. Silver proofs, which at one time were thought to be shillings, are also known to exist.

Fig. 84—Farthing, St Patrick's issue, c. 1670. *SNC*, May 1994, No. 3495

The obverse of the farthing coin similarly features a king playing a harp with a crown above the central design. The obverse legend, which forms the border, reads 'FLOREAT REX' (May the king flourish). The reverse design features St

Patrick holding a long double cross in his left hand, and with his right hand he is seen driving away snakes and reptiles. A cathedral or church building is to be found to the right of the saint. The reverse legend reads 'QVIESCAT PLEBS' (May the people be at peace).

A number of varieties of the St Patrick farthing are also known, including one which incorporates star designs in the legend and others which include an annulet or martlet design, or both, below the figure of the king on the obverse.

Proofs of the farthing coin struck in silver and gold are also known to exist.

The edges of both the halfpenny and farthing coins are grained or 'milled', although examples of both coins with plain edges are also known.

The St Patrick's coins were not only to see circulation in Ireland but were also used in the Isle of Man until a Tynwald Act of 24 June 1679 forbade their use, along with Irish 'butchers tokens' from Limerick and Dublin. In 1681 Mark Newby, the leader of a group of Irish emigrants, brought about 10,800 St Patrick's coins to New Jersey in the American colonies, where a year later they were authorised as legal tender by the New Jersey general assembly in a bid to remedy a shortage of small coin in the colony.

In October 1673 the Irish authorities once again issued a proclamation in a bid to stop the manufacture and issuing of trade tokens: 'Whereas divers persons, in all or most of the cities, corporate and market towns in this kingdom, have taken a liberty without any restraint, to make in very great quantities a kind of brass or copper tokens, with such stamps as they pleased, and vented them to the people, some of the said tokens for a penny, and some others for a halfpenny each piece, to the great grievance of his majesties subjects; we thereby doe by this our proclamation, in his majesties name, strictly charge and require all persons whatsoever, from henceforth to forbear to make or stamp, or cause to be made or stamped, any brass or copper, or other tokens whatsoever, without special licence from his majesty in that behalf, and hereof they may not fail, as they will answer the contrary at their perils' (Simon 1749, 133–4).

This proclamation, like the previous proclamations, seems to have had little effect, and corporations and traders continued to issue their tokens.

At long last, in 1675, the lord lieutenant proposed to address the problem of the illegal tokens by sanctioning the issuing of an official farthing, but this proposal was to come to nothing!

Fig. 85—Farthing, Charles II, pattern.
Spink Irish Coin Values (1979), 3601

It is possible that a pattern halfpenny identified in Patrick Finn's *Irish coin values* (1979) with an intricate crowned royal 'CR' cypher on the obverse and an elegant crowned harp on the reverse might belong to this period.

In 1679 the Dublin Corporation issued its own Dublin halfpenny, which again shows how little weight the 1673 and earlier proclamations outlawing tokens carried. The Dublin halfpenny features on the obverse a crowned harp with the legend 'LONG LIVE THE KING' forming the border, and the reverse features the arms of Dublin on a shield with the date '1679' above the shield. The reverse legend reads '+ THE DUBLIN ● HALFPENNIE'. Like the St Patrick's halfpenny and farthing, the edge of the coin is milled.

The 1670s saw a further expansion of the Irish economy in spite of the scarcity of coin. Exports of grain, wool, hides, cattle and sheep increased, and when England prohibited the import of Irish livestock Irish merchants looked to the Continent to sell their salted beef and dairy products. The towns and cities also saw rapid expansion and economic development. The population of Dublin trebled during this period, and four new bridges were to be 'thrown' across the Liffey to cope with the increased traffic and trade in the city. The continued issuing of trade tokens by merchants and shopkeepers throughout the 1670s, as in the Commonwealth period, was yet another indicator of this prosperity.

In 1680 the authorities finally recognised that the only way to deal with the illegal trade tokens was to issue an officially sanctioned coin which would be more readily accepted by the general population than the tokens issued by corporations or traders. It is possible that the larger Dublin halfpenny of 1679 served as a model in terms of weight and size, being much larger and heavier than the trade tokens issued during the 1660s and 1670s.

In the early part of 1680 the son of Sir Thomas Armstrong, another Thomas, petitioned the king to grant him a new patent for the minting of coins, arguing that the lord lieutenant's failure to authorise the new farthing coins in 1661 had meant that his father had not enjoyed the full benefits of the grant despite investing in minting equipment and supplies of metal.

A new patent was granted to Armstrong and a business associate, Colonel George Legge of County Louth, on 18 May 1680 to produce copper halfpennies for a period of 21 years. The king as in the previous patent was to receive an annual payment of £16 13s 4d. This time Armstrong was to ensure that the patent had the endorsement of the lord lieutenant and this was to be emphasised in the preamble: 'We do hereby, with the advice and consent of our beloved cozen and counsellor James duke of Ormonde, our lord lieutenant general and our general governor of Ireland ... give unto the said Sir Thomas Armstrong and Colonel George Legg, their heirs, executors, administrators and assigns, full power during the terme of twenty-on years from the date herof to make and coyn such quantity of copper half-pence to be made of copper by engines, having on one side the figure or effigies of our head stampt thereon, and on the other side the impression of an harpe crowned, with this inscription round before and on the obverse, Carolus secondus dei gratia magn. Brittan, Franc Hibern Rex, and each to weigh one hundred and seven grains' (Simon 1749, 138–9).

The obverse of the regal halfpenny struck by Armstrong and Legge was to follow closely the design set out in the patent, featuring a bewigged portrait of the king wearing a laurel wreath facing right and the legend 'CAROLVS II DEI GRATIA' (Charles II by the grace of God). The reverse features a crowned harp with a divided date nestling below the crown on either point of the harp and the legend 'MAG BR FRA ET HIB REX' (Great Britain, France and Ireland, king). This halfpenny was to be issued in 1680, 1681 and 1682.

Fig. 86—Halfpenny, Charles II, 'Large Lettering', 1680. *SNC*, February 2001, IM 0006

Three varieties of this halfpenny are known to exist for 1680 — one which features a cross after the words 'Carolvs' and 'Dei' on the obverse, another in which there are pellets after 'Carolvs' and 'Dei' on the obverse, and a third in which the word 'Gratia' reads 'GARTIA' on the obverse. A proof version of the halfpenny in silver also dates from 1680.

In 1681 a second type of the halfpenny was issued; it followed essentially the same design as the 1680 halfpenny but with smaller lettering. This coin was to be issued in 1681, 1682, 1683 and 1684. Again a silver proof version dates from 1681. One variety of this later Charles halfpenny is known from 1683 in which the lettering of 'MAG BR FRA' on the obverse is larger than the 'ET HIB REX' on the reverse.

Fig. 87—Halfpenny, Charles II, 'Small Lettering', 1681. *SNC*, May 1996, No. 2234

Minor variations in the reverse design have been identified on both types of halfpenny, with the harp having between twelve and seventeen strings. It is thought that the variation in the number of strings might have been used as some sort of internal coding system within the mint.

On 19 July 1680 a proclamation was issued by the lord lieutenant authorising the use of the new halfpennies and also forbidding the making or counterfeiting of the halfpennies and 'any other halfpenny tokens, pence or farthing tokens, or copper pieces or brass pieces, or pieces of any other metal which have been or shall be made for tokens' (Simon 1749, 140).

This proclamation finally brought an end to the unofficial production of trade tokens, although its success probably owed more to the new halfpennies being much more readily acceptable than the old trade tokens rather than to any newly acquired respect for the weight of the law.

Within weeks of receiving the patent Armstrong and Legge were to sell it on to John Knox, a Dublin city alderman, 'in consideration of the sum of one thousand five hundred pounds of lawfull money &c well and truly paid &c by the said John Knox all such power &c to coin, stamp, disperse, either &c of copper halfpence within the kingdom of Ireland' (Simon 1749, 144).

Whilst Armstrong and Legge's, and later Knox's, halfpennies were to meet the needs for small change, the Irish continued to rely on foreign gold and silver coins for many of their larger monetary transactions. On 6 June 1683 a further proclamation was issued regulating the value and circulation of some fourteen foreign gold coins and 44 foreign silver coins. It also laid down acceptable weights for the foreign coins and arrangements for the production of coin weights so that traders could check the weight of foreign coins presented to them. The production of all official coin weights was granted to Henry Paris and John Cuthbeard of Dublin, who were to manufacture weights 'stamp't with the number of penny weights it bears on one side and the crown and harp on the other side' (Simon 1749, 143).

The last years of Charles II's reign were characterised by a tightening of the penal laws following the so-called 'Popish Plot' which was to see Oliver Plunkett, the Catholic archbishop of Armagh, executed at Tyburn.

Attempts were also made to exclude Charles's heir, the Catholic James, duke of York, from the succession. On 6 February 1685 James II ascended the English throne on the death of his brother, Charles II. His accession was viewed with suspicion by most of the English population, but was generally welcomed in Ireland. In England some consolation was found in James's two daughters, Mary and Anne, who despite their father's conversion had been brought up as Protestants — England was assured a Protestant succession. This assurance had been reinforced when Princess Mary married her cousin, the Protestant William of Orange. James's accession was immediately challenged by the ill-fated rebellion led by Charles II's illegitimate son, James, duke of Monmouth. The Monmouth Rebellion was brutally suppressed and James, now secure on his throne, began his programme of advancing Catholics in the army and at court which was to bring him into increasing conflict with the English parliament and the established church.

In October 1685 John Knox, now lord mayor of Dublin, surrendered his patent to King James II and requested a new patent for the unexpired period of the old one. Knox's request may have been prompted by the fate of the two previous patent-holders, Armstrong and Legge, and uncertainty about the status of the patent he had purchased. Armstrong had been closely associated with the intrigues of the duke of Monmouth and after the Monmouth Rebellion was declared a traitor by James II, whilst Legge, who had become the governor of Portsmouth, master of the King's Ordnance and a peer of the realm, had died earlier in 1685.

On 23 October 1685 a new patent was granted to John Knox, and confirmed by the king on 29 December 1685, in which 'the said halfpence (were) to be made of copper by engines, having on one side the figure or effigies of our head, and on the other side the stamp of an harp crowned; with this inscription round before and on the reverse Jacobus secondus Dei gratia magnae Britanniae Franciae et Hiberniae Rex' (Simon 1749, 145). Knox was required to pay the king an annual fee of £16 13s 4d and in turn was assured 'all the proffits ariseing from the sayd coinage'.

The halfpennies struck by Knox in the name of James II were to follow the same design as those of Charles II. The obverse featured a portrait of the king looking left with the legend 'IACOBVS II DEI GRATIA' (James II by the grace of God) forming the border. The reverse featured a crowned harp with the divided date and the legend 'MAG BR FRA ET HIB REX' (of Great Britain, France and Ireland, king) forming the border. Again the harp on the reverse of the coin has been identified as having between twelve and sixteen strings. The halfpenny has been found with milled, partially milled and plain edges.

Fig. 88—Halfpenny, James II, 1688.
SNC, February 2002, No. IM 0126

The halfpenny was to be issued in 1685, 1686, 1687 and 1688. A proof version dated 1685 is known. Whilst halfpennies from the first two years are relatively common, the 1687 halfpenny is rare and an example of this coin in 'Good Fine' condition sold at the Whyte's Millennial Collection Sale (April 2000) for £IR900.

In Ireland the Catholic Richard Talbot, later earl of Tyrconnell, was appointed lord lieutenant by James II. Under his lieutenancy a policy of recruiting and promoting Catholics in the army and in civil positions was vigorously promoted. Irish Catholics looked to James to restore their properties and to overturn the 1662 Act of Settlement, and with it to end the Protestant Ascendancy over land and parliament. James's position in England by the autumn of 1688 was, however, under threat. The birth of a Catholic prince and heir to the throne in the summer and the trial of seven Anglican bishops prompted a group of leading English noblemen to write to William of Orange, inviting him to England to restore the position of parliament and the Church of England.

On 5 November 1688 William landed at Torbay in the west of England and advanced on London. James's friends and supporters, including his daughter Anne, deserted him. James initially moved to challenge William, but then panicked. He packed his wife and infant son off to France and followed a few days later. He was, however, recognised and captured on the English coast and brought back to London, much to the embarrassment of his son-in-law. William was to ensure that James escaped successfully to France a few days later.

In England, parliament declared the throne vacant following James's flight and offered the crown to Princess Mary and her husband, William of Orange.

13. THE WAR OF THE KINGS
The origins of the Gun Money coinage of James II
(1689–90)

In the early spring of 1689 a small French fleet dropped anchor in the harbour town of Kinsale on the south-east coast of Ireland. Aboard one of the ships was the deposed James II, who had sailed from France a week or so earlier to reclaim his crown from his son-in-law, William of Orange.

The events of the next two years have become known in Ireland as the 'War of the Kings'. They were to have major consequences, some of which still touch the lives of Irish people over 300 years later.

These events, which culminated in the Battle of the Boyne, also saw one of the most remarkable episodes in Ireland's thousand-year-old numismatic history with the issuing of the so-called 'Gun Money' coinage of James II.

While England had welcomed William in the autumn of 1688, Ireland remained loyal to James. Most of the country was under the control of James's lord deputy, the earl of Tyrconnell. Only the Ulster towns of Enniskillen and Londonderry had declared for William. Tyrconnell, however, was uncertain as to whether he should remain loyal to James or throw in his lot with William in the hope of retaining his position as lord deputy and the advances Irish Catholics had enjoyed over the last three years. Eventually, after much deliberation, he decided to send an embassy to Versailles led by two prominent Irish nobles, one to argue that James should come to Ireland and the other to convince him to remain in France. The argument that James should come to Ireland won the day. James left his palace at St Germain on 15 February, leaving Lord Mountjoy, who had been sent to argue the case against his coming to Ireland, locked in the Bastille for his efforts.

James arrived in Kinsale on 12 March accompanied by a small French force; his twelve-day journey to Dublin was to turn into a triumphal progress as he was welcomed in every town and village by cheering crowds.

He arrived at Dublin Castle on 24 March 1688, the last day of the old year. Britain and Ireland at that time were still using the Old Style or Julian calendar with the new year starting on Lady Day, 25 March — hence 24 March 1688 was followed by 25 March 1689. In adhering to the Julian calendar rather than to the Gregorian calendar, which had been adopted by the rest of Europe, Britain and Ireland were eleven days adrift — for example, 1 July 1690 was 12 July 1690 in the rest of Europe. In 1752 the Gregorian calendar was finally adopted in Britain and Ireland by an act of parliament which moved the calendar forward twelve days and the start of the new year to 1 January.

One of James's first acts was to issue a proclamation the following day (25 March 1689) to regulate the value of 'foreign and outlandish coyn' circulating in Ireland. During the latter months of his reign large amounts of gold and silver had been sent out of Ireland to England for safekeeping by Protestant merchants and landowners, and the news of his arrival in Kinsale had seen what little gold and silver was still in circulation quickly disappear.

The proclamation sought to regulate the exchange rates of French, Spanish, Portuguese and English coins; the guinea was tariffed at £1 4s 0d, the silver crown at 5s 5d, and the shilling at 1s 1d. The effect of the proclamation was that the value of gold coins was raised by 20% and silver by 8%.

James almost immediately directed his efforts against Londonderry and marched his French and Irish troops north. He arrived outside the walls of Londonderry on 19 April 1689; the 'Apprentice Boys' slammed the city gates shut in his face, and so began the Siege of Londonderry. James quickly tired of the siege and returned to Dublin, where on 7 May 1689 he summoned the Irish parliament. Almost overwhelmingly Catholic, it passed 35 acts in ten weeks, many of them directed against the Irish Acts of Settlement of 1662 and 1665 which had confirmed Protestant rights to land confiscated from Catholic landowners by Oliver Cromwell. Ironically, James as duke of York had received some 120,000 acres of Irish land in the early 1660s under the early Act of Settlement!

Meanwhile the siege of Londonderry continued. It was finally lifted on 31 July 1689, when ships sent by William III got through to the beleaguered city and its people. This major blow for James was compounded by the news of the defeat of a detachment of his troops at Newton Butler by Protestant volunteers from Enniskillen the previous day. This defeat and the relief of Londonderry led to the collapse of support for James in the north, and his army withdrew to Athlone and Dublin. Within three months of his arrival in Ireland most of the north had been lost to William.

On 13 August 1689 a force of 10,000 men loyal to William landed at Bangor under the command of the German Marshal Schomberg and advanced to Dundalk without difficulty before settling in for a prolonged encampment over the winter.

It was against this background that the first moves took place to introduce a coinage to meet the needs of James's army and the civilian population. The king had brought with him supplies of French silver three-sous coins with a face value of 1½d to pay his French troops. In a proclamation of 4 May 1689 the three-sous coin was declared 'current money within this our kingdom' at a value of 3½d. The supplies of revalued sous did not, however, even begin to meet James's coinage needs — a more radical solution was required.

In the same month James laid aside the patent granted to John Knox to mint halfpennies, which had been subsequently transferred to Colonel Roger Moore. An order of 19 June 1689 signed by Lord Melfort, the secretary of state, authorised the seizure of Colonel Moore's minting equipment, tools and supplies of copper.

The order stated that 'our will and pleasure is that forthwith goe to the severall place or places where stamps, presses or coyning mills are, which with the several instruments belonging to the coynage you are to secure under your respective seales, in some safe place soe as none can come at or meddle with the same without your consent' (Simon 1749, 148).

A mint was established at 61 Capel Street, Dublin, with the two coin presses confiscated from Colonel Moore, known as the Duchess and James presses. The mint was placed under the control of six commissioners. The staff consisted of four comptrollers, two secretaries, two warders, one treasurer, four tellers, four feeders, eight labourers at the fly, two porters, a messenger, a storekeeper and two doorkeepers — a set of men were obliged to work at each press for twelve hours night and day.

Minting was to begin slowly at Capel Street — most of Dublin's engravers were Protestant and were reluctant to assist James's cause.

According to contemporary sources, 'the man that King James trusted the management of his mint to' was William Bromfield, the other five commissioners 'being men of no knowledge in such matters'. Bromfield, an English Quaker from Hitchin, was in turn a surgeon, businessman, politician and spy, and is credited with the idea of issuing a token coinage to support James's army.

On the same day as the order to seize Moore's minting equipment, a royal proclamation was issued authorising the minting of copper and brass sixpences. The proclamation described the coin as 'each piece having of one side the effigies or figure of our head with the inscription round — Jacobus II dei Gratia and upon the other side the stamp or impression of cross sceptres and a crown between JR with VI above, the month wherein they are coyned below with this inscription round "Mag Brit Fran et Hiber Rex 1689" and fringed round' (Simon 1749, 149).

The proclamation went on to state that the coins were to be 'accepted as current money among our subjects within our realm', with the exception of first sale of foreign goods, payment of customs and excise duties, money left in trust, payment of mortgages, bills, bonds and debts due by record. 'Any subject refusing to receive the said pieces of copper and brass shall be punished according to the utmost rigour of the law as conteminers of our royal prerogative and command'.

The proclamation made clear that the coinage was temporary and would be replaced as soon as the emergency was over by gold and silver coinage. It is thought that the inclusion of the month was to allow a system whereby coins would be redeemed in phases at a later date.

It is interesting to note that James retained his technical claim to the throne of France in his royal titles on these coins despite being wholly dependent on financial and military support from Louis XIV!

The sixpence was to be struck in Dublin from June 1689 to February 1689 (1690) with the exception of the month of October. The design of the coin closely followed the description set out in the proclamation. The obverse features the bust of the king looking left with the legend 'IACOBVS II DEI GRATIA' (James II by the grace of God) forming the border. The reverse features a crown over two crossed sceptres with the royal cypher of a 'J' and an 'R' on either side of the crown. The value of the coin is denoted in Roman numerals 'VI' above the crown and the month of issue is found below the crown. The reverse legend reads 'MAG BR FRA ET HIB REX 1689' (Great Britain, France and Ireland king 1689), with the date '1690' appearing on later coins.

Fig. 89—Sixpence, James II, 'Gun Money', July 1689. *SNC,* May 1994, No. 3540

The design of the crown and crossed sceptres may have been inspired by the Kilkenny halfpennies and farthing of the Confederate Catholics issued during the Great Rebellion or by the earlier Harrington and Lennox farthings.

Fig. 90—Shilling, James II, 'Gun Money', December 1689. *SNC,* May 1994, No. 3528

On 27 June 1689 a second proclamation was published authorising the issuing of shillings and half-crowns following the same design as the sixpence. The shilling, with a simpler portrait of James II, was struck in Dublin from July 1689 to April 1690, the shillings dated March 1689 and March 1690 being struck within days of each other at the turning of the old year. The half-crown, which had a similar portrait to that found on the sixpence, was similarly struck from July 1689 to April 1690; again there are examples of March 1689 and March 1690 half-crowns. All the half-crowns at the Dublin mint were struck on the James press.

Fig. 91—Half-crown, James II, 'Gun Money', August 1689. *SNC*, February 1998, No. IM 0030

It is believed that the brass coins were engraved by Jan Roettier or a member of his family. Despite the high standard of the early coins, the design and quality of engraving was to deteriorate significantly over time, particularly with the later pewter coins. The coins at the time were popularly known as 'brass money'. The term 'Gun Money' was first used to describe these coins in a sales catalogue of 1764 and was probably inspired by Archbishop King's description of the coins as being made 'of a mixture of old guns, old broken bells, old copper, brass, pewter, old kitchen furniture (utensils) and the refuse of metals molten down' (Simon 1749, 61).

The potential for counterfeiting was recognised in this second proclamation, which stated that the counterfeiting of the new coins constituted high treason. Mint employees found counterfeiting coins at Capel Street in November 1689 were duly dispatched on the gallows. The proclamation also promised a reward of £20 to anyone informing on counterfeiters.

In July 1689 the French ambassador reported to Louis XIV that the new brass coinage was being generally accepted, much to the relief of King James. The continued success of the whole financial scheme and the new coinage was, however, dependent upon supplies of metal. Not only were there shortages of gold and silver but also of scrap metal. On 4 July 1689 the first of many orders was sent out to collectors of revenue to procure as much copper and brass as they could find at the best rates and send it to the mint in Capel Street. A week after this first order, Lord Melfort was reduced to writing to the master general of ordnance, asking him to deliver up two brass cannon lying in the courtyard of Dublin Castle. Even James's exiled queen, Mary of Modena, was pressed into service to locate scrap metal in France. Tyrconnell writing to the French king on one occasion requested 'forty guns to coyne money', and on another requested 80 to 90 tons of copper, stressing that the copper was more important than arms or ammunition. James's war expenses at the time were £100,000 per month. Thirteen tons of copper were required each month to produce the necessary coins.

Cannon from Limerick, Athlone, Dublin and from Brest in France were literally 'pressed' into service.

In August 1689 the first reports of people refusing to accept the new brass money occurred when country people bringing goods into the markets in Dublin refused to accept payment in this coinage. The problem was further exacerbated when it was learned that James's lord chancellor was himself refusing to accept payment of rent from his tenants in brass money. These uncertainties were to lead to the relative value of the brass money falling and prices rising — inflation was to set in.

The official actions of James's government similarly did not inspire confidence in the new coinage. The controllers of revenue accepted brass money reluctantly and only if taxpayers could demonstrate that they had no gold or silver; James's French officers likewise refused to accept payment in brass. The coinage was increasingly foisted onto the civilian population and James's Irish soldiers.

Faced with growing concerns about the value of and confidence in brass money, the government announced their intention to limit the production of brass money and to restore confidence by offering to receive loans of brass money at 6% interest and later 10% interest. Despite these assurances there is no evidence that minting activities were reduced.

Some 250 die varieties exist in the Gun Money series. This does not take account of the bewildering number of minor die varieties, with differences in the size of lettering or the script used for the month, the presence or absence of dots, the size of the Roman numerals used to denote the value of the coin, as well as the angles at which the cross sceptres point.

The wide range of varieties are attributed to three possible reasons. The first, and most probable, is that the range of die varieties, in particular the variations in the abbreviated rendering of the month, was a method of production or batch control. Different reverse dies differentiate the Duchess and James presses in Dublin, one having beads or pearls on the bands of the crown, the other having foliage. In other cases stops or the absence of stops and cinquefoils may also have been used to distinguish batches.

The month with the widest range of die varieties is October 1689. On the shilling, for example, the month is represented in eight different ways, four abbreviated spellings using capitals or italics and four incorporating the number eight, October under the old-style calendar being the eighth month of the year.

Fig. 92—Shilling, James II, 'Gun Money', October 1689, '8BER'. *SNC*, May 1994

A variation of the December 1689 shilling has the number 10, December being the tenth month of the old-style year.

A variety of the November 1689 shilling features a castle and two pellets below the bust on the obverse, and a rarer version has the castle without the accompanying pellets. The reason behind the use of this castle mint mark is not known. An example of this rarer version sold for £IR650 at the Whyte's Millennial Collection Sale in April 2000.

Other die varieties in the series can be explained as being due to poor engraving and mistakes in the construction of the dies, with misspellings such as RIX instead of REX on some crowns, ERA instead of FRA on some shillings, and MAO instead of MAG on some half-crowns. Some die varieties are also probably due to the retouching or re-engraving of old dies.

Coupled with the varieties in the regular series, there are a number of silver and gold proofs, some of which may be contemporary while others are more likely to be later restrikes. There are also examples of 'sports' or overstrikes on coins, including English, Scottish and French coins.

On 4 February 1689 (1690) a proclamation was issued extending the use of Gun Money to cover a range of payments previously excluded by the 15 June proclamation. The proclamation restated earlier pledges about the temporary nature of the coinage, promising 'all our loving subjects within this kingdom ... full satisfaction for the same in gold and silver' (Simon 1749, 152).

This proclamation was to be the first in a series in which the officials of the exiled king attempted to remedy the growing shortage of scrap metal needed for coin to pay James's troops. New and increasingly desperate measures were, however, required if James was to keep his army in the field and have some chance of regaining his crown.

14. TINKERLY TREASURE
The later Gun Money and pewter coinage of James II (1690–1)

On 1 March 1689 (1690) a proclamation was issued by James II from his court at Dublin Castle authorising the issuing of two new coins, 'one the bigness of a shilling to be made of white mix'd metal having of one side the effigies of figure of our head with this inscription around out "Jacobus II dei gratia" and on the other side having a piece of prince's metal (brass) fixed in the middle with the stamp or impression of the harpe and crowne with this inscription around it "Mag Brit Fra et Hib Rex" with the year of Our Lord which piece is to pass for a penny' (Simon 1749, 156).

A smaller coin, about the size of a sixpence, was also authorised to pass as a halfpenny. A further proclamation was issued four weeks later, on 28 March 1690, stating that those refusing to accept the two new coins would be punished according to the utmost rigour of the law.

The new pewter penny featured a portrait of the king looking left, similar to that found on the shilling, with the legend 'IACOBVS II DEI GRATIA' (James II by the grace of God) forming the border. The reverse featured a crowned harp with the year above and the legend 'MAG BR FRA ET HIB REX' (of Great Britain, France and Ireland king) forming the border. Examples dated both 1689 and 1690 exist, although the 1689 coin is rarer than the 1690 version.

Fig. 93—Penny, James II, pewter penny (first type), 1690. *SNC,* February 2001, IM 0065

A second type of penny, dated 1690, was also issued which featured on the obverse a portrait of the king with short hair, similar to that found on the obverse of his English maundy coins, with '1D' behind the head and the legend 'IACOBVS II DEI GRATIA' (James II by the grace of God) forming the border, and on the reverse a crowned harp with the divided date '16' and '90' on either side of the harp and the legend 'MAG BR FRA ET HIB REX' (of Great Britain,

France and Ireland king) forming the border. A slightly corroded version of this coin in fine condition sold at the Whyte's Millennial Collection Sale for £IR550.

Fig. 94—Penny, James II, pewter penny (second type), 1690. *SNC*, February 2001, IM 0066

The halfpenny likewise is found dated 1689 and 1690 and features the short-haired portrait of the king, similar to that found on the second penny. A variety of the halfpenny features a slightly smaller portrait of the king with a leaf below his head. The reverse of both varieties of halfpenny follows essentially the same design as the penny although the date is found on the reverse, divided by the crown rather than the harp. A halfpenny with the leaf below the king's head in very fine condition was to sell for £IR550 at the Whyte's Millennial Collection Sale in April 2000.

Fig. 95—Halfpenny, James II, leaf below bust, 1690. *SNC*, May 1994, No. 3554

James Simon in his essay on Irish coins (1749) includes an illustration of a possible design for a halfpenny with King James on horseback which was never issued. Silver versions of the first type of halfpenny are known which were struck over French silver five-sous of Louis XIV dating from 1643 and 1644.

Fig. 96—Halfpenny, James II, silver sport on half-écu, 1690. *SNC*, February 1998, No. 157

A pewter groat was also issued prior to 25 March 1690 with the legend 'IACOBVS II DEI GRATIA' (James II by the grace of God) forming the border. The coin, the size of a sixpence, featured a similar portrait to that found on the sixpence, while the reverse features a crowned harp with two Roman numeral 'II' on either side of the harp and the legend 'MAG BR: FRA ET HIB REX' (of Great Britain, France and Ireland king) with the date above the crown. This coin is one of the rarest in the Gun Money series.

On 25 March 1690 a mint in Limerick was established at the Deanery under Commissioner Walter Plunkett. It is thought that as early as January 1689 plans were in hand to establish a second mint. Consideration was given to establishing a mint at Athlone in the Irish midlands, but Limerick was finally chosen probably because it was more accessible for supplies of metal from France. The Duchess press was sent to Limerick with a set of obverse and reverse dies and punches. The obverses and reverses of the coins struck at Limerick are distinguishable from the coins struck at Dublin from 1690.

At the Limerick mint sixpences were only struck in May 1690 (having ceased to be struck in Dublin in February 1689), large shillings in March 1690 and large half-crowns from March to May 1690.

On 21 April 1690 a fourth new pewter coin was introduced — a white metal crown with a portrait of the king on horseback and the legend 'JAC II DEI GRA MAG BRI FRA ET HIB REX' (James by the grace of God king of Great Britain, France and Ireland). The reverse has a brass plug with the crown in the centre and four crowned shields with the legend 'CHRISTO VICTORE TRIUMPHO ANNO DOM 1690' (I exalt in the victory of Christ, Year of Our Lord 1690) and around the edge the inscription 'MELIORIS TESSARA FATI — ANNO REGNI SEXTO' (an improved token uttered in the sixth year of the reign).

It was certainly not viewed as an improved token by the Irish of the time. They disliked the pewter metal used in the crown and other coins, which they called 'soft copper' or 'uim-bog' in Irish, from which is derived the English word 'humbug', meaning a sham, an imposter or a deception.

It is thought that a large crown-sized pattern coin dated 1689 may belong to this period. This coin, which is struck in pewter with a brass plug, features the king on horseback facing left on the obverse with the legend 'IACOBVS II DEI GRATIA' (James II by the grace of God). The reverse features a large crown in the centre with the legend 'MAG BR FRA ET HIB REX 1689' (of Great Britain, France and Ireland, king 1689). This pattern coin is extremely rare; an example is known in the British Museum collection, and even official electrotypes or copies command high prices.

The same proclamation also announced the decision, for 'publick convenience', to reduce the size of shillings and half-crowns in an attempt to make supplies of metal go further. A proclamation of 15 June 1690 called in all large shillings and half-crowns struck before May 1690 to be replaced by the new smaller coins. It was announced that the old large shillings and half-crowns would be demonetised on 30 June 1690 in Dublin and throughout the rest of Ireland on 31 July 1690.

A second proclamation on 15 June 1690 announced the issuing of a copper and brass crown, similar in design to the pewter crown but without an edge inscription. These crowns were to be struck over the returned large half-crowns. The brass crowns did not bear a month of issue and all were struck at the Dublin mint.

Fig. 97—Crown, James II, Gun Money crown, 1690. *SNC*, February 2001, No. IM 0025

The obverse of the crown coins featured the king on horseback facing left and holding a sword, with the legend 'IAC II DEI GRA MAG BRI FRA ET HIB REX' (James II by the grace of God king of Great Britain, France and Ireland). The reverse features the four shields of England, Scotland France and Ireland set out in a cruciform arrangement with a crown in the centre with the words 'ANO' 'DOM' in the upper part of the design and the divided date '16' '90' in the lower part. The legend on the reverse reads 'CHRISTO VICTORE TRIUMPHO' (I triumph in the victory of Christ). The edge of this crown piece was milled.

As with other Gun Money coins, versions of the crown pieces were struck in gold and silver and these may have been presentation pieces for James II and senior officials.

These coins are much cruder than the early Gun Money coins and most examples show traces of the underlying half-crown coins on which they were struck. Varieties include the misspelt 'RIX' crown and the 'chubby horseman' version. Variations also occur with differences in the size of lettering and the starting-point or break-up of the legend.

Fig. 98—'Chubby horseman' crown, James II, 1690. *SNC* May 1994, No. 3503

Small half-crowns were struck in Dublin in April and May 1690, and from May 1690 to October 1690 at Limerick. These coins followed essentially the same design as the old half-crowns, although a simpler portrait of the king, similar to that found on the large shillings, was used.

Fig. 99—Half-crown, James II, Gun Money, 'Small Type', May 1690. *SNC*, May 1994, No. 3516

Small shillings were struck at Dublin in May and June 1690 and in April, May and September 1690 at Limerick. Again, these coins follow essentially the same design as the large shillings but have a slightly modified portrait of the king on the obverse.

Fig. 100—Shilling, James II, Gun Money, 'Small Type', April 1690. *SNC*, May 1994, No. 3536

The decision to reduce the size of the coinage further diminished public confidence in James's brass money; people were increasingly desperate for gold and silver and seem to have been prepared to pay any price for it. In an attempt to bolster confidence in Gun Money a third proclamation on 15 June 1690 forbade the payment of more than £1 18s for a gold guinea or 7s 6d for a silver crown under pain of death. It is questionable whether this proclamation had any real effect as gold guineas by this stage were commanding the equivalent of £4 10s in brass money.

At this juncture, however, political and military events were to come to a head.

Early in 1690 William III decided to take personal charge of the Irish campaign. Schomberg's encampment at Dundalk the previous autumn had proved disastrous; his troops were ill-equipped for the long winter and over 5,000 of his soldiers died before he withdrew to Belfast. On 14 June 1690 William landed at Carrickfergus and rapidly moved his forces south.

William had a total of 36,000 men under his command, a mixture of English, Ulster Protestants, Dutch, Danish, German and French Huguenots. By 30 June 1690 William had arrived on the northern bank of the Boyne; James's army of 25,000 Irish and French soldiers was encamped on the southern side of the river near Oldbridge. The following day, in the words of an Irish folk song, 'Two foreign old monarchs in battle did join, each wanting his head on the back of a coin'. By the end of the day about 1,500 men lay dead. William's superior generalship had triumphed.

James fled the field and was among the first back in Dublin. Within days he had departed for France from Waterford. The bulk of his forces withdrew to Limerick and the western towns of Galway and Athlone. William pursued James's supporters to Limerick, where he laid siege to the city; but in August, as heavy rains set in, he raised the siege and returned to England. A month later the southern towns of Cork and Kinsale were to fall to William's forces under John Churchill, the future duke of Marlborough, bringing the south and east of Ireland under William's control. Only Limerick, Athlone and Galway continued to hold out.

It is thought that a series of counter-marked coins, including copper tokens issued by James Ballard in 1677, with a stamp including the word 'CORKE' below a lion's head and above two sprigs or branches, which at one time were attributed to the Great Rebellion, may have been counter-stamped and circulated in the besieged city of Cork at this time.

Following James's defeat at the Boyne, William had seized Dublin and the Capel Street mint, where £22,489 in newly minted brass money was found. On 10 July 1690 William issued a proclamation from his camp at Finglas on the outskirts of Dublin reducing the value of brass and mixed metal money 'for the value of copper money formerly currant in the kingdom' (Simon 1749, 162). The large half-crowns and the new crowns were to circulate at one penny, the small half-crown at ½d, the large shilling at ½d, the small shilling and sixpence at ¼d. The pewter penny was devalued to ½d and the halfpenny to ¼d.

The effect of the proclamation reduced the £22,489 at the Dublin mint to £641 19s 3¼d; the wider effect of this proclamation on traders and the civilian population was to be disastrous.

Brass money, shillings and half-crowns, continued to be struck at the Limerick mint until October 1690 but confidence in the brass money had disappeared; even in areas where James's forces still held sway the brass money was increasingly viewed with suspicion. In January 1690 (1691) James's supporters devalued their own coinage, the crown being devalued to 5d, the half crown to 2½d, the shilling to a penny. The situation went from bad to worse when the Irish leaders announced their intention to demonetise their own brass coinage from 15 March 1690 (1691), the only compensation promised being a receipt from the Jacobite treasury with a pledge of full repayment when James was restored to his throne.

The irony of this action was that the brass money was potentially worth more in the areas of Ireland held by William III and his forces. Large amounts of brass money began to flow into these areas as people desperately tried to salvage something from their savings. On 23 February 1690 (1691) William's government in Dublin issued a proclamation against 'the Irish in rebellion' (Simon 1749, 161) who sought to use their brass coin in 'secret and cunning ways' to supply 'their wants and necessities'. The brass money was demonetised throughout the rest of Ireland three days later. Considering the condition in which some of the Gun Money coins are found today, it seems likely that these coins did, however, continue to circulate for some time after demonetisation. Gun Money half-crowns and shillings were to find their way to the Isle of Man, where they circulated unofficially as halfpennies and farthings, and Gun Money shillings and sixpences are also known to have circulated on Guernsey in the Channel Islands during the eighteenth century.

The final stage in the collapse of the hopes of James's supporters began in the summer of 1691 when forces supporting William advanced from Dublin. Athlone was taken in late June. The French General St Ruth with 25,000 men withdrew to the tiny town of Aughrim, where they faced the Dutch General Ginkel with a mixed force of English, Danish, Dutch, Huguenot and German mercenaries numbering 20,000. The Battle of Aughrim, fought on 12 July 1691, was the greatest pitched battle to take place on Irish soil. Whilst the numbers were smaller than those at the Boyne it was much more bloody — some 11,000 men died in the battle. A supporter of William described the fallen Irish as 'the flower of their army and nation'. At one stage it seemed that the Irish might carry the day, but then St Ruth was killed by a stray cannonball and the Irish infantry collapsed in confusion.

Aughrim was the last great battle of the War of the Kings. The remnants of the Irish army, about 15,000, fled to Limerick to make a last stand under the Irish commander Patrick Sarsfield. Ginkel followed and blocked the River Shannon to ensure that supplies could not reach the city. The second siege of Limerick had begun, and heralded the final stage in the numismatic history of James II's emergency coinage.

Behind the walls of Limerick the Duchess press re-coined large shillings and small shillings into halfpennies and farthings to meet the needs of the besieged city. The coins, which are known as 'Hibernias', featured a portrait of James II on the obverse and the figure of Hibernia on the reverse, the design possibly reflecting the nationalist aspirations of the city's defenders. These were the first coins to feature the figure of Hibernia, which later appeared on coins of George I and George III.

The obverse features a crude portrait of the king and the legend 'IACOBVS II DEI GRATIA' (James II by the grace of God) forming the border. The reverse features a rather crude engraving of Hibernia facing left with her left hand resting on a harp and holding a cross in her raised right hand, with the legend 'HIBERNIA' (Ireland) to the front of the figure and the date '1691' behind her.

Fig. 101—Halfpenny, James II, Limerick, 1691. *SNC,* February 2001, No. IM 0069

The Limerick Hibernias were crudely engraved and struck, the features of the overstruck coin often being seen. The halfpenny has a reversed 'N' in the word 'Hibernia'. Three varieties of the farthing exist which all follow the same design as the halfpenny — one with the reversed 'N', a rarer version with a normal 'N', and a variety with the spelling 'GRAVTIA' on the obverse.

Fig. 102—Farthing, James II, Limerick, 1691. *SNC,* February 2001, No. IM 0071

The siege of Limerick ended on 3 October 1691 when Patrick Sarsfield surrendered. The Treaty of Limerick, negotiated by Ginkel, guaranteed Catholic rights and allowed James's Irish supporters to leave for France in an event that is one of the defining moments of Irish history — some 11,000 Irish soldiers and their commanders left in what is known as the 'Flight of the Wild Geese'. Ginkel's treaty was overturned by the now Protestant-dominated Irish parliament in Dublin and the series of anti-Catholic laws known as the Penal Acts were passed, depriving the Irish Catholic population of civil and economic rights for almost a century. The War of the Kings was over, but with tragic consequences for James's Irish supporters, who were left impoverished and leaderless.

A regal Irish coinage was restored in 1692 with the issuing of a copper halfpenny with the conjoined portraits of William and Mary and a crowned harp on the reverse. The Irish experience with Gun Money, however, left an understandable suspicion of base metal coinage. On 17 February 1692 the Dublin authorities were required to issue a proclamation 'in order to quiet the minds of the people' (Simon 1749, 165), who refused to accept the new halfpenny and its English tin and copper equivalents. The suspicion was to continue well into the next century and probably accounts for the widespread rejection of Wood's Bath-Metal halfpennies and farthings in the reign of George I. It was not until the reign of George II that copper coinage was to become widely accepted again.

When William III seized the Capel Street mint in Dublin, the dies and punches were sent to London. They eventually came into the hands of John White, who was responsible in the mid-eighteenth century for the production of a series of restrikes — including some fantasy months. An avid collector of these restrikes was the Hanoverian King George III, who, safe on his throne from Jacobite pretenders, was in turn to donate his collection of Gun Money coins to the British Museum.

A Protestant commentator at the time of the Williamite campaigns described the brass money contemptuously as 'tinkerly treasure'. One of the questions which has been the subject of speculation and debate amongst numismatists is how much of this tinkerly treasure was actually produced. The brass coinage of James II was the largest regal issue of a completely token coinage in Europe since Roman times. It has been described as the fulfilment of the alchemist's dream — a pound weight of base metal costing between 3d and 4d could be transformed into £5.00 worth of coin, and from June 1690 with the reduction in the size of the coins £10 worth of coin could be produced from 4d worth of metal!

Estimates vary as to the value of coinage produced. Fairly accurate records were kept at the Dublin mint from its establishment until 1 July 1690 and suggest that some £965,375 worth of Gun Money coins were produced. James's treasury officials estimated that £1,100,000 was produced in total. Other records show that 10,451,099 coins were produced in Dublin between 3 August 1689 and 17 May 1690, with a value of £779,759 14s 11d. This would equate to £18,000 worth of coins being produced a week. These figures do not include the output of the Limerick mint, for which there are no records. A reasonable estimate, however, would be that a total in the region of £1,100,000 to £1,500,000 worth of coinage was struck during the period June 1689–October 1690 at the two mints, Limerick continuing to operate for a further four months after the Battle of the Boyne.

The immediate legacy of James's Gun Money was inflation and impoverishment for his many Irish supporters and in that sense Bromfield's scheme could be seen as a failure. James Simon in his essay on Irish coins (1749) was to write of this seeming failure some 60 years after the events '[what] glorious recompense for so much blood spilt in his [James's] service'.

More recent writers, however, have pointed to the fact that the Gun Money scheme did allow James to maintain an army in the field against William III for a year, and with the exception of a few dips it was generally accepted as long as there was some prospect that James might regain his crown.

With the hindsight of history, writers now see that Bromfield's scheme was to influence the founding of the Bank of England in 1696 and the issuing of paper money and bonds, which in turn have formed the basis of modern international monetary and financial systems whereby paper money and plastic credit cards are backed by central reserves and the vagaries of currency trading and stock market performance.

15. THESE USELESS TOKENS
The coinage of early Ascendancy Ireland and William Wood (1692–1725)

The defeat of James's army at the Boyne on 1 July 1690 was to set in train a series of measures known as the Penal Laws which were ultimately to deprive Irish Catholics of almost all of their civic and economic rights. Political and economic power in Ireland for the next 150 years was to be in the hands of a small Protestant élite of landlords and professional classes in the cities and towns. This period in Irish history, which was to roughly coincide with the reigns of the four Georges, is known as the Protestant Ascendancy or the Ascendancy Years.

The Ascendancy period was to see a flowering of Irish arts, literature and architecture and, as the eighteenth century progressed, increasing demands for the Dublin parliament to be independent of Westminster. Dublin was to be transformed into a city of elegant Georgian townhouses and classical public buildings. The Irish capital was increasingly recognised as the second city of the British Empire. Commerce, trade and manufacturing also flourished. Despite the growing economic prosperity of Dublin and other Irish cities and towns, one of the most pressing problems of daily life for most of the Irish population, irrespective of social class or religion, was the absence of a sound and reliable coinage.

One of the first acts of the victorious William III was to issue a proclamation devaluing the Gun Money coins issued by James II to fund his military campaign, with dire consequences for the Irish population. On 23 February 1691 a further proclamation was issued, 'decrying and totally abolishing the brass and copper money lately coined by James II' (Simon 1749, 165). With the defeat of the Jacobite forces in Ireland in October 1691, the authorities in Dublin were able to return to the more routine matters of governing Ireland, including the reintroduction of a new regal coinage.

In 1692 the first of a series of halfpennies was issued. They featured on the obverse the conjoined busts of William III and Mary II facing right and the legend 'GVLIEMVS ET MARIA DEI GRATIA' (William and Mary by the grace of God) forming the border. On the reverse a crowned harp dividing the date formed the central design, with the legend 'MAG BR FR ET HIB REX ET REGINA' (Great Britain, France and Ireland king and queen). The minting

Fig. 103—Halfpenny, William III and Mary II, 1692. *SNC*, August 2000, No. 3309

of these coins was granted to a patentee, according to James Simon (1749). It is probable that Colonel Roger Moore, who had previously held the patent up until 1689 (before his equipment was seized by James II to mint the Gun Money coins), had his patent renewed or confirmed by William III.

The restoration of the regal Irish coinage did not pass without problems. Perhaps it was the Irish experience of Gun Money which had left an understandable suspicion of base metal coinage, or perhaps it was the fault of political agitators, but on 17 February 1692 the Dublin authorities were required to issue a proclamation in order 'to quiet the minds of the people', who were refusing to accept the new copper halfpenny and the English tin halfpennies and farthings.

The new coins were eventually accepted, and further issues were made in 1692, 1693 and 1694. Four varieties are known: two from 1692 with minor variations or mistakes in spelling — one in which the 'A's in 'GRATIA' are represented by an unbarred 'A' or inverted 'V' and a second in which 'GVLIELMVS' is spelt 'GVULELMVS' — and the remaining two varieties dating from 1694. The first had been struck with a plain rather than a milled edge and the other was struck on a thicker flan, although it is thought that this latter variety might be a forgery. As with the early Charles and James issues, the harps on the reverse of the coin contain between twelve and eighteen strings.

Following the death of Mary II in 1694 a further issue of copper halfpennies was made under William III; these were all dated 1696 and are presumed to have been minted in Dublin.

Two types of halfpenny were struck in the name of William III. The first type features a clothed or draped bust of the king facing right with the legend 'GVLIELMVS III DEI GRA' (William III by the grace of God). The reverse featured the crowned harp and divided date with the legend 'MAG BR FRA ET HIB REX' (of Great Britain, France and Ireland, king). The quality of the design

Fig. 104—Halfpenny, William III, draped bust, 1696. *SNC*, February 2001, No. 0080

is much cruder than the 1692–4 coins. Two variations of the reverse design are known, the second slightly cruder and more cluttered. This first type of halfpenny was only to be struck in 1696. Again a variety exists in which the king's name is spelt differently, reading 'GWLIELMVS'. Despite the crude design and striking of the coins, proofs in silver and silver-gilt are known.

The second type of halfpenny, which was also struck in 1696, features a cruder undraped portrait of the king with the legend 'GVLIELMVS III DEI GRATIA' (William III by the grace of God) on the obverse and the crowned harp/divided date device on the reverse with the legend 'MAG BRI FRA ET HIB REX' (of Great Britain, France and Ireland, king). A silver proof version of this second type of halfpenny is also known.

Fig. 105—Halfpenny, William III, undraped bust, 1696. *SNC*, February 2001, IM 0080

Again, harps with between ten and fourteen strings have been identified. The William III halfpennies, in particular the undraped type, are much scarcer than those of William and Mary.

It is generally thought that these halfpennies were the last Irish coins to be struck in Ireland for another 280 years.

As in previous reigns, with the exception of the regal copper halfpennies, the Irish were largely dependent for most of their coinage needs on the range of English and foreign gold and silver coins that circulated across the country. Fluctuations in the value of gold and silver, particularly when its value as bullion was higher than its notional monetary value, led to coin being melted down or sent abroad for sale as bullion. This presented major problems for the authorities and the economic stability of the country. On 29 May 1695 a proclamation was issued increasing the current rate and value of a range of Spanish, French and Portuguese gold and silver coins. In 1701 a second proclamation reduced the monetary value of the same range of coins following a fall in gold and silver prices.

William's officials in Ireland also had to tackle counterfeiting, in particular the importation of large quantities of counterfeit halfpennies from Scotland. Despite the issue of regal halfpennies, there were still chronic shortages of coinage, and in particular in Northern Ireland the only small change in circulation were these 'raps' or counterfeit coins. A proclamation of 13 August 1697 commanded justices of the peace, mayors and other magistrates to seize and secure all quantities or parcels of the said counterfeit halfpence. Counterfeiting was not, however, limited to copper coins. A proclamation issued four months later on 10 December 1697 tried to put 'a stop to another growing evil of a much more dangerous consequence: the importing or making counterfeit pieces of gold and silver' (Simon 1749, 166).

In order to combat this counterfeiting of gold and silver coins and to regulate more easily the use of foreign gold and silver coins, a proclamation issued on 21 February 1698 set the standards of weights to be used for weighing gold and silver coins, 'forbidding any person to make, sell or adjust the said weights except Vincent Kidder', a Dublin goldsmith. A further proclamation, dated 23 May 1698, promised a reward of £10 for 'several coiners of counterfeit money ... lately fled from England and other parts, and are come into this kingdom, where they have again set up and exercise the same wicked course and practice' (Simon 1749, 167). Proclamations to tackle counterfeiting and the regulating of the value of foreign gold and silver coins were to be a regular feature of eighteenth-century Ireland.

The reign of Queen Anne was to see no Irish regal coins issued, but the now-familiar proclamations regarding the regulation of weights, the value of foreign gold and silver coins and counterfeiting, including a proclamation of 1714 which declared counterfeiters, their aiders and abettors guilty of high treason, continued to be issued. Whilst no Irish coins were to be issued with the portrait of Queen Anne, it is the view of some numismatists that the portly figure of the queen inspired the representation of Hibernia that appeared on her successor's halfpennies and farthings!

Fig. 106—Irish coin weight for eight escudos, Queen Anne. *SNC,* May 1996, No. 2369

The next Irish regal coin was not to be issued until 1722, a gap of 26 years since the last coin. These coins were probably the most controversial ever issued in Ireland, the infamous Wood's Halfpennies.

In 1722 a patent for minting copper coins for Ireland and the American colonies was granted by George I to his German mistress, the duchess of Kendal, who in turn sold the patent for £10,000 to William Wood, a wealthy mine-owner from Wolverhampton. The patent, or contract, was to run for fourteen years. A handsome profit was assured for the patentee, who was allowed to coin the equivalent of 30 pence from one pound of copper, as opposed to 24 pence from one pound which was the standard in England. The price of copper at that time was about twelve to thirteen pence a pound. The quantity of coins to be struck under the patent was limited to 360 tons of metal, 100 tons to be used in the first year and 20 tons in each of the thirteen remaining years. It was estimated that the total value of the contract was about £100,800, with Wood retaining a profit of about £46,000.

William Wood, as soon as he received the patent, began manufacturing at a foundry in Phoenix Street, Seven Dials, in London and later at a foundry in Bristol in late 1722. In the first year he was to produce some six and a half million halfpennies and a million farthings, an output of 20,000 coins a day.

Two main types of halfpenny were produced. The first type has a portrait of George I on the obverse looking right and the legend 'GEORGIUS DEI GRATIA REX' (George by the grace of God king). The reverse featured the figure of Hibernia holding a harp to her left and the legend 'HIBERNIA 1722' (Ireland 1722). An earlier pattern had Hibernia looking right at a mass of rock. A farthing dated 1722 features a similar design but with the obverse legend shortened to 'GEORGIUS DG. REX' (George by the grace of God king).

Fig. 107—Halfpenny, George I, William Wood first type, facing Hibernia, 1722. *SNC,* February 1998, No. 166

The second type of halfpenny was issued from 1722 through to 1724. It features a similar obverse to the first type, whilst the reverse design features a seated Hibernia holding a branch in her right hand with her right arm resting on a harp to her right and with the word 'Hibernia' and the date forming the border in the upper part of the coin. This version of Hibernia is believed to have been based on a figure of Britannia from a copper pattern from the reign of Queen Anne, who probably inspired the portrait. A number of varieties of this halfpenny were to be issued with minor variations in the placing of stops and the layout of the reverse legend.

Fig. 108—Halfpenny, George I, William Wood second type, 1724. *SNC,* April 1992, No. 1943

As with earlier regal issues, harps have been identified with between seven and twelve strings. The second type of halfpenny is much more common than the first type.

Farthings of the type with Hibernia resting on a harp to her right were also issued in 1723 and 1724. A number of patterns were to be associated with this series, as well as silver proof versions of halfpennies and farthings.

Wood's coins were struck in Bath Metal — a mixture of brass or copper and zinc with a small trace of silver. The metal content and the design of the coins were generally considered to be superior to any Irish coin previously issued, or indeed to the copper coinage of George I that circulated in England. Their arrival in Ireland was, however, met with political uproar.

Fig. 109—Farthing, George I,
William Wood second type, 1723.
SNC, February 1998, No. 109

The authorities in England had failed to consult the Irish authorities or the Irish parliament about the granting of patent to mint coins for Ireland. In retaliation the Irish privy council and the commissioners of revenue refused to accept the coins or to use them to make payments. Wood responded by saying that he would put an end to their 'stupid objections' and make the Irish swallow his coins 'in fireballs'. It was at this stage that Jonathan Swift, the dean of St Patrick's Cathedral in Dublin and the author of *Gulliver's Travels*, stepped into the fray. In a series of anonymous letters, the so-called Drapier Letters, he warned the tradesmen, shopkeepers, farmers and common people in general of Ireland to reject 'these useless tokens'. Swift's vitriol was not limited to the coins: in a stinging attack he described Wood as 'a mean, ordinary man, a hardware dealer', and later likened him to an insect! Whilst directed at Wood's coinage, the underlying arguments of Swift's letters related to the relationship between the Irish and English parliaments.

Wood, in an attempt to remedy the situation, called for an official assay of his coins. Sir Isaac Newton, the master of the mint in London, was responsible for assaying Wood's halfpence and farthings. Despite reporting on 27 April 1724 that the coins fulfilled the contract, he could not allay Irish concerns about the profits that Wood was making from producing lightweight coins. The Irish parliament formally petitioned George I to end Wood's patent and offered 'as our humble opinion, that the reserving the coinage of Halfpence and Farthings to the Crown, and the not trusting it with any private person, body politick or corporate' (Simon 1749, 171).

In August 1725 Wood eventually surrendered his patent and received compensation of £3,000 a year for the rest of his life. By the time of his death in 1730 he had received £42,000. Wood's Irish coinage was withdrawn from circulation. The generally accepted view was that it was gathered in and shipped across the Atlantic to meet the currency needs of the American colonies. Modern research, however, suggests that this did not happen. No documentary or legislative evidence seems to exist that points to the export of any large quantities of these coins, and in North America archaeological evidence has not thrown up significant numbers. The largest concentration, some eighteen coins, were excavated at Perinaquid in Maine, which was occupied by 50 Irish families in about 1729, the likelihood being that these coins were carried in the pockets of early Irish immigrants.

Whatever the fate of Wood's halfpennies, it was to be another 80 years before coins of as good a quality as those produced by William Wood were to circulate in Ireland again.

16. FOR WANT OF GOOD COPPER
The coinage of the Ascendancy in Ireland and the Union (1728–1826)

The political débâcle over William Wood's halfpennies and farthings saw the Irish authorities withdraw probably the finest regal coinage ever produced for the country. For the next ten years some of the coinage needs of Ireland were once again filled principally by the token issues of merchants and grocers.

In the north-east of Ireland a range of tokens, including copper twopences and silver threepences, were struck in Antrim, Armagh, Down, Londonderry and Tyrone in the early 1730s. The issue of a small copper twopence was a legacy of the Scottish coins, including the demonetised Scottish 'turner' or twopence, which had circulated for centuries in Ulster because of its close geographical and commercial links with the west of Scotland. Further down the east coast, pennies and halfpennies from the Isle of Man were to circulate.

As with the tokens issued from the 1650s to the 1670s, some of the designs reflected the issuer's trade (the Lurgan draper James Greer included a roll of linen on his silver threepence of 1736) or made a play on the name of the issuer (Thomas Fisher of Newtownards issued a copper twopence with a kingfisher with a fish in its beak on the reverse of his token coin).

Fig. 110—Twopence token, Thomas Fisher, Newtownards, c. 1760. *SNC*, February 1998, No. 286

In Dublin James Maculla, a foundry-owner, was to issue a series of large copper token pennies and halfpennies between 1728 and 1731. The issuing of these tokens was, however, opposed by Dean Swift as they did not contain their

Fig. 111—Penny token, James Maculla, Dublin, 1731. *SNC*, February 1998, No. 287

Fig. 112—Halfpenny token, James Maculla, Dublin, 1729. *SNC*, February 1998, No. 289

intrinsic value in copper. Swift in turn proposed his own scheme for issuing copper tokens, but this was to come to nothing. A Dublin merchant, Ben Bower, was to issue a silver threepence sometime in the 1730s.

The economy of the country, particularly the linen industry, inevitably began to suffer for 'the want of good copper money'. In 1736 the lords justice and privy council of Ireland petitioned George II to have 50 tons of coins struck from 'fine copper, which when heated red hot, would spread thin under the hammer without cracking' (Simon 1749, 172–3). The Irish authorities proposed that the order should be made up of one-sixth part in farthings and five-sixths in halfpences, 52 halfpences or 104 farthings being made from a pound of copper. The petition went on to describe the desired design of the coin: 'his majesties effigies with the inscription Georgius II Rex — should be stamped on one side of each piece, the Irish harp crowned on the other side, and over it the word 'Hibernia' with the date of the year under it'. The new coins were struck at the mint in the Tower of London and sent over to Ireland in April 1737, and were declared legal tender in a proclamation of 6 May 1737.

Fig. 113—Halfpenny, George II, 'Young Head' type, 1736. *SNC*, May 1996, No. 2253

The halfpennies, in line with the petition, featured on the obverse a youthful portrait of the king facing left with the legend 'GEORGIUS II REX' (King George II). The reverse featured a crowned harp with the word 'HIBERNIA' (Ireland) in the upper border of the coin and the year divided by the base of the harp at the bottom of the coin.

The halfpenny was to be struck between 1736 and 1738 and again from 1741 to 1755, with the exception of 1745 and 1754. Three types of halfpenny exist, all following essentially the same design; those struck between 1736 and 1738 have small lettering in the legend, while those from 1741–6 have large lettering. The halfpennies from 1747 read 'GEORGIVS' rather than 'GEORGIUS'. Farthings

Fig. 114—Farthing, George II, 'Young Head' type, 1737. *SNC*, May 1995, No. 2907

similar in design to the halfpenny were struck in 1737 and 1738 with small lettering and in 1744 with large lettering. Proofs of the first type of halfpenny dated 1736 exist in copper and silver, and again in copper for some later dates. Proofs of the 1739 farthing in copper and silver are also known.

Between 1736 and 1753 three contracts for the production of 189 tons of copper coinage were processed. A rare pattern halfpenny of 1742 has an older laureate portrait of George II with long curling hair.

Whilst the shortage of copper coinage was remedied through this series of contracts, there remained an ongoing problem with supplies of foreign gold and silver coinage. The rise in bullion prices once again saw gold and silver coins exported abroad to the extent that the only silver left in the country by 1737 was 'some English money, not worth melting, shilling pieces hardly worth nine pence or ten pence and sixpenny pieces not worth a groat' (Simon 1749, 175). A contemporary numismatist of the time, a Mr T. Prior, wrote that 'All these difficulties would be effectively removed by having a mint established in Ireland, and several pieces of copper, silver and gold coins made of such a standard, weights and value compared with the English as should be thought proper and convenient for us' (*ibid.*). The proposal for an Irish mint and the establishment of a proper Irish coinage, however, was to go no further.

In September 1760 a further shortage of copper coinage prompted the authorities to issue a fourth contract for a further 50 tons of copper coinage to be struck at the mint in London. The death of George II a month later was to delay the processing of this contract, which was not completed until April 1762.

Fig. 115—Halfpenny, George II, 'Old Head' type, 1760. *SNC*, February 1998, No. 170

The delay in completing this order saw the gap created by the absence of regal coins once again filled by private tokens. In Dublin a button-manufacturer named Roche of South King Street was responsible for the issuing of a series of token halfpennies and farthings known as the 'VOCE POPULI' series ('voice of the people' or 'the people's choice') because of their obverse legend. The coins dated 1760 are presumed to have been issued after the death of George II. At least nine different types of halfpenny are known, the quality of the portrait being better on some of the earlier types. Some of the later ones are much cruder and are known to numismatists as 'square-head', 'long-head' or even 'mouse-face' types. The reverse design of these tokens featured the figure of Hibernia holding a staff or spear with one arm resting on a harp, with the word 'HIBERNIA' above the figure and the date below a line in the exergue or bottom part of the coin.

Fig. 116—Halfpenny, George II, 'Voce Populi', 1760. *SNC*, May 1996, No. 2259

The portrait on the earlier coins and the letter 'P' on some of the later coins are believed to represent the Jacobite pretender James III or his son, Prince Charles Edward Stuart (the Young Pretender), suggesting that Roche may have been a Jacobite sympathiser — an unlikely political allegiance for the man responsible for manufacturing the buttons for King George's army in Ireland!

Some other sources have, however, suggested that the portrait on the obverse of the Voce Populi coins is that of Hely Hutchinson, the provost of Trinity College, the 'P' behind the portrait standing for provost. John Hely Hutchinson was to become a prominent Irish statesman, but in 1760 he had only recently taken his seat in the Irish House of Commons as MP for Lanesborough and was not to be installed as provost of Trinity until 1774, some fourteen years after the Voce Populi tokens are believed to have been issued.

The weight and size of the halfpennies vary considerably and, like many other Irish tokens, a number were to find their way across the Atlantic to the American colonies, who were experiencing similar shortages of regular coinage. Two types of farthings are also known in the series but these are both very rare.

Fig. 117—Farthing, George II, 'Voce Populi', 1760. *SNC*, May 1996, No. 2260

In April 1762 the first copper coins to be issued in George III's reign arrived in Ireland. They featured the Old Head portrait of his grandfather George II and bore the date 1760. These halfpennies and farthings feature the dead king with short-cropped hair and a laurel wreath looking left with the legend 'GEORGIVS II REX' (King George II) forming the border. The reverse, like the earlier coins of George II, featured a crowned harp with the word 'HIBERNIA' and the date '1760' below the harp.

The first coins to feature the portrait of George III were issued in 1766 and formed part of a contract for 50 tons of copper halfpennies. These first halfpennies feature a portrait of the king looking right with short hair and the legend 'GEORGIVS III REX' (King George III) on the obverse and a crowned harp with the legend 'HIBERNIA' and the date below the harp. A further issue was made in 1769.

Fig. 118—Halfpenny, George III, first type, 1766. *SNC*, June 2001, No. 3274

A second type of halfpenny was also issued in 1769, featuring a portrait of the king with slightly older features; these two types of halfpennies may have made up a further contract of 50 tons made in 1769. A third type of halfpenny was issued in 1775. It featured a more youthful portrait of the king with long hair. This halfpenny was also issued in 1776, 1781 and 1782. All these halfpennies were struck at the Tower mint in London.

Fig. 119—Halfpenny, George III, third type, 1775. *SNC*, May 1995, No. 2913

A pattern halfpenny of 1733 also exists which shows a slightly more mature portrait of the king with long curling hair and a much finer representation of a crowned harp on the reverse.

One of the most interesting pattern coins of the early part of George III's reign is the Condordia penny of 1789. The pattern was engraved by William Mossop, an Irish die-engraver. On the obverse it featured a portrait of the king with short hair and a harp below the bust with the legend 'GEORGIVS III REX' (King George III). The reverse, based on a design by Sir Joshua Reynolds, featured Britannia and Hibernia clasping hands before an altar with the legend

'CONCORDIA' (unanimity) and the date 1789 in the exergue. Six specimens of the coin were struck, of which two were presented to George III.

Fig. 120—Penny, Mossop's 'Concordia' pattern penny, 1789. *SNC*, May 1995, No. 2918

The Condordia penny was struck at a time of growing national consciousness. Sometimes known incorrectly as the Union penny, it preceded the Act of Union with Great Britain by twelve years.

In the absence of a regal coinage during the 1780s, unofficial tokens were once again issued to meet the need for small change. Large quantities of imitation Irish halfpennies were struck in foundries in Birmingham and exported to Ireland, where they circulated alongside the regal coins of George III. These coins featured the laureate bust, similar to that of the king, with spurious legends, including the king's name and titles and those of popes, and even one which featured the name of 'Georgeivs Washington'. The reverse of the tokens featured crowned harps with a variety of legends or slogans, including blundered renderings of 'Hibernia'.

From the 1790s merchants, principally in Dublin, again issued their own copper trade tokens, mainly halfpennies and farthings. Two mining companies, the Associated Irish Mine Company which mined copper in Avoca, Co. Wicklow, and the Hibernian Mining Company which mined near Arklow, were responsible for the production of a large number of copper trading tokens which were to circulate widely across Ireland. The Associated Irish Mine Company featured the head of St Patrick on the obverse of their token, while the Hibernian Mining Company, or Camac Kyan and Camac (the names of the company directors), issued tokens popularly known as 'commacs' which included a figure of Hibernia on the reverse. Alongside the copper tokens some grocers, principally in Cork and Dublin, issued lead farthing tokens which tended to circulate in the immediate vicinity of their shops. In Dublin, some 29 grocers or traders from fifteen streets, including C. Colgan of 13 Thomas Street, issued their own lead farthings between 1780 and 1820. The largest concentration of issuers of these farthings were to be found in Church Street and Pill Lane (now Chancery Street behind the Four Courts). In Cork City at least nine grocers issued lead farthings in the same period.

The 1780s saw the Irish Patriot Parliament under the leadership of Henry Grattan attempt to reassert its independence from Westminster in the wake of the American Revolution. It was, however, revolution in France, with two attempted invasions by French forces and the United Irish Rebellion of 1798, which was to leave a more lasting legacy on Irish history. Against a background of invasion and rebellion William Pitt, the British prime minister, pressed for union between Great Britain and Ireland on 31 January 1799. A Bill for Union was put before the Irish parliament on 21 May 1800. Promises of patronage and peerages ensured that the bill abolishing the Irish House of Commons and House of Lords was passed on 1 August 1800. The formal union of Great Britain and Ireland took place on 1 January 1801. For the next 121 years Ireland was to be ruled from Westminster.

Despite political union with Britain, the shortage of coinage in Ireland continued. The rise in silver prices saw the little silver coin that remained in the country melted down and exported to England, where silver bullion commanded higher prices.

In 1804 two Dublin companies, Clark, West and Company and the Irish Bullion Company, produced and sold hall-marked silver shilling tokens with a weight of 2dwt 20 grains in an attempt to remedy the shortage of silver coins.

On 2 March 1804 a committee of the House of Commons was established to consider the state of the currency of Ireland. The committee found the coinage to be in an appalling condition. Only 2% of the circulating silver coinage was officially minted silver. The remaining 98% consisted of counterfeit base silver shillings and sixpences worth half their notional value. Very little of the official mint copper coinage, last struck in 1782, was also in circulation. The bulk of copper coinage was private tokens, and increasing use was being made of promissory 'silver' notes.

The Irish currency system by 1804 was a mixture of worn copper coins, merchants' tokens, counterfeit base silver coins and promissory notes issued by banks or traders. The counterfeit coins had some legal status since government offices accepted them in payment and in turn the government paid its troops in the same counterfeit coins. The system could have continued, but in the spring of 1804 the Irish Post Office refused to accept counterfeit coin. This action brought the whole monetary system to the point of collapse, and there was a real fear that the coinage crisis could lead to political unrest and possible rebellion.

The parliamentary committee's response was to propose the withdrawal of all 'bad silver', counterfeit coins, and their replacement by new silver and copper coins. It was proposed that the shortage of silver coinage could be addressed by the issuing of officially sanctioned silver tokens by the Bank of Ireland, which had been founded in 1782.

A silver dollar coin similar to the Bank of England dollar was proposed. The privy council authorised the striking and circulation of a Bank of Ireland dollar with a value of six shillings, taking into account the difference in the English and Irish currencies; in 1804 thirteen Irish pence were equivalent to twelve English pence. The Bank of England dollar valued at five English shillings was equivalent to five shillings and fivepence (Irish). An additional 7d was added by the Bank of Ireland to ensure that the monetary value of the coin was higher than its bullion value in order that the coins remained in Ireland rather than being melted down or exported for their bullion value.

The design of the new Bank of Ireland dollar was set out in a letter of 21 April 1804 from the directors of the Bank of Ireland to Matthew Boulton at the Soho mint in Birmingham who was tasked with producing the new coin on new steam-powered mint presses. The coin was designed and engraved by Konrad Heinrich Kuchler (d. 1810). The obverse featured a laureate and draped bust of the king facing right and the legend 'GEORGIUS III DEI GRATIA REX' (George III by the grace of God king). The reverse featured the figure of Hibernia (initially consideration had been given to a harp), with the legend 'BANK OF IRELAND TOKEN' and '1804' 'SIX SHILLINGS' in the exergue. The new Irish 'dollar' coins were overstruck on Spanish dollar or eight-real pieces. The coining of the new Irish money commenced on 31 May 1804 and was completed by 19 June. Some 790,509 Spanish dollars were overstruck into Bank of Ireland dollars at Boulton's mint. The 132 casks of new dollars were then placed on a canal barge for Liverpool with an armed escort of twelve soldiers and a sergeant before being transferred onto a man-of-war for their journey to Dublin.

Fig. 121—Six shillings, George III, Bank of Ireland token, 1804. *SNC*, February 1998, No. 194

In addition to the circulation coins, Boulton decided to produce 1000 proof 'dollars', writing on 17 May 1804 that he was 'persuaded the Irish dollar will be thought a more beautiful coin than the English one ... I am desirous that every cabinet of coins in the kingdom should have one and therefore I propose to coin a few hundreds, put them into proper preserving cases and offer them to sale in some other shops about Charing Cross or Pall Mall or St James Street' (Vice 1994). The proof dollars were to be sold at 8s 6d. Nearly 200 years later a silver proof dollar sold at the Whyte's Millennial Collection Sale for £IR825 in April 2000.

A number of varieties of the Bank of Ireland dollar exist, including silver, gilt and copper proofs, as well as some copper patterns struck at a later date by W. J. Taylor of London.

Alongside this official overstriking of Spanish dollar coins, the countess of Ormonde at about this time had Spanish eight-real coins counter-marked with a small stamp bearing the value of '5s 5d' and the legend 'PAYABLE AT CASTLE COMER COLLIERY' to pay the miners working in the Butler family's collieries.

Whilst the issuing of the Bank of Ireland dollars went some way towards alleviating Ireland's coinage problems, the lord lieutenant's office was already writing to Boulton in June 1804 to explore the possibility of his acquiring Spanish half-dollar coins or other small foreign coins to use in the production of smaller silver token coins. By the end of 1804 the chancellor of the exchequer for Ireland was pressing the parliamentary committee for authorisation to issue a new smaller coinage.

In February 1805 authorisation was granted for the issuing of a token valued at 1/6 dollar. After further consideration it was decided that a 10d token would be more appropriate (thirteen tokens at 10d equalling two English dollars). The Royal Mint was commissioned by the Bank of Ireland to strike a new 10d token and a new 5d token.

The new tokens were designed by Lewis Pingo (1743–1830) and featured a bust of the king draped and in armour facing right with the legend 'GEORGIVS III DEI GRATIA' (George III by the grace of God) on the obverse. The reverse featured the following legend in six lines: 'BANK TOKEN TEN PENCE IRISH 1805'. The coin was also to be issued in 1806. The smaller 5d token followed a similar design and was also to be issued in 1805 and 1806.

Fig. 122—Tenpence, George III, Bank of Ireland token, 1805. Patrick Finn List 17/1999, No. 479

The legislation authorising the issuing of these new 10d and 5d tokens had stipulated that the date on these coins should be 1805. Technically the coins issued with the date 1806 were an illegal issue!

Whilst the Royal Mint in London was striking the new silver tokens, Matthew Boulton's mint in Birmingham was tasked with the production of a new copper coinage for Ireland consisting of a penny, halfpenny and farthing. Unlike the silver coins, the copper coins were official Irish regal coins rather than bank tokens.

The three coins all follow the same design and were designed by Küchler. The obverse features a laureate and draped portrait of the king facing right with the legend 'GEORGIUS III D.G. REX' (George III by the grace of God king), and the reverse a crowned harp with the date below and the legend 'HIBERNIA' above the crown. The penny and halfpenny were struck in 1805 and the farthing in 1806. A range of proofs in copper, bronzed copper, gilt copper, silver and gold exist. A pattern halfpenny with a larger portrait than that which appeared on the regular coinage also exists.

Fig. 123—Penny, George III, 1805. *SNC,* February 1998, No. 184

In 1808 a 30d token was issued by the Bank of Ireland. The coin, which was struck by the Royal Mint, was designed by Pingo. The obverse featured a portrait of the king similar to that found on the earlier 10d and 5d tokens issued in 1805 and 1806 and the legend 'GEORGIVS III DEI GRATIA REX' (George III by the grace of God king). The reverse featured the figure of Hibernia with the legend 'BANK TOKEN' forming the upper border and 'XXX PENCE IRISH' in the exergue. The date '1808' is to be found below the bust on the obverse. Two varieties of this coin exist, the first where the top of the harp on the reverse points between the 'O' and 'K' in 'TOKEN' and the second where the top of the harp points to the 'O' in 'TOKEN'.

Fig. 124—Thirty pence, George III, Bank of Ireland token, 1808. *SNC,* February 1998, No. 200

A final issue of Bank of Ireland tokens was to be made in 1813 with the issuing of a new 10d token. This new coin was struck at the Royal Mint from silver rupees coined from Spanish dollars in India by the East India Company, which were shipped to England, melted down, struck into new coins and sent to Ireland! Some £200,000 of these new tokens were to be produced. The coin was designed by Thomas Wyon (1792–1817). The obverse design had been originally intended for a Bank of England 9d token which was never issued. The obverse featured a laureate portrait of the king facing right with the legend 'GEORGIUS

III DEI GRATIA REX' (George III by the grace of God king). The reverse featured the words 'BANK TOKEN 10 PENCE IRISH 1813' in five lines within a wreath of shamrock. Proof versions of this coin were also struck.

Fig. 125—Tenpence, George III, Bank of Ireland token, 1813. *SNC*, February 1998, No. 4937

The range of silver tokens issued by the Bank of Ireland were to continue to circulate in Ireland until about 1817, when they were withdrawn from circulation as Imperial gold and silver coins resulting from the 1816 British coinage reforms became more readily available in Ireland.

Two types of pattern pennies designed by Thomas Wyon and dating from 1813 exist, featuring obverse portraits of the king used on his coinage in Demerara and Essequibo and Ceylon — the reverse featuring a more ornate smaller crowned harp than that to be found on the 1805 copper coinage.

As in previous reigns, the issuing of official regal pennies and halfpennies in 1805 and farthings in 1806 brought an end to the production and acceptance of unofficial trade tokens. However, by 1810 the growth of the agricultural economy and flourishing trade with Britain led to further demands for a regular supply of good coinage, in particular small change. In the absence of any official response, merchants in Strabane, Coleraine and Dublin once again began to issue unofficial copper pennies and halfpennies.

A number of these tokens were issued by the merchant Edward Stephens of James Street, Dublin, between 1813 and 1822. Many of his tokens include a portrait of the victor of the Peninsular Wars and Waterloo, the Irish-born duke of Wellington, combined with the slogan 'ERIN GO BRAGH' (Ireland for ever) on the obverse and a crowned harp on the reverse.

A later penny token without an issuer's name reflects the changing political climate with demands for Catholic emancipation. It features a laureate portrait of Daniel O'Connell with the legend 'IRELANDS ADVOCATE', whilst the reverse features a crowned harp and the legend 'MAY OUR FRIENDS PROSPER'.

The production of unofficial tokens was to continue until the early 1820s, when an officially sanctioned regal coinage was once again struck.

The last Irish regal coins were issued under an order in council of George IV on 5 July 1822 and consisted of a penny and halfpenny. The bust of the king on the obverse was modelled by Beneditto Pistrucci (1784–1855) and engraved by William Wyon (1795–1851), who also modelled and engraved the reverse.

The last Irish coins to bear the portrait of a British monarch were struck at the Royal Mint in London. The design for both coins was the same; the obverse featured a laureate and draped bust of the king facing left with the legend 'GEORGIUS IV D:G: REX' (George IV by the grace of God king) and the reverse an ornate crowned harp with the legend 'HIBERNIA' above the crown and the date below the harp. The penny and halfpenny were issued in 1822 and 1823. A pattern penny dated 1822 with a smaller harp by Wyon also exists.

Fig. 126—Penny, George IV, 1822. *SNC*, February 1998, No. 213

A farthing was also ordered to be issued under the 1822 order in council, and a pattern farthing dated 1822 with the same design as the circulating penny and halfpenny is known but was never to be issued. It is thought that as few as six of these pattern farthings exist. In 1997 an example sold for £IR1,000.

Proof versions of the penny and halfpenny were also to be struck, including some with a special bronzed finish.

In 1826 probably one of the most important events in Ireland's monetary and numismatic history took place. Despite political union in 1801, the economies of the two countries and their monetary systems remained separate. Thirteen Irish pence were still the equivalent of twelve British pence. The differences in the currencies dated back as far as 1460, with the 13:12 ratio dating from 1701. On 20 December 1825 this position was finally remedied when a proclamation was issued assimilating the gold and silver coinages in Great Britain and Ireland. The proclamation stated that as from 5 January 1826 silver and gold coins of Great Britain would 'circulate and be current in Ireland at the same nominal as well as real value as in other parts of the United Kingdom ... that is to say that the British silver sixpence shall circulate and shall be taken, accepted, paid and computed as current for and divisible into and representing six pence only, and not sixpence and one halfpenny; the British silver shilling as twelve pence and not as thirteen pence...' (Royal Mint 1915, 42–4).

With this proclamation, the Irish regal coins of George IV and his predecessors were formally withdrawn from circulation on 12 July 1826 and replaced by the Imperial coinage of the United Kingdom, which was to remain the official coinage of Ireland for the next 100 years.

17. A NATION ONCE AGAIN
The early coinage of modern Ireland (1928–66)

In the tense early hours of 6 December 1921, the British cabinet, led by Prime Minister David Lloyd George, and an Irish Republican delegation, led by Arthur Griffith and Michael Collins, signed the Anglo-Irish Treaty which signalled the end of almost 700 years of British rule over most of Ireland.

The Treaty was the culmination of a century of political activity to repeal the 1800 Act of Union with Britain. The campaign for Repeal or Home Rule was first led by 'the Liberator', Daniel O'Connell, in the 1830s and the famine years of the 1840s, and later in the 1880s by the 'uncrowned king of Ireland', Charles Stewart Parnell.

Home Rule for Ireland was eventually achieved on 18 September 1914, but its implementation was suspended for the duration of the war. The suspension led to a split in the nationalist movement, resulting in the 1916 Easter Rising led by Padraig Pearse and his Republican supporters. The suppression of the rising saw the political struggle against British rule turn into a national campaign of civil resistance and eventually open warfare against the forces of the Crown from 1919 to 1921.

The Anglo-Irish Treaty signed that December morning established *Saorstat Éireann*, the Irish Free State, in the 26 counties of the south and a separate administration in the six northern counties. The Treaty, which gave the Irish Dominion status within the British Empire, was to divide the Republican movement. Within weeks of the provisional government of the Irish Free State formally taking power in January 1922 the country was plunged into a vicious civil war.

It was to be another four years before the new state began to give serious consideration to its coinage. In the meantime, British Imperial coins continued to circulate. On 13 April 1926, a century after Ireland's last distinctive coinage was abolished, Dáil Éireann passed the Coinage Act which allowed for the introduction of a new Irish coinage. The Irish Free State government established a committee to advise them on the designs for a new coinage; it was chaired by the poet William Butler Yeats (1865–1939), who had a particular interest in ancient Greek coinage. At the suggestion of the Irish artist Sir William Orpen, it was agreed that the designs should reflect the natural products of the country, and eventually these were limited to the animals and birds of the Irish countryside.

Yeats, in his report 'The designing of Ireland's coinage', outlined the approach the committee adopted to designing its new coinage. Whilst political independence had been achieved, there was no intention to break with the pound sterling or £sd monetary system, or indeed to withdraw British coins from circulation; it was intended that the new Irish coins would circulate alongside British coins.

In his opening remarks Yeats wrote: 'As the most famous and beautiful coins are the coins of the Greek colonies, especially those of Sicily, we decided to send photographs of some of these and one coin of Carthage, to our selected artists, and to ask them as far as possible to take them as a model. But the Greek coins have two advantages that ours could not have; one side need not balance the other, and either could be stamped in high relief, whereas ours must pitch and spin to please the gambler, and pack into rolls to please the banker' (Yeats 1928).

The committee short-listed ten artists who were offered a payment of £50 to design the new Irish coinage, having collected examples of modern coinage from various foreign embassies and private individuals.

Each of the artists was sent details of the designs to appear on the new coins, and photographs of examples of ancient Greek coins and pictures of some of the animals to feature on the coins. The committee agreed that the following animals or birds should be represented on the new coinage: a woodcock on the farthing, a ram or a pig on the halfpenny, a hen and chicks on the penny, a hare on the threepence, an Irish wolfhound on the sixpence, a bull on the shilling, a salmon on the florin and a horse on the half-crown. Yeats was to write: 'What better symbols could we find for this horse riding, salmon fishing, cattle raising country?' All the coins were to be the same size as their British counterparts with the exception of the sixpence and threepence, which were to be slightly larger.

Fig. 127—Florin, shilling, sixpence and threepence, group of Morbiducci patterns, 1927. Patrick Finn List 2000

Fig. 128—Half-crown Morbiducci pattern, 1927. *Coin News,* March 2000

Seven artists eventually submitted designs, including the Irish sculptors Albert Power, Oliver Shepherd and Jerome Connor, the English medallist Percy Metcalfe, the American Paul Manship, the Swedish sculptor Carl Milles and the Italian medallist Publio Morbiducci, who alongside his plaster casts had a series of pattern coins struck in silver and bronze. A magnificent collection of six Morbiducci pattern coins, all dated 1927, including a half-crown, florin, shilling, sixpence, threepence and penny, were to sell at the Whyte's Millennial Collection Sale for £IR28,000.

The Yugoslav sculptor Ivan Mestrovic did not submit his design in time, the committee having sent his letter of invitation to the wrong address. Mestrovic did, however, donate his powerful obverse design to the Irish Free State. Mestrovic's design was never used on any Irish coin although it was adopted by the Central Bank of Ireland for use as their official seal in 1965. A simplified version of the design was to appear in 1971 on the Central Bank of Ireland's commemorative wallet containing a set of the new decimal coins.

Fig. 129—Mestrovic pattern, obverse, 1927. *Coin News,* March 2000

Some 66 plaster casts of the designs were submitted to the committee. Originally it was envisaged that one of two designs from each designer would be chosen, but in Yeats's words, 'One set of designs seemed far to exceed the others'; these were the designs of Percy Metcalfe (1895–1970). The designs were subsequently submitted to the Ministry of Agriculture for their observations, and they proposed changes to some of Metcalfe's original designs. As Yeats later described, 'the first bull had to go, though one of the finest of all designs because it might have upset ... the eugenics of the farmyard. I sigh, however, over the pig, though I admit the state of the market for pigs' cheeks made the old design impossible; with the round cheek of the pig went the lifted head, the look of insolence and wisdom'.

An original plaster cast of the reverse of Metcalfe's threepence, measuring 4½ inches in diameter, was also to be sold at the Whyte's Millennial Collection Sale for £IR1,500.

Metcalfe's harp design, based on the fifteenth-century Brian Boru harp in Trinity College, was also to feature on the obverse of all the new coins, with the legend 'SAORSTAT EIREANN' and the date divided by the harp. The farthing, halfpenny and penny were struck in bronze, the threepence and sixpence in nickel, and the shilling, florin and half-crown in .750 silver as compared to the British .500 silver. All the coins were to be struck by the Royal Mint in London. The new coins were put into general circulation on 12 December 1928. Some 6,001 proof sets were also struck, of which 4,001 were released for sale.

Fig. 130—Shilling and halfpenny, Metcalfe's original designs, 1927. *Coin News*, March 2000

The reverse of the half-crown featured a hunter looking left, with the legend 'LEAT CHOROIN' (half-crown) forming the border and '2s 6d' and Metcalfe's initials 'PM' in the exergue of the coin.

The reverse of the florin featured a leaping salmon facing right, with the word 'FLOIRIN' (florin) and '2s' to the right of the salmon.

The reverse of the shilling featured a bull facing right, with '1s' above the bull and the word 'SCILLING' (shilling) in the exergue.

Fig. 131—Shilling, Saorstat Éireann, 1937. *Coin News*, March 2000

The sixpence featured a wolfhound facing left, with '6d' above the dog and the word 'REUL' (sixpence) in the exergue. The threepence complemented the sixpence design with a hare. The reverse featured the hare with the legend 'LEAT REUL' (threepence or half-sixpence) forming the border and '3d' in the exergue.

In 1969 it was suggested that the hare portrayed on Metcalfe's threepence was not the native Irish hare but an English brown hare! The edges of the sixpence and threepence coins were both plain rather than milled.

The reverse of the penny featured a hen and her clutch of chicks facing left. The hen is thought to be holding an arrowhead in her claw. The value of the coin '1d' is to be found above the hen and the word 'PINGIN' (penny) in the exergue.

,**Fig. 132**—Halfpenny, Saorstat Éireann, 1933. *SNC,* February 1998, No. 249

The halfpenny similarly featured a family group, in this case a sow and her piglets facing left, with the value '½d' above the pig and the words 'LEAT PINGIN' (halfpenny) in the exergue.

The farthing, like the florin, was to have a much freer design with no exergue; it featured a woodcock in flight facing left, with the value '¼d' above the bird and the word 'FEOIRLING' (farthing) below the woodcock in the lower part of the coin.

All three bronze coins, like the nickel coins, were to have plain edges.

The 1928 Royal Mint Report was somewhat dismissive of the new Irish coins, commenting that 'The originality of the designs seems to have had a direct appeal to the Irish sense of humour' (Young 1969, 32), but the *Manchester Guardian* wrote that 'The Irish coinage will be acknowledged as the most beautiful in the modern world. I doubt if any country ... would have had the imagination and freedom to lay down the conditions that would have made such designs possible' (*ibid.*).

Fig. 133—Half-crown, Éire, 1939. *SNC,* July 1998, No. 4964

The new coins were all to be issued in 1928 and then at different intervals for each coin from 1930 through to 1937.

In June 1937 the government of Eamon de Valera adopted a new constitution, changing the name of the state from Saorstat Éireann to Éire. The position of the Crown was finally abolished and the office of governor general replaced by that of *an t-Uachtarain* or president. On 25 June 1938 the elderly Gaelic scholar Dr Douglas Hyde was sworn in as Ireland's first president at Dublin Castle, the former seat of British viceregal power. Ireland was a republic in all but name.

Fig. 134—Sixpence, Éire, 1939. Threepence, Éire, 1939. *SNC,* February 1998, Nos. 238, 240

The change in the Irish constitution in 1937 was reflected in the Irish coinage from 1939 onwards. The obverse design was changed, with the word 'EIRE' replacing 'SAORSTAT EIREANN' and the date being moved to the border, presenting a less cluttered appearance. The detailed design of the harp was also simplified, and the number of strings reduced from sixteen to fourteen. Minor modifications were also made to the reverse designs of the penny and the half-crown.

Fig. 135—Farthing, Éire, 1939. *SNC,* February 1997, No. 364

Trial strikings of a half-crown and penny dated 1938 were made from the modified dies of the half-crown and penny. An example of the trial 1938 half-crown and the trial 1938 penny were held in the archives of the Department of Finance until July 2000, when both coins were presented to the National Museum of Ireland. These two coins are the rarest in the modern Irish series. The 1938 trial half-crown is thought to be unique, and only two examples of the 1938 penny are known.

Éire, although a member of the British Commonwealth, was to remain neutral during the Second World War. The war years were known in Ireland as 'the Emergency'. Ireland's coins throughout this period continued to be produced at the Royal Mint. The shilling, florin and half-crown continued to be struck in .750 silver up until 1943, but in 1942 the metal composition of the threepence and sixpence was changed from nickel to cupro-nickel. The 1943 florin and half-crown are the two scarcest coins in the modern Irish series. It seems that normal quantities of both these coins were produced by the Royal Mint and shipped to Dublin, where they were placed in the vaults of the Central Bank of Ireland. The coins were to remain in the bank's vaults until 1951, when some of the bags containing the 1943 coins were accidentally released into general circulation. Estimates vary on the number of coins released, but it is believed that about 7,000 half-crowns and 1,000 florins may have been issued. The remaining bags of the 1943 coins were returned to the Royal Mint to be melted down.

A brilliant uncirculated example of a 1943 florin, one of only four known in this condition, was sold at Whyte's Auction House on 23 February 2001 for £IR15,000.

One curious numismatic legacy of the Emergency years was the production of officially sanctioned brass and white metal tokens, including a penny, a sixpence, a shilling and two shillings for use by prisoners of war or internees in the Curragh internment camp. All the tokens are dated '1940' and were used by both Allied and Axis prisoners who were captured or found in neutral Ireland!

Whilst bronze and cupro-nickel coins continued to be struck throughout the 1940s, no half-crowns, florins and shillings were struck after 1943 until 1951, when the metal composition was changed under the Coinage Act of 1950 from .750 silver to cupro-nickel.

The uncertain constitutional position between Britain and Ireland was finally resolved with the passing of the Republic of Ireland Act by the Irish Dáil and the passing of the 1949 Ireland Act by the Westminster parliament. On 18 April 1949 the Republic of Ireland broke its last link with the British Crown by leaving the British Commonwealth. Despite these political changes Ireland's monetary system remained linked to sterling and her economy, through the 1948 Anglo-Irish Trade Agreement, closely interdependent with that of Britain. In 1973 both countries were to join the European Economic Community. The constitutional changes of 1948 and 1949 were not to lead to any changes in the design or wording of Ireland's coinage.

Fig. 136—Florin, Éire, proof version, 1955. *SNC*, February 2002, IMI 263

Regular issues of all Ireland's coins were to be made from 1951 onwards up to 1968, with the exception of the half-crown and the halfpenny which were last struck in 1967 and the sixpence which was struck up to 1969. The farthing was last struck as a circulating coin in 1959, although 96,000 were struck in 1966 for commemorative sets.

The modern Irish series only has a few minor die varieties. Most of the variation that has been identified tends to relate to very minor differences in the spacing between the numbers in the date or the letters in the legend. However, one major variety dates from the early 1960s — the 1961 'mule' half-crown. These half-crowns circulated for almost seven years before the numismatist Derek Young noted that two types of 1961 half-crown were in circulation. Whilst both coins had the same obverse, there were minor differences in the reverse designs. It eventually transpired that one coin featured the normal reverse design which had been used since 1939 (some parts of the design were modified in 1938) whilst the others had been struck from the earlier 1928 reverse die!

Fig. 137—Penny, Éire, proof version, 1968. *SNC*, February 2002, IMI 295

April 1966 saw the introduction of the first Irish commemorative coin, a dished ten-shilling coin struck in .833 silver to mark the 50th anniversary of the 1916 Easter Rising. In a departure from previous modern Irish coins, the obverse featured a portrait of Padraig Pearse, the leader of the 1916 Rising, by T. H. Paget, looking right with the word 'EIRE' to the left of Pearse and the date '1966' to the right. The reverse featured the figure of the legendary Irish hero Cuchulainn, based on the statue by Oliver Sheppard in the General Post Office in Dublin, with the value of the coin 'DEIC SCILLING' forming the border. The edge of the coin was engraved with the legend 'EIRI AMAC NA CASCA 1916' (The Easter Rising 1916), although varieties exist with 'NA CASCA' spelt 'NASCA' and 'NACASCA'.

Fig. 138—Ten shillings, 'Easter Rising Commemorative', 1966. Central Bank of Ireland

It was envisaged that the coin would be a circulating coin as well as a commemorative piece. Two million of the coins were put into circulation and 20,000 proofs were issued. The coin, because of its weight, proved unpopular, however, and 1,270,000 were subsequently withdrawn and melted down.

The use of a dished or double concaved coin was a major departure in coin design, and the Royal Mint, who struck the Irish ten-shilling coin, were to experiment through 1966 and 1967 with trial strikings of this coin in silver, nickel and cupro-nickel using a range of dies, including the unlikely combination of a portrait of Queen Elizabeth II on the obverse and the figure of Cuchulainn on the reverse!

By the end of 1966 the Department of Finance and the Central Bank of Ireland's attempt to introduce a new denomination to replace the ten-shilling bank note was generally thought to have failed as the general public rejected the new coin and consigned it to the melting pot. Three years later, however, the general public were to face a far greater challenge with the introduction of Ireland's first decimal coins.

18. A CHRISTENING OR A WAKE
Decimalisation to the Euro (1969–2002)

In the early 1960s the Irish government began to consider the introduction of a decimal system. Initially a system based on the ten-shilling unit was proposed, but in 1968 it was decided that the Irish decimal system would be the same as that of the United Kingdom, with 100 new pennies to the pound, and that the shape, size, weight and metal content of coins would be the same in both countries. The changeover to decimalisation which was set out in the Decimal Currency Acts of 1969 and 1970 was to take place on 15 February 1971.

In autumn 1969 the first decimal coins, new ten pence and five pence coins, were introduced, featuring the Percy Metcalfe salmon and bull design. In 1970 a new equilateral curved heptagon-shaped 50 pence coin was issued, with the Percy Metcalfe woodcock design from the old farthing on the reverse.

All three of the new coins featured the by now traditional harp design on the obverse. The reverse of the new ten pence coin featured the salmon facing right and '10P' below the salmon; the new five pence featured the bull facing left and '5P' above the bull; and the new 50 pence featured the woodcock in flight facing left with '50P' above the bird. The overall impression was of a cleaner and simpler design than the coins they were replacing. The ten pence was to be issued at intervals until 1986 and the five pence until 1990. The 50 pence was to be issued at intervals until 2000.

In 1971 the three cupro-nickel coins were joined by new bronze halfpenny, one penny and two pence coins. The obverse of the new coins again retained the traditional harp design, but the reverse designs featured a series of Celtic bird designs by the Irish artist and sculptor Gabriel Hayes (1909–78). The halfpenny was based on an ornamental bird from a manuscript in the Cathedral Library in Cologne, the penny from an illumination in the Book of Kells in Trinity College, Dublin, and the two pence from the bible of Charles the Bald in the Bibliothèque Nationale in Paris.

The reverse of the halfpenny featured a stylised bird with an elongated neck circling around the coin with '½P' below the bird. The penny featured a peacock-like bird with elaborate tail feathers with '1P' to the right of the bird, and the two pence an intricate stylised rendering of a bird with a large beak with '2P' above the bird. The two pence and the penny were to be issued at intervals until 2000.

Fig. 139—Two pence, penny and halfpenny. Reverse design of decimal coins, 1971. Central Bank of Ireland

The halfpenny was similarly to be issued at intervals until 1982, with a small number being produced in 1986 for inclusion in special proof or specimen sets. Nearly 3,000,000 halfpennies were struck in 1985, although they were never issued. It is thought that the entire issue was melted down, although rumours persist that a few may have escaped the melting pot.

Proof and uncirculated sets were issued in 1971 by the Central Bank of Ireland to mark the introduction of the new coinage.

In the run-up to decimalisation the half-crown, halfpenny and farthing had been formally withdrawn and demonetised on 31 December 1969. The sixpence, threepence and penny were to be withdrawn on 18 February 1971.

In 1976 a mint was established at Sandyford near Dublin and there began a gradual process of an increasing proportion of Ireland's coinage being struck in Ireland rather than at the Royal Mint. At times the continued reliance on the Royal Mint for the production of some of Ireland's coinage requirements has led to some controversy and political debate.

In March 1979 the Irish government took the Irish pound into the EMS (European Monetary System), breaking the link with sterling that had been in place since 1826. With British coins and Irish coins now having different values, British coins were withdrawn from circulation in the Republic, and in the North of Ireland Irish coins ceased to circulate alongside British coins. One numismatic legacy of the 'Troubles' and the system of the two coinages circulating side by side is the series of counter-marked Irish coins with loyalist political slogans that are to be found.

The break between the two currencies meant that Irish coins no longer needed to conform to the shape, size, weight and metal content of their British counterparts. The first departure occurred in 1986 when a new nickel bronze twenty pence coin was issued, slightly larger than a two pence, with the edge having three smooth and three grained segments for ease of identification. The reverse of the coin featured the Percy Metcalfe hunter from the old half-crown facing left with '20P' above the horse.

It is thought that some trial pieces of this new coin, dated 1985, were produced and that some of these may have found their way into general circulation. If this is the case, the 1985 twenty pence is probably the rarest coin in the modern Irish decimal series.

A proof or specimen version of the 1986 twenty pence was also produced as part of a special coin set produced by the Central Bank of Ireland. The set was to contain three coins, the halfpenny, the ten pence and the 50 pence, which were struck specifically for inclusion in the set. These three coins are amongst the scarcest in the modern decimal series.

In 1988 a second Irish commemorative coin was issued, a 50 pence to mark the Millennium of the city of Dublin. The reverse, by the Irish artist Thomas Ryan (b. 1929), featured the coat of arms of the city of Dublin with the ceremonial mace, sword and cap of maintenance traditionally worn by the lord mayor of Dublin, with the dates '998' and '1998' on either side of the shield and a scroll below with '1000'. Some 50,000 proof coins were also struck alongside the coins issued for general circulation.

Fig. 140—Fifty pence, Éire, 'Dublin Millennium', 1988. Central Bank of Ireland Information Leaflet (1988)

The passing of the 1990 Decimal Currency Act on 1 March 1990 allowed for the introduction of a new one pound coin, which was issued for the first time on 20 June 1990. On the day before the formal launch of the new coin, the Irish finance minister, Albert Reynolds, said: 'It is not beyond the bounds of possibility that before the end of the decade my successor will be introducing a Euronote and Euro coinage that will be legal tender everywhere from Tory Island to Rhodes' (Young 1990).

Fig. 141—Pound, Éire, 1990. Central Bank of Ireland Information Leaflet (1990)

The new one pound coin, which was struck in cupro-nickel, featured an Irish red deer by Thomas Ryan, who had previously designed the Dublin Millennium 50 pence. The coin, which was about the size of the old half-crown although much lighter, was to have a unique engrailed edge — a milled edge with inset beading. The coin was not launched without controversy when it was discovered that the initial issue of 20,000,000 coins had been struck at the Royal Mint and not the Dublin Mint.

The reverse of the new pound coin featured an Irish red deer facing left with the word 'PUNT' in the border above the deer and '£1' in the exergue.

Some examples of the one pound coin are found with a milled edge rather than an engrailed edge. Whilst these coins command higher prices from a collector's perspective, they are mint errors or misstrikes, where the coin has not been properly engrailed, rather than a specific variety. Examples of one pound coins with milled edges are known for every year of issue.

On the same day as the launch of the Irish one pound coin, a set of three commemorative ECU coins to mark Ireland's presidency of the European Community was also launched. The set included a sterling silver five ECU and ten ECU and a 22 carat gold 50 ECU coin.

Fig. 142—Ten ECU, Éire, 1990. Central Bank of Ireland Information Leaflet (1990)

The coins, which were issued only as 'proofs', featured on the obverse a harp surrounded by the twelve stars of the European Community and the value of the coin beneath the harp. The reverse featured Thomas Ryan's red deer against a backdrop of Kerry mountains with the word 'EIRE' in the border and the date '1990' in the exergue. Twenty thousand proof pieces of the silver five ECU and ten ECU coins were issued, and 5,000 of the gold 50 ECUs.

Fig. 143—Fifty ECU, Éire, 1990. Central Bank of Ireland Information Leaflet (1990)

The gold 50 ECU was the first Irish gold 'coin' to be issued since the 1646 Ormonde 'double-pistole' and 'pistole' coins, and only the third gold coin in the Irish series dating back to 997. These coins were similarly not without controversy since their issue seemed to imply an endorsement by the Irish government led by Charles Haughey of a single European currency, when a formal decision still had to be made.

The introduction of the new one pound coin heralded a number of other changes in Ireland's coinage as outlined in the Decimal Currency Act of 1990. In 1992 a smaller five pence coin was introduced, with Metcalfe's bull being turned to face left; this was followed in 1993 by the introduction of a small ten pence coin with the salmon similarly facing left. Albert Reynolds at the time of the launch of the new one pound coin (June 1990) also indicated that a round, smaller 50 pence would replace the existing 50 pence in 1991 and that the Percy Metcalfe designs of the Irish wolfhound from the old sixpence and the hare from the old threepence would replace the Gabriel Hayes 'Celtic bird' designs on the new bronze-coated steel penny and two pence coins (the old halfpenny having been demonetised on 31 December 1986) which were to replace the existing bronze coins.

Fig. 144—Ten pence and five pence, Éire, 1993 and 1992. Central Bank of Ireland Information Leaflet (1992)

These proposed changes were not, however, to take place. The 50 pence was to continue to be issued in its old form, and the Gabriel Hayes designs likewise continued to feature on Ireland's 'bronze' coins.

The plans to further modernise Ireland's coinage were put on hold following the signing of the Maastricht Treaty in February 1992 and the referendum to endorse the Treaty on 18 June 1992 which committed Ireland to the single currency if it met the appropriate economic criteria. In 1998 the European Council confirmed that Ireland would qualify to join the European Monetary Union.

A year earlier the millennium of Ireland's coinage was marked by the issuing of a commemorative medal and a special philatelic numismatic cover on 3 April 1997. The 32p stamp featured a silver penny of the Norse king of Dublin, Sitric III, who issued the first Irish coin in 997. The commemorative medal featured the Sitric penny with a legend in English and Irish reading 'Millennium of Irish coinage'. The postal cover, designed by Thomas Ryan, featured coins covering the period from 1190 to 1990.

The year 1997 also saw one of the most curious episodes in Ireland's recent numismatic history. In 1995, to mark the 50th anniversary of the founding of the United Nations, an international coin programme was launched. The programme was to see commemorative coins launched over the next three years by 36 states, including Ireland. Whilst dated 1995, the first Irish United Nations commemorative coin was presented to Mr Charlie McCreevy, the minister for finance, on 16 December 1997.

The coin was a crown-sized silver proof one pound struck at the Royal Mint, and was issued as part of a twenty proof coin collection set marketed by the Royal Mint. The obverse features the harp with the word 'EIRE' above it and the dates '1945–1995' below it. The reverse followed a standard design prepared for all coins issued in the United Nations Coin Programme and featured a dove in flight holding a banner in its beak, with the dates '1945' '1995' with the United Nations symbol and '50' to the right of the dove. The value of the coin '£1' is to be found below the dove and the inscription in Celtic lettering 'NATIONS UNITED FOR PEACE' above it. The coin was designed by David McGrail.

Fig. 145—United Nations Proof Pound, Eire, 1995. Central Bank of Ireland

There is some speculation as to how many of these silver proof coins were produced. The 'authorised limit' for this new coin was to be 25,000, but it is thought that just over 3,000 were produced for the Royal Mint sets. The Central Bank was only to order an additional 500 examples of the coin to be sold through its Currency Issue Department, and of these some were sent abroad to Irish embassies to be presented as official gifts. Whilst the coin had been around since late 1997, it did not come to the attention of many collectors and dealers until early 2001!

It is thought that less than 4,000 of these proof silver one pound coins were produced, making it the lowest mintage in the Irish decimal series.

The Euro became the official currency of Ireland, and of another ten European Union countries, on 1 January 1999, with 78 Irish pence equal to one Euro, although for the first three years of its existence the Euro could only be used in cashless transactions.

On 14 January 1998 the Department of Finance issued the second edition of Ireland's *National Plan for the Changeover to the Single Currency*. The Plan, whilst principally focusing on the changeover arrangements, was to include the designs for the new Euro notes (which had been agreed at the Dublin European Council in December 1996) and the new Euro coins. It also included the design for the Irish face of the Euro coins, an Irish harp within a border of twelve stars with the word 'EIRE' and the date on either side of the harp, which had been devised by Jarlath Hayes following a national competition. Ireland is one of only two Euro Zone countries which have the same national design on all their coins, as most other states opted for two or three different designs for their 'national' side.

In all, eight new Euro coins were proposed, consisting of one, two, five, ten, twenty and 50 Euro cent coins and one and two Euro coins. The 'European' side of all eight coins was designed by Luc Luycx of the Royal Belgian Mint. The 'bronze' one, two and five Euro cents, which are struck in copper-plated steel, feature a globe with a map of Europe highlighted, symbolising Europe's place in the world. Six European stars are to be found below and above the globe, linked by parallel lines. The value of the coins, '1 EURO CENT', '2 EURO CENT' and '5 EURO CENT', is to be found to the left of the globe. The 'brass' ten, twenty and 50 Euro cent coins, which are struck in a yellow metal known as 'Northern Alloy' or 'Nordic Gold', feature a map of Europe with the national borders clearly defined. Again six European stars linked with parallel lines are to be found below and above the map, with the value — '10 EURO CENT', '20 EURO CENT' and '50 EURO CENT' — placed to the right. The bi-metallic one and two euro coins feature a map of Europe without boundaries, with the star and line device over and below the map and the value of the coin, '1 EURO' or '2 EURO', to the left of the map.

Fig. 146—One Euro, Éire, national reverse and common obverse, 2002. Central Bank of Ireland (2000)

The one Euro coin has a 'silver' inner nickel-plated centre with an outer yellow metal ring, whilst the two Euro has a yellow metal centre and a 'silver ' nickel-plated outer ring.

Fig. 147—Two Euro, Éire, national reverse and common obverse. Central Bank of Ireland (2000)

All the coins are round with the exception of the 20 cent, which has seven small indentations and is described as 'Spanish Rose'.

Production of Ireland's new Euro coins officially commenced at 1.40 pm on 13 September 1999. It was estimated that 950 million coins would be required to meet the country's needs from 1 January 2002. In the end a billion coins were produced. Across Europe a staggering 56 billion new coins were required to replace the old national coins in the twelve Euro Zone countries.

At the official reception to launch the production of the new Euro coins, Mr Maurice O'Connell, the governor of the Central Bank of Ireland, commented: 'As we mark the start of the production of Euro coins in Ireland, we should spare a thought for our distinctive Irish coins, which will soon be consigned to history. I am not entirely sure whether this occasion is more akin to a christening or a wake. Perhaps there is an element of both in it' (*Irish Times*, 13 September 1999).

By the end of December 1999, 128 million Euro coins had been produced at Sandyford.

In order to meet the demands for the new Euro coins the Central Bank of Ireland commenced a major £IR35 million investment in new coining and note production equipment in 1996, and an additional 40 staff were recruited alongside the 210 permanent staff who work at Sandyford, the modern-day equivalents of Eole the Viking moneyer. During 2000 the staff at the mint, as in the time of James II and his Gun Money coinage, were placed on a double shift system to produce their 'tinkerly treasure'. At the height of operations the mint was producing 850 Euro coins a minute.

Alongside the production of Euro coins the production of the national coinage continued, and during 2000 6.8 million Irish coins were to be produced, as well as 420 million Euro coins.

Earlier, in 1999, the Department of Finance had authorised the striking of a fourth commemorative coin to mark the Millennium. A competition was held in March 1999 for this new coin, which was later to be described by the taoiseach as the 'last of the distinctive Irish coins' to be produced before the introduction of the Euro. The competition was won by Alan Ardiff, a Dublin jeweller, and Garrett Stokes of a Dublin-based design and communications company. The new one pound coin was to feature the standard obverse harp design with the date '2000'. The reverse design was based on the Broighter boat in the National Museum of Ireland in Dublin. This six-inch miniature gold boat, which is over 2000 years old, was part of a hoard of gold artefacts found in County Derry in 1896. Two stars representing the two millennia since the birth of Christ are to be found to the right of the boat, with the word 'MILLENNIUM' beneath the boat and the value of the coin '£1' to its left.

A silver proof version of the one pound coin was launched by the taoiseach, Bertie Ahern, on 29 November 1999 at the National Museum. A reporter for the

Fig. 148—Millennium Pound,
Eire, 2000.
Central Bank of Ireland

Irish Times was to liken the design of the coin to a slice of melon speared by several
cocktail sticks!

As with many Irish coins over the centuries, this new coin was not to be issued
without some controversy. News programmes on the radio on the night before
the proof coin was released for sale reported that traders and shopkeepers were
complaining about shortages of coins in the run-up to Christmas. The blame for
these shortages was placed on the Central Bank of Ireland and the Irish mint for
having switched their production efforts to the minting of new Millennium
£1 coins.

Some 95,000 silver proof piedforte (double thickness) one pound coins were
to be produced for sale to collectors, and a further five million cupro-nickel
Millennium coins were to be issued for general circulation in January 2000.

Inevitably, the demise of Ireland's distinctive national coinage has prompted a
renewed interest in Irish coins. The Central Bank of Ireland in recent years has
issued uncirculated sets of its circulating coins for collectors, and 10,000 sets of
circulating coins in a special commemorative folder, including the Millennium
pound, were released in April 2000 for sale at £IR10. The complete issue of sets
was sold out within weeks. Such was the interest in this special commemorative
cover that a set of the seven coins, no different from the millions of 2000 coins in
general circulation, with a total face value of £IR1.88p, sold at Whyte's in
February 2001 for £IR93!

No distinctive Irish coins were to be issued after 2000. Whilst it was originally
proposed that Irish bank notes and coins would circulate alongside new Euro
notes and coins until July 2002, the date for their withdrawal was brought forward
to 9 February 2002. In 2001 the Central Bank issued a 'Nostalgia' set for sale to
collectors to mark the passing of the punt, which included an uncirculated
example of the last Irish pound note and a proof version of the first Irish pound
coin.

As the Central Bank bade farewell to the punt, the general public prepared to welcome the Euro. On 14 December 2001 Euro 'starter packs' containing eighteen Euro coins worth €6.35 went on sale in banks and post offices for £IR5. The starter packs were to sell out in Ireland and the rest of Europe almost immediately. 'Euro-phoria', as it was described, had gripped Ireland and Europe.

On 1 January 2002 the new Euro coins and notes officially entered circulation across the Euro Zone area. For the first time since the Roman Empire, almost all of western Europe — nearly 300 million people in twelve nation states — shared the same currency. In Ireland, the eve of E-day (Euro-Day) was marked by government ministers and Central Bank officials handing out chocolate Euros in Grafton Street. At the stroke of midnight, the first of Ireland's one billion Euro coins entered circulation. Some twelve hours later the Euro was 'officially' launched in Ireland when Bertie Ahern walked into his local newsagents in Drumcondra in Dublin and bought a sultana cake, some milk, two pears and a lottery scratch card.

The next phase in Ireland's thousand-year numismatic history had just begun...

A NORTHERN POSTSCRIPT

Following partition in 1922 the people of Northern Ireland continued to use the coins of the United Kingdom which had been used throughout Ireland since 1826.

The Union of 1801 had seen little immediate change to Britain's coinage. The harp had first appeared on English and Scottish coins in 1603 and has continued to feature as part of the royal arms on British coins ever since. The first officially sanctioned coin to allude to the new union of the kingdoms of Great Britain and Ireland was curiously not struck in the British Isles but in India when, in 1803, the British East India Company ordered the striking of a gold mohur coin and a year later a silver rupee which included a border with a wreath of roses, thistles and shamrock. It was some 20 years after the Union that a British coin first featured a shamrock in its design, and this was the elaborate 'garnished shield' silver series of coins issued for George IV in 1821. For the next 150 years the shamrock device was to be regularly incorporated into the designs of British coins, its last most prominent use being on the florins and sixpences of Elizabeth II issued from 1953 to 1967.

Fig. 149—Garnished Shield half-crown of George IV, 1821. *SNC,* August 2000, No. 3514

It has been suggested that some thought was given in the late 1960s to including a coin in Britain's decimal series with a Northern Ireland design or motif, but none was produced. It was to be fifteen years after decimalisation, in 1986, that the first British coin was struck, for use throughout the United Kingdom, with a Northern Ireland-inspired design.

The 1986 coin formed part of a series of pound coins which had been initiated in 1984 to honour the four constituent countries of the United

Kingdom and which in each case included a national flower or plant encircled by a royal diadem or tiara on the reverse of the coin.

Fig. 150—United Kingdom 'Northern Ireland' design one pound coins. *Spink* 1999

With the 'troubles' in Northern Ireland, particular consideration had to be given to the national plant which would represent the province. The flax plant, which has long been associated with the Irish linen industry, was eventually chosen as the plant to represent Northern Ireland. The official description of the reverse design by Leslie Durbin is 'a Flax Plant eradicated enfiling a representation of Our Royal Diadem'. The edge inscription also had to be carefully considered, and whereas the two previous coins had included the motto from the Scottish Order of the Thistle or words from the Welsh National Anthem, it was decided to retain the 'DECUS ET TUTAMEN' (An ornament and a safeguard) wording which had been used on the newly issued pound coin in 1983 and on English and British coins dating back to the 1660s. The flax plant was to feature again on the British pound coin in 1991.

In 1994 a new series of British pound coins was introduced featuring heraldic devices associated with the constituent parts of the United Kingdom. Again, the choice of an appropriate heraldic device for Northern Ireland had to be carefully considered. The harp and the red hand of Ulster were both too loaded with symbolism for the two traditions in Northern Ireland. Instead, the designer Norman Sillman broke with his two earlier heraldic designs and produced a design for Northern Ireland in 1996 which drew heavily on its Celtic past for inspiration. The reverse design featured an ancient ornate collar superimposed upon an intricately carved Celtic cross with a pimpernel flower at its centre. The edge inscription for this coin was again to read 'DECUS ET TUTAMEN'. The Celtic cross and collar design was again used on a United Kingdom pound coin in 2001.

A year earlier a sort of 'unity', at least in terms of coin design, had been achieved in Ireland with the issue of the Irish Millennium pound coin. Both the Irish Millennium pound coin and the 1996/2001 United Kingdom pound coin draw on a common source for the inspiration of their designs — the Broighter treasure which was discovered in County Derry in 1896. The British pound coin features the Broighter collar and the Irish pound coin the Broighter boat, both of which are to be found in the same display case in the National Museum of Ireland in Dublin.

BIBLIOGRAPHY

ACKERMAN, J.Y. 1840 *A numismatic manual.* Taylor and Walton, London.

BECKETT, J.C. 1989 *The making of modern Ireland 1602–1923.* Faber and Faber Ltd, London.

BRADLEY, H.W. 1978 *A handbook of coins of the British Isles.* London.

BRADY, G. 1976 The plaster casts for the design of the Irish coinage. *Spink Numismatic Circular* (December 1976), 460–1.

BRADY, G. and DOLLEY, M. 1970 A parcel of Irish 'White Money' from Co. Tipperary. *Numismatic Society of Ireland Occasional Papers* **10–14**, 15–19.

BRADY, G. and GALLAGHER, C. 1996 Munster 'Siege Pieces' or 'Early Tokens': evidence from a Cork scattering. *Spink Numismatic Circular* (April 1996), 75–7.

BRADY, G., GALLAGHER, C. and BRADY, F. 1995 The Lambert Simnel coinage — an enquiry. *Spink Numismatic Circular* (October 1995), 301–2.

CENTRAL BANK OF IRELAND 1999 *Launch of £1 Millennium coin.* Press Release, Dublin, 29 November 1999.

CHALLIS, C.E. 1971 The Tudor coinage for Ireland. *British Numismatic Journal* **40**, 97–119.

CHOWN, J. 1980 Hiberno-Norse coins in the name of Aethelred with enigmatic reverse. *Spink Numismatic Circular* (October 1980).

CONNOLLY, S.J. (ed.) 1998 *The Oxford companion to Irish history.* Oxford University Press.

DENTON, C.J. 2001 *Ireland's unknown crown: the 1995 Eire £1 silver proof.* Orpington, Kent.

DOLLEY, M. 1970 A pattern shilling Irish of Mary Tudor. *British Numismatic Journal* **39**, 98–110.

DOLLEY, M. 1972 *Medieval Anglo-Irish coins.* B.A. Seaby Ltd, London.

DOLLEY, M. and HACKMAN, W.D. 1969 The coinages for Ireland of Henry VIII. *British Numismatic Journal* **38**, 84–107.

DOLLEY, M. and LANE, S.N. 1970 A parcel of three-crown groats probably from a find of 1838. *Numismatic Society of Ireland Occasional Papers* **10–14**, 11–14.

DOLLEY, M. and MOORE, C.N. 1973 Some reflections on the English coinages of Sihtric Caoch, king of Dublin and of York. *British Numismatic Journal* **43**, 45–9.

DOLLEY, M. and SEABY, W.A.1967 Le Money del Oraylly. *British Numismatic Journal* **36**, 114–17.

DOLLEY, R.H.M. 1966 *The Hiberno-Norse coins in the British Museum*. Trustees of the British Museum, London.

DOWLE, A. and FINN, P. 1969 *The guide book to the coinage of Ireland from 995 AD to the present day.* Spink and Son Ltd, London.

DUFFY, S. 1997 *Ireland in the Middle Ages.* MacMillan Press Ltd, Basingstoke and London.

DYKES, D.W. 1963 The Irish coinage of Henry III. *British Numismatic Journal* **32**, 99–116.

DYKES, D.W. 1976 The Anglo-Irish coinage of Edward III. *British Numismatic Journal* **46**, 44–50.

ELLIS, S.G. 1978 The struggle for control of the Irish mint, 1460–*c.* 1506. *Proceedings of the Royal Irish Academy* **78**C, 18–35.

FINN, P. 1975 The position of the sceptres on the Irish pennies of John as king. *Spink Numismatic Circular* (May 1975).

FINN, P. 1996 The third known Irish coin of Henry VI. *Spink Numismatic Circular* (September 1996), 3.

FINN, P. 1999 *List of coins* **17** (1999).

FOSTER, R.F. 1989 *Modern Ireland 1600–1972*. Penguin Books, London.

GALLAGHER, C. 1967 Neglected documentary evidence for the currency of 14th century Scottish coins in N.E. Ireland. *British Numismatic Journal* **36**, 93–5.

GLENDININGS 2000 Ancient English and world coins and historical medals. *Auction Catalogue Sale 30, 889* (19 July 2000).

GLENDINNING, V. 1998 *Jonathan Swift*. Hutchinson, London.

HOLMES, G. (ed.) 1988 *The Oxford illustrated history of medieval Europe.* Oxford University Press.

IRISH TIMES 1999 First Irish Euro coins minted. *The Irish Times* (13 September 1999).

JONES, G. 1984 *A history of the Vikings.* Oxford University Press.

KELLY, E.M. 1976 *Spanish dollars and silver tokens.* Spink and Son, London.
KENNY, M. 1987 A hoard of Irish coins of John, found in France. *Spink Numismatic Circular* (September 1987), 219.

LOBEL, R., DAVIDSON, M., HAILSTONE, A. and CALLIGAS, E. 1999 *Coincraft's standard catalogue of the coins of Scotland, Ireland, Channel Islands and the Isle of Man.* Coincraft, London.
LYNDON, J. *The making of Ireland.* Routledge, London and New York.

MACCARTHY, J.J. 1996 *"The Last King" inc "The State of Ireland under Elizabeth Tudor". An Account by Don Philip O'Sullivan Beare.* The MacCarthy Clan Society, Cork.
MORRIESON, H.W. 1923–4 Some entries of numismatic interest in the Masters Accounts of the Merchant Tailors Guild of Dublin 1553–61. *British Numismatic Journal.* London
MOSSMAN, P.L. 2000 The circulation of Irish coinage in pre-federal America. *The Web of Time, Pages from the American Post* 2 (4), 1–6.

O'SULLIVAN, W. 1964 The only gold coins issued in Ireland 1646. *British Numismatic Journal* 33, 141–50.
O'SULLIVAN, W. 1964 *The earliest Anglo-Irish coinage.* National Museum of Ireland, Dublin.
O'SULLIVAN, W. 1981 *The earliest Irish coinage.* National Museum of Ireland, Dublin. [First published 1961.]

PARSONS, H.A. 1921–2 An Irish eleventh century coin of the southern O'Neil. *British Numismatic Journal* 16, 59–71.
PERRY, B.S. 1985 Hiberno–Norse imitations of the English coinage of William I. *Spink Numismatic Circular* (November 1985), 294–6.
POWELL, J. S. 1978 The Irish coinage of Armstrong and Legge. *Seaby's Coin and Medal Bulletin* (June 1978), 174–6.

REMICK, J.H. 1967 *The coinage and banknotes of Ireland 1928–68.* Almanzar's Coins of the World, San Antonio, Texas.
RICE, G. 1994 The gun money of James II. *Spink Numismatic Circular* (May 1994).
ROYAL MINT 1915 *Statutes and statutory rules and orders relating to coinage.* H.M. Stationery Office, London.

SEABY, P.J. 1958 The Armstrong Farthings. *Seaby's Coin and Medal Bulletin*

(November 1958), 443–4.

SEABY, P. 1970 *Coins and tokens of Ireland*. Seaby's Standard Catalogue Part 3. B.A. Seaby Ltd, London.

SEABY, P. and PURVEY, P. F. 1984 *Coins of Scotland, Ireland and the Islands*. Standard Catalogue of British Coins Vol. 2. B.A. Seaby Ltd, London.

SEABY, W.A. 1970 Forgery of John Mascle farthing. *Numismatic Society of Ireland Occasional Papers* **10–14**, 20–3.

SEABY, W.A. and BRADY, G. 1976 The extant Ormonde Pistoles and Double Pistoles of 1646. *British Numismatic Journal* **43**, 80–95.

SEABY, W.A. and KENNY, M. 1988 The Stacpoole Collection of Hiberno-Norse coins in the National Museum of Ireland. *Spink Numismatic Circular* (April 1988), 75–8.

SIMON, J. 1749 *An essay towards an historical account of Irish coins and of the currency of foreign moneys in Ireland*. Dublin. (Reprinted Andrew Publishing Company, London, 1975.)

STAFFORD-LANGAN, J. http://www.irishcoinage.com

STAFFORD-LANGAN, J. 2000 A review of the Irish coinage of Edward IV. Unpublished paper, Dublin, June 2000.

STAFFORD-LANGAN, J. 2001 A revised date for the Irish Cross on Rose coinage of Edward IV. Unpublished paper, Dublin, July 2001.

STEVENSON, D. 1967 The Irish emergency coinage of James II 1689–1691. *British Numismatic Journal* **36**.

VICE, D. 1994 *The 1804 Bank of Ireland six shilling token*. Format List No. 50, Birmingham.

WHYTE'S in association with FINN, P. 2000 *The Millennial Collection*. Dublin, 29 April 2000.

WILLSON YEATES, F. 1919–20 The coinage of Ireland during the rebellion 1641–1652. *British Numismatic Journal* **15**, 185–223.

WILLSON YEATES, F. 1921–2 Further notes on Irish coinage 1641–1652. *British Numismatic Journal* **16**, 189–94.

YEATS, W.B. 1928 *The coinage of Saorstat Éireann*. Irish Government Publication, Dublin.

YOUNG, D. 1969 *Coin catalogue of Ireland 1692–1969* (4th edn). Stagecast Publications, Dublin.

YOUNG, D. 1990a Plans for Ireland's new coinage. *Coin News* (May 1990), 26–7.

YOUNG, D. 1990b Launch of the new Irish £1 coin. *Coin News* (August 1990), 36.

Index